Understanding desistance from crime
Theoretical directions in resettlement and rehabilitation

Understanding desistance from crime

Emerging theoretical directions in resettlement and rehabilitation

Stephen Farrall and Adam Calverley

Open University Press
McGraw-Hill Education
McGraw-Hill House
Shoppenhangers Road
Maidenhead
Berkshire
England
SL6 2QL

email: enquiries@openup.co.uk
world wide web: www.openup.co.uk

and Two Penn Plaza, New York, NY 10121–2289, USA

First published 2006

A catalogue record of this book is available from the British Library

ISBN-10: 0335 21948 9 (pb) 0 335 21949 7 (hb)
ISBN-13: 978 0335 21948 3 (pb) 978 0335 21949 0 (hb)

Library of Congress Cataloguing-in-Publication Data
CIP data applied for

Typeset by YHT Ltd, London
Printed in the UK by Bell & Bain Ltd, Glasgow

Contents

For Katie and Emma,
with love from Stephen and Adam

Preface and acknowledgements: Society's stories about change and reform: *not* an optimistic place from which to start...

1st Parole Board Member:	We gotta name for people like you, H. I. That name is called 'recidivism'.
2nd Parole Board Member:	Re-peat O-ffender.
1st Parole Board Member:	Not a pretty name, is it H. I.?
H. I.:	No, sir, that's one bonehead name. But that ain't me anymore.
1st Parole Board Member:	You're not just telling us what we want to hear?
H. I.:	No, sir, no.
2nd Parole Board Member:	'Cause we just wanna hear the truth.
H. I.:	Well, then I guess I *am* telling you what you want to hear.
2nd Parole Board Member:	Boy! Didn't we just tell you not to do that!
H. I.:	Yes sir.
2nd Parole Board Member:	Okay then.

(H. I. McDonnough's third appearance at the Parole Board, from *Raising Arizona*, Ethan and Joel Cohen, 1987)

Brian Field, born in 1932, was a solicitor's clerk. He rose through the legal profession to become the managing clerk at John Wheater & Co., a firm of London solicitors. Prior to working at Wheater & Co., he had held a post at Probyn Deighton and was widely expected to be a 'high-flyer'. Having served in the army, he was also a married man, his wife being the ballet-dancing daughter of a German judge. To all intents and purposes a very ordinary man.

And yet, numerous of the accounts of the 1963 Great Train Robbery (e.g. Donaldson, 2003: 257) suggest that Brian Field had been the 'mastermind' behind the botched robbery. Certainly Field was heavily involved in the robbery, buying Leatherslade Farm, the hide-out used by the gang.

The criminal 'mastermind' had used his own firm of solicitors when buying the farm, had signed the lease himself and had placed his share of the proceeds in a holdall cunningly marked 'Brian Field', (see Donaldson, 2003; Morton, 2001: 201–5; Reynolds, 1995 – Reynolds himself was another of the applicants from a strong field of candidates vying for the title 'mastermind of the Great Train Robbery'). For his part in the robbery, Field received five years' imprisonment.

After his release from prison, Field first worked as a salesman (Morton, 2001: 205), before marrying a British Airways air hostess in 1969 and opening a restaurant in Cornwall. Both his marriage and his cooking failed to stand the test of time[1] and Field moved on to a new relationship and new employment (working for a publishing company). Having changed his name to Carlton, in 1979 both he and his wife were killed in a road accident. His new family were shocked to discover his real identity and learn of his past as a criminal 'mastermind'. Field was described by his father-in-law, Edgar Hope, as being a 'charming and accomplished man'.[2]

Aside from the sorry tale of another of the ex-train robbers and their descent into reduced circumstances, what ought we to take from this tale? For us, having studied why people stop offending and how they go about building themselves a new life, it is the tail-end of the story that is of most interest. Field changed his name and (at least in the eyes of his new family) became a different person. Not only that, but so mundane had his life become that no one amongst his new family had even the slightest suspicion, it would appear, that he had once been involved in one of the most notorious crimes of the twentieth century. And indeed, when we first came across the case (by virtue of it being listed in Donaldson, 2003), we too were curious. One hears little of the great train robbers other than accounts of the millions they stole, their daring exploits, escapes from prison and the years they spent on the run overseas boozing away the time and playing international hide-and-seek with Nipper Read. The idea that one of them had quietly got married, settled down and got himself a 'straight job' just seemed implausible. The impossibility of change, or at least society's reluctance to provide very many commonly available ways of describing it, can be found amongst many of the documents of life (be they religious texts, sayings or famous quotations). Take, for example, the following, all culled from either (a) *The Oxford Dictionary of Quotations* or (b) *The Oxford Dictionary of Phrase, Saying & Quotation*:[3]

- 'Even a God cannot change the past', Agathon (a, 6:20).
- 'The leopard does not change his spots', mid-sixteenth century saying (a, 605: 16).
- 'Semper eadem' (Latin, 'ever the same'), the motto of Elizabeth I (b, 67: 11).
- 'An ape's an ape, a varlet's a varlet, though they be clad in silk or scarlet', mid-sixteenth century saying meaning that inward nature cannot be changed cosmetically (b, 69: 1).

- 'Once a ____, always a ____', early seventeenth century saying (b, 69: 10).

And, finally, this from Al Capone:

- 'Once in the racket you're always in it' (b, 106: 44).

Of the quotations that we found in just these two volumes, only two implied that change was possible ('It is never too late to mend' and the somewhat odd 'There's many a good cock come out of a tattered bag'), whilst 16 suggested that change was impossible. We also found a further three that implied that death was the only route to redemption (and all of these were associated with Christianity in some way). True, there are also some full-blown stories about change, the Road to Damascus being the most famous of them, but, as a rule, there is an in-built tendency on the part of society to view people as stable and individual-level change as uncommon. As Christina Odone, in her *Thought for the Day* for BBC Radio Four on 18 December 2003 said in relation to Maxine Carr,[4] 'Everyone is reduced to cartoon strip figures, capable of no complex emotions, U-turn, or reform.'

Those who do experience dramatic change in the full glare of attention – think if you will of Jonathan Aitken or Jeffery Archer – often withdraw from public life for some considerable time during or after this change. Quite why it ought to be the case that societies prefer to view people as stable entities remains both puzzling and beyond the scope of the present study. It could be that societies find it easier to maintain classificatory schema and that change implies that the schema is challengeable or at least unfinished. Or it could be that once labelled or identified in some negative way, one is deemed as untrustworthy and it then becomes impossible to ever fully 'de-label' oneself, especially in the absence of de-certification agencies (see also Braithwaite, 1989). Or it could be that, put crudely, people don't change and that the 'once a thief always a thief' doctrine is valid.

However, it is not our experience that the 'once a thief always a thief' approach is warranted. Nor is it the experience of many of the men and women who embark upon short-lived criminal careers only to end them in a matter of years. Amongst the, by now familiar, statistics which crim-inologists, policy-makers and government officials frequently remind each other of are that:

- approximately one-third of males have a criminal conviction by the age of 30; and
- around half of all community rehabilitation orders and prison sen-tences result in a further conviction within two years.

Despite the rather disappointing image that these statistics paint, we ought to remind ourselves that this still means that for very, very many of the people who are found guilty of crimes, their involvement with the criminal justice system is short-lived. Again, we concede that there are some individuals for whom the criminal justice system represents a perpetual feature of their lives, but there are a great deal more who serve their punishment, move on and are (thankfully for all concerned) never to appear before a judge again. These people, however, are rarely given much thought, other than as a comparison group against which to assess just *how* bad the *really bad* recidivist bunch are. The processes by which people stop offending and are 'resettled', 'reintegrated', 'rehabilitated', 'reformed' and so on have only of late received very much attention. All of these 're' words imply that this group of people are in some way returned (another 're' word) to some state that previously they had occupied. However, the 'reintegrated' probably were never fully 'integrated' in the first place and the 'reformed' often need to 'form' themselves completely afresh. Often, it would appear, these people have had to create themselves and their lives anew. These are not always tasks without their heartaches and bruises, as H. I. McDonnough, the fictional character in *Raising Arizona*, found for himself. Yet sometimes, also, people move back into their old haunts and their old habits without either reoffending or undergoing a major reorganization of 'who' they are.

In what follows we chart a group of these men and women. These people represent the traffic of the criminal justice system, or at least a portion of it, from the late 1990s. Between late 1997 and early 1998 they all shared one experience: the commencement of what was then called a probation order.[5] For some this was the first time they had been in trouble with the law, for others it was just another of the sentences which they would receive as they zigzagged between 'the community' and imprisonment. For some it was the outcome of just another court appearance, while for others it was the last time they ever committed a crime, and for others still – and indeed the majority – it was the start of the end of their involvement in crime. These, then, are the stories of the people that have not obeyed society's laws twice: they have broken both the formal law (as it pertains to criminal statutes) and the informal law that suggests that change is uncommon.

We extend our thanks to...

We owe a debt of thanks to a vast number of people. The Leverhulme Trust was generous enough to provide the monies (as grant F/00130/G) which allowed us to retrace and interview the original members of the *Tracking Progress on Probation* study. Tracing the cases was easier than we had imagined it would be, and this is in part due to the excellent help that we received from the Home Office Prisons Department, and in particular Tony Bullock, Mike Elkins, Jonathan Barbour and Farid Guessous. Jonathan and Farid were patient enough to check the prison database not once but twice for our sample members. Staff working in 'community corrections' (that is, the probation service) were also kind enough to check and recheck their own databases for our sample members. We accordingly thank Christine Knott, Steve Stanley, Imogen Brown, Diana Fulbrook, Mary Archer, Patrick Williams, Stella Newell, Julia Ramsden, Vicky Baker and Tracy Murray for their help in providing us with an updated list of addresses. The previous team of interviewers, we found as we started to return to our recontact sheets and the data in general, had done a wonderful job of recording salient details and facts which made our jobs all the easier – hence we thank them all. The transcribing of the interviews – a task daunting enough just to contemplate – was undertaken by Kath Pye, Claire Sillitoe, Emma Calverley and AC Consultants. Mike Maguire as Series Editor and Chris Cudmore as Commissioning Editor at the Open University Press were supportive throughout our writing schedule.

We have been fortunate enough to benefit from comments on various draft chapters from our friends and colleagues who share our interest in desistance: Fergus McNeill, Ros Burnett, Peter Raynor and Lorraine Gelsthorpe each provided thoughtful views on our work as it pertained to the long term impacts of probation supervision. Anne Worrall, Ian O'Donnell, Fergus McNeill, David Gadd, Jason Ditton, Shadd Maruna and Joseph Kotarba all provided interesting comments on our chapter on the existential aspects of desistance. So too did attendees at a conference held in September 2004 in Onati, Spain, on crime and the emotions organized by Susanne Karstedt, Ian Loader and Heather Strang. Tim Hope took the time to discuss victimization with us and in so doing greatly shaped Chapter 7. Roger Hood provided help in tracking down references to 'ancient' materials from the dim and distant 1970s. Rob Evans, who, like Stephen Farrall, is a former inmate of 'HMP Basingstoke', and who worked for a while as a probation officer, provided stimulating ideas from the perspective of a practitioner. Comments from the attendees at two two-day seminars on 'Life After Punishment' held at Keele University and supported by the Department of Criminology helped refine some of our thinking with regards to citizenship and desistance, and also in a general way. Clare Hoy did a wonderful job of commenting upon a near-complete draft of this book before we finally let go of it. Naturally enough, our final word of thanks goes to the 51 men and women who we interviewed (again).

Notes

1. Proof then, perhaps, that Ludwig van Beethoven was correct in his assertion that 'Anyone who tells a lie has not a pure heart, and cannot make a good soup', cited in Ratcliffe, 2003: 85.
2. Readers who wish to learn more about the circumstances of Brian Field's death

are referred to the *Daily Telegraph*, 1st May 1979, page 3, 7th September 1979, page 19 and 8th September 1979, page 17. The last of which the quote from Edgar Hope was taken.

[3] We report quotations as (volume, page number, entry number).

[4] Maxine Carr was found guilty of perverting the course of justice for her part in protecting Ian Huntley, himself found guilty of the murders of two school children.

[5] Probation orders are now called community rehabilitation orders, whilst what was once called community service is now known as community punishment. Combination orders are community punishment and rehabilitation orders.

Stephen Farrall
Adam Calverley
Summer 2005

Dramatis personae

In the previous discussion of this project (Farrall, 2002), only some cases were given names. The remainder were referred to by their case numbers. For this book, with far fewer cases (51 instead of 199), we have been able to provide each case with a first name, and it is by these names that we distinguish between cases. So that readers can trace the development of cases between this and the previous publications that draw from this data set, we list here case numbers and names. In some instances we use data from earlier interviews with cases who, in the previous publications, were not given names and who were not reinterviewed for this book. For these cases we simply list their case numbers. All cases were given names that reflected their gender and ethnicity.

Case number	Name	Case number	Name	Case number	Name
007	Lucy	076	Clive	127	Geoff
013	Ben	077	Ron	146	Al
017	Michael	080	Ian	151	Martin
019	Damien	081	Tony	158	Frank
024	Fred	092	Jules	164	Ken
025	Richard	093	Will	165	Paul
043	Meera	094	Anthony	167	Patrick
049	Tim	095	Barry	172	Matthew
050	John	098	Bernard	180	Malcolm
051	Bill	105	Sally-Anne	198	Vincent
059	Peter	108	George	199	Terry
062	Andrew	110	Ann	202	Gary
063	Sandra	114	Justin	212	Danny
064	Mark	115	Jamie	218	Gordon
065	Mickey	120	Nick	220	Don
070	Edward	121	Jimmy	223	Niall
073	Tom	122	Rajeev	227	Dominic

chapter one

Getting to grips with desistance

Desistance from crime: what is it and what do we know about it?
What are the current theories used to explain desistance?
Recent theoretical developments in desistance research
'Rethinking what works with offenders'
Topics for exploration

The purpose of this book is to familiarize the reader with the main pre-occupations of research on desistance from crime and the processes associated with it, and to introduce them to new strands of research and theorizing in this field. We do this via summaries of previous theoretical and empirical work, as well as presenting some new data and analyses based on our research into one cohort of ex-offenders whom we have followed for the past seven years. Desistance from crime, that is to say the process of ending a period of involvement in offending behaviour, is something of an enigma in modern criminology. It is the implicit focus of much criminological and criminal justice work and yet is an area that has been relatively neglected in terms of research. However, the last 10 or 20 years have greatly extended what we know about the reasons why people cease offending.

Early forays into the field have led on to more rigorous and sustained efforts at charting the processes and factors associated with desistance (for recent reviews of this literature, see Laub and Sampson, 2001, 2003; Farrall, 2000, 2002; Maruna, 2001). During this time, we have also seen a renewed optimism about the outcomes of probation supervision and the development of the 'What Works' programme in North America and the UK. This book continues, and builds upon, this general work and upon one study in particular. In the late autumn of 1997, researchers started to follow the progress of a small cohort of men and women made subject to probation and combination orders (respectively now community rehabilitation and community punishment and rehabilitation orders). In all, 199 men and women were recruited into the study and, over the next two years, were reinterviewed at various points during the remainder of their periods of supervision. Fieldwork for the original study ended over the summer of 1999, and the results of the research eventually published (as Farrall, 2002). Four or five years after they were interviewed for the last time, we embarked upon a process of retracing and reinterviewing as many of these cohort members as we could find, up to a maximum of 50. In fact, we did slightly better than this, and this book reports on the results of these interviews and provides an update on the lives of 51 of these men and women.

This chapter provides an introduction to the literature on desistance and an outline of the main theories used to explain desistance. Following this, we explore recent developments in the study of why people stop offending which have been published since the original study was published. Here our focus is on the development of new *ideas* and the use of new concepts to explore, 'make sense' of and understand desistance. There are four key texts which we review herein (Maruna, 2001; Giordano *et al.*, 2002; Laub and Sampson, 2003; and Bottoms *et al.*, 2004). Following this, we will provide an outline of the study to which this book is a follow-up and an outline of the remainder of this book, introducing to the reader the topics we shall return to in subsequent chapters and our rationale for focusing upon these topics.

Desistance from crime: what is it and what do we know about it?

Desistance is usually defined as the end of a period of involvement in offending. Most researchers therefore think of desistance as meaning that an individual has given up offending permanently, rather than just ceasing to offend for a short while before continuing to commit further offences. As Maruna and Farrall (2004: 174–5) note, we are therefore not interested in short term crime-free lulls (which they refer to as 'primary desistance'), but rather we are concerned with charting 'secondary desistance' – a process by which individuals often assume a role of non-offender or 'reformed person'. In many cases, but not all, this sort of change is associated with a reorganization on the part of the desister of 'who' they are and the sort of person they now wish to be.

As Maruna and Farrall (2004: 171) remind us, although it is true that most adult offenders exhibited many of the telltale signs of being delinquent children, the majority of juvenile delinquents do *not* go on to become adult offenders. For most individuals, participation in 'street crimes' (such as burglary, robbery and drug sales) generally begins in the early teenage years, peaks in late adolescence or young adulthood and dissipates before the person reaches 30 years of age (Holden, 1986; Barclay, 1990; Blumstein and Cohen, 1987; Weitekamp *et al.*, 2000).

From the early twentieth century, which witnessed the development of interest in why people started to offend, through to the work of 'correctional' officers and the more recent interventions in situational crime prevention and cautioning (such as 'target hardening' and restorative justice), we can trace a series of attempts to understand and deal more effectively with offending behaviour in such a way that it can be slowed down, reduced or halted altogether. Yet, despite this interest in understanding why people offend and how best to reduce the needs and opportunities associated with offending, the *systematic* investigation of desistance is a relatively recent development in criminology.

The origins of research into desistance

The Gluecks must take most of the credit for initiating interest in why people stop offending. Publishing, as they did, most of their works between the 1930s and 1960s, the Gluecks were amongst the few criminologists during that period who were interested in the termination of offending careers. Most criminologists at that time were engaged in developing theories designed to account for the *onset* of offending rather than its termination. One critic, Gove (1985: 118), even goes as far as to argue that 'all of these theoretical perspectives [labelling theory, conflict theory, differential association, control theory and strain theory] either explicitly or implicitly suggest that deviant behaviour is an amplifying process that leads to further and more serious deviance'.

It was not until the 1970s and 1980s that interest in desistance increased dramatically. The growth of interest in this field at this time was partly the result of a wave of longitudinal research projects that had been initiated several years earlier. In the UK and North America a number of longitudinal research programmes were started in the 1960s.[1] The respondents in these studies were generally school children aged between 8 and 15. As they aged during the late 1960s and early 1970s, some of them embarked on offending careers. Many of the cohort members who did engage in offending behaviours – following what is now known to be a typical pattern – would have ceased their involvement in crime as they left their teenage years behind during the 1970s and early 1980s. Thus by the mid-late 1970s a sizeable proportion of these cohorts consisted of people who had either never offended or who had offended but whose offending had decelerated or who had ceased offending altogether. The result was that many researchers, who had been anticipating studying involvement in crime over the life course, were left having to explain the cessation of involvement in crime by many of their cohort members. In addition to this, researchers relying on qualitative interview data started to publish the results of their own enquiries at around this time (Neal Shover and Thomas Meisenhelder being two such researchers who contributed to the growing interest in desistance).

By the mid-1980s the investigation of desistance was not merely an appendage to research on criminal careers, but represented a legitimate topic for research in its own right (e.g. Cusson and Pinsonneault, 1986; Mulvey and LaRosa, 1986). Since then several studies have been undertaken with the specific aim of exploring the ending of criminal careers rather than their onset (e.g. Shover, 1983, 1996; Burnett, 1992; Rand, 1987; Leibrich, 1993; Graham and Bowling, 1995; Maruna, 1997, 2001; Uggen and Kruttschnitt, 1998; Uggen and Pilliavin, 1998; Farrall, 2002).

Factors and processes associated with desistance

Drawing on the insights of earlier work on criminal careers, this body of work has pointed to a number of correlates of desistance. The literature on desistance is commonly based on longitudinal data sets (e.g. Knight and West, 1975; Loeber *et al.*, 1991; Sampson and Laub, 1993) or on one-off retrospective research (e.g. Shover, 1983; Cusson and Pinsonneault, 1986; Graham and Bowling, 1995). In a few cases (e.g. Leibrich, 1993; Burnett, 1992; Farrall, 2002), data have been collected by following the careers of persons after they have been made subject to criminal justice interventions. The research undertaken so far has shed light on the role of social and personal factors in desistance (for outlines of this body of work, see Adams, 1997; Farrall, 2000; Laub and Sampson, 2001).

A number of researchers (e.g. Uggen and Kruttschnitt, 1998; Mischkowitz, 1994; Farrall, 2002) have provided evidence that desistance is associated with gaining employment, although the precise causal links between engaging in legitimate employment and desistance from offending have yet to be satisfactorily established. Meisenhelder (1977) noted that the acquisition of a good job provided the men in his sample with important social and economic resources, whilst Shover (1983: 214) reported how a job generated '... a pattern of routine activities ... which conflicted with and left little time for the daily activities associated with crime'.

Similar sentiments were expressed by Robert Sampson and John Laub (Sampson and Laub, 1993; Laub and Sampson, 2003). They wrote that desisters were characterized as having '... good work habits and were frequently described as "hard workers"' (Sampson and Laub, 1993: 220). Farrington *et al.* (1986: 351) reported that 'proportionally more crimes were committed by ... youths during periods of unemployment than during periods of employment', a finding supported by the later work of Horney *et al.* (1995). However, as researchers such as Ditton (1977) and Henry (1978) have shown, full-time employment does not preclude either the opportunities to offend or actual offending. Graham and Bowling (1995: 56, Table 5.2) found that for young males employment was not related to desistance, as did Rand (1987) when she investigated the impact of vocational training on criminal careers.

Another of the most common findings in the literature on desistance is that individuals cease to offend at about the same time as they start to form significant life partnerships (e.g. Chylicki, 1992). One of the clearest statements in support of this line of reasoning came from Shover (1983: 213), who wrote that, 'The establishment of a mutually satisfying relationship with a woman was a common pattern ... [and] ... an important factor in the transformation of their career line.' Cusson and Pinsonneault (1986) and Mischkowitz (1994) followed West (1982: 101–4) in arguing that what was important (in terms of facilitating desistance) was not marriage *per se*, but rather the *quality* of the relationship and the offending career of the person whom the would-be desister married. The work of Laub *et al.* (1998) supports this contention: as marriages became stronger amongst the men in their sample, so these men's offending began to be curtailed. A number of studies have suggested that the experience of becoming a parent is also associated with desistance from offending (see, for example, Trasler, 1979: 315; Irwin, 1970: 203; Sampson and Laub, 1993: 218; Caddle, 1991: 37; Leibrich, 1993: 59, Jamieson *et al.*, 1999: 130; Uggen and Kruttschnitt, 1998: 355; Hughes, 1997, 1998: 146; Parker 1976: 41).

Despite the evidence suggesting that forming a life partnership may result in desistance, some researchers have questioned this rather simple cause and effect model.[2] Rand (1987: 137) tested the hypothesis that '... young men who marry are less criminal than those who never marry' and found no support for this in her data. Knight *et al.* (1977: 359) found no significant differences (in terms of the number of subsequent convictions) between the married and unmarried groups from the Cambridge Study in Delinquent Development. Similarly, Mulvey and Aber (1988) reported finding no connection between partnership and desistance; nor were they able to find any firm link between parenthood and desistance. Rand (1987: 143) also found no support for the idea that men who became fathers were less criminal than those who did not.

However, at least some of these negative findings can be reassessed following the findings of Uggen (2000) and Ouimet and Le Blanc (1996), which suggest that the impact of various life events upon an individual's offending is age-graded. For example, Ouimet and Le Blanc (1996: 92) suggest that it is only from around the mid-20s that cohabitation with a woman was associated with desistance for the males in their sample. In a similar vein, Uggen (2000: 542) suggests that work appears to be a turning point in the criminal careers of those offenders aged over 26, whilst it has a marginal effect on the offending of younger offenders. When findings like these are taken into consideration, the importance of structuring the enquiry by age is made apparent. However, many of the earlier studies concerning the factors associated with desistance were unaware of this caveat and as such their findings that there was no impact of employment or partnership on desistance must be treated accordingly.[3]

Various other factors have been identified which appear to be related to desistance. Amongst members of the Cambridge Study in Delinquent Development cohort, Osborn (1980) found that leaving London (where they had grown up) was associated with reductions in subsequent offending (both self-reported and official). Similar findings using alternative data sets have been made by Sampson and Laub, (1993: 217) and Jamieson *et al.* (1999: 133). The break-up of the peer group has been another, and more commonly, cited factor. Knight and West (1975: 49) and Cromwell *et al.* (1991: 83) both referred to cases in which peer group disintegration was related to subsequent desistance (as did Warr, 1998). Experiencing a shift in identity (Shover, 1983: 210; Meisenhelder, 1982; Maruna, 1997, 2000; Burnett, 1992) and feeling shame at one's past behaviours (Leibrich, 1993: 204, 1996) have also been posited as processes associated with desistance.

An individual's motivation to avoid further offending is another key factor in accounting for desistance. Shover (1983), Shover and Thompson (1992), West (1978), Pezzin (1995), Moffitt (1993) and Sommers *et al.* (1994) have all pointed to a range of factors which motivated the desisters in their samples. Burnett (1992: 66, 1994: 55–6) and Farrall (2002: 99–115) have both suggested that those who reported that they wanted to stop offending and felt they were able to stop offending were more likely to desist than those who said they were unsure if they wanted to stop offending.

Others have pointed to the influence of the criminal justice system on those repeatedly incarcerated. Cusson and Pinsonneault (1986), employing data drawn from in-depth interviews with ex-robbers, identified the following as influential factors in desisting: shock (such as being wounded in a bank raid); growing tired of doing time in prison; becoming aware of the possibility of longer prison terms; and a reassessment of what was important to the individual. Similar findings have been made by other researchers. Leibrich (1993: 56–7), Shover (1983: 213) and Cromwell *et al.* (1991: 83) reported that desisters experienced a period of re-evaluation before coming to their decision to desist. Within a perspective heavily influenced by rational choice models, Shover and Thompson wrote that '... the probability of desistance from criminal participation increases as expectations for achieving friends, money, autonomy and happiness via crime decrease' (1992: 97).

Hughes' (1998) study of ethnic minority desisters living in the USA reported how fear of serious physical harm and/or death was cited by 16 of her 20 respondents. Similar fears were reported by those interviewed by Sommers *et al.*, (1994) and Cusson and Pinsonneault, (1986), and amongst Maruna's (1997) study of published autobiographies of desistance. Work by Meisenhelder (1977) and others (e.g. Shover, 1983; Hughes, 1998; Burnett, 1992) has revealed that some of those repeatedly incarcerated say that they have become tired of prison and feel that they can no longer cope physically and emotionally with the experiences of prison life. In effect, some offenders reach a point in their lives when they can 'take no more' from the criminal justice system and 'burn out'.

As such, it appears that, when we talk about the processes associated with desistance, we need to consider the extent to which an individual has been engaged in offending. Work by Moffitt (1993) – which we outline in more detail below – suggests that there are two ideal types of offending careers. Adolescent-limited offenders start to offend as they enter their teenage years and end as they make the transition to adulthood. Life-course persistent offenders start to become involved in trouble early in life (often before they are 10 years old) and offend well into their 30s, 40s and 50s. These two groups appear to have different modes of exit. The adolescent-limited cease to offend as they leave school, start work, establish their own homes, form life partnerships and start families (Sampson and Laub, 1993; Farrington *et al.*, 1986; Farrall and Bowling, 1999; Bottoms *et al.*, 2004). As such, they do not undergo a radical reorganization of self, but rather drift away from crime. These processes, as mentioned above, strengthen after the mid-20s.

On the other hand, the life-course persistent, when they do cease to offend, often report a differing set of motivations and processes of desistance. Fear of death and witnessing terrible harms done to others, exhaustion from imprisonment and the finding of a religions faith litter their accounts (Cusson and Pinsonneault, 1986; Sommers and Baskin, 1998; Shover, 1983; Maruna, 1997, 2001; Cromwell *et al.*, 1991, Adler, 1993; Farrall, 2002). This group also report several 'false starts' as they try to put crime behind them and experience many obstacles to their eventual reform. Marriage and employment, when they do come, often serve to reinforce desires and motivations to cease offending.

Gaps in our knowledge

Inevitably, some gaps in our knowledge base exist. Very few of the investigations undertaken so far have considered female desisters, for example. Graham and Bowling's (1995) study was one that did. They found that the processes leading to desistance for men and women appeared to be quite different. For women, becoming 'an adult' (e.g. leaving home, finishing schooling and starting a family) was related to desistance. Yet the same was not true for men. As this study was not longitudinal and as all respondents were aged between 15 and 25, it is hard to assess the significance of this finding. It could be due to males needing longer to mature – so that if older males had been included in the sample, the gender differences in the processes of desistance may have been less pronounced – or it could be that the processes of desistance for males and females actually *are* quite different.

A similar study by the Home Office, which extended the upper age limit to 30 (Flood-Page *et al.*, 2000), has since suggested that males *do* need longer to desist, but it did not comment on the processes of desistance for older males and females. However, the factors associated with female desistance from 'street crime' (as reported by Sommers *et al.*, 1994) were very similar to those reported in studies of male 'street offenders' (e.g.

Shover, 1983; Cusson and Pinsonneault, 1986; Cromwell *et al.*, 1991). This could, however, be due to the similarities in desistance from such *crimes*, rather than *gender* similarities.

Only a few studies have addressed the issue of ethnicity and desistance, and the data that exist have a number of drawbacks. In the UK, Farrall (2002: 175) found that there was no variation in rates of desistance between white and ethnic minority probationers in his sample. However, this study did not look at how the processes of desistance might differ according to ethnicity. In the USA, Elliott (1994) found that black offenders had longer violent careers than white offenders except when employment and living arrangements were taken into account, but his study was limited to serious violent offenders. Rand (1987) indicated that there was not as strong an association with early desistance for those offenders who were not white as compared to whites, yet her categorization of ethnic groups is blurred and (like Elliott) relies on official records. Hughes (1997) identified fatherhood and mentorship as the key factors promoting desistance, but relied upon a small sample of 20 black and Latino men. Besides these limitations, the fact that many of these studies were conducted in the USA under a different justice system means that it cannot be assumed that their conclusions apply to ethnic groups in other countries. In England and Wales almost nothing is known about the differences in desistance from crime between white and other ethnic groups.

Another group of offenders that have not been considered in full are sex offenders. Most of the literature on sex offenders details the various intervention programmes run by probation services and prisons and their outcomes (e.g. Friendship *et al.*, 2003). However, Kruttschnitt *et al.* (2000) suggest that informal social controls (such as employment) do help to aid desistance amongst this group of offenders. Similar findings are reported by Brogden and Harkin (2000), who point to the role of family members in helping ex-sex offenders from committing further crimes of this nature. White-collar offenders are also largely absent from our research agenda (although see Weisburd *et al.*, 2001; Hunter, 2004).

Summary

In summary, the desistance literature has pointed to a range of factors associated with the ending of active involvement in offending. Most of these factors are related to acquiring 'something' (most commonly employment, a life partner or a family) which the desister values in some way and which initiates a re-evaluation of his or her life, and for some a sense of who they 'are'. Others have pointed to the criminal justice system (in most cases imprisonment) as eventually exerting an influence on those repeatedly incarcerated. This body of work suggests that any attempt to investigate the impact of probation on offending careers needs also to consider the role of various social processes, *viz.* employment, marriage, ageing and so on. Conversely, the literature on desistance has often not paid sufficient attention to criminal justice interventions, although this is starting to change. Researchers studying desistance are now increasingly starting to forge the connections between the research literature on this topic and policy implications (see Farrall, 2002; McNeill, 2003; Maruna *et al.*, 2004, Burnett and Maruna, forthcoming). This book extends those arguments and debates (see Chapters 3 and 8 in particular).

What are the current theories used to explain desistance?

In this section – and the one that follows – we outline some of the key theoretical positions which criminologists have adopted in order to account for desistance. This section deals with those theories that were developed from the mid-1980s to the mid-1990s, whilst the next section deals with theoretical positions and modifications to existing theories which have emerged since the turn of the century.

One of the earliest approaches to desistance championed the idea that ex-offenders made a rational decision to cease offending. The work in this area was theoretically driven by Clarke and Cornish (1985). Clarke and Cornish touched on desistance only briefly (1985: 172–3), producing a hypothetical decision tree to show how a burglar may decide to stop burgling. Although they acknowledged the existence and influence of wider social factors which may impact upon the (hypothetical) burglar's decision to desist, these factors are portrayed as helping the offender come to a decision rather than constraining the decision-making capabilities or influencing the offender in ways which were unacknowledged by them.

Whilst Cornish and Clarke did not present any data to support or illustrate their theoretical model of desistance, a study which did illustrate some of the issues raised by them was that by Cusson and Pinsonneault (1986). The data from which their analysis was drawn came from qualitative interviews with 17 ex-robbers. The influential factors identified by the authors included: shock (such as being wounded in a bank raid); growing tired of doing time in prison; becoming aware of the possibility of longer prison terms; and a reassessment of what is important to the individual. All of these are described in terms of a 'decision' to give up crime.

Similar findings have been reported by other researchers. Leibrich (1993: 56–7), Shover (1983: 213) and Cromwell *et al.* (1991: 83) all reported that desisters experienced a period of re-evaluation before coming to their decision to desist. Shover and Thompson, for example, wrote that '... the probability of desistance from criminal participation increases as expectations for achieving friends, money, autonomy and happiness via crime decrease' (1992: 97). Pezzin (1995) came to similar conclusions: those with higher earnings were found to be those most likely to disengage from offending; however, future expectations were not found to be related to decisions to desist from crime. The interest in rational choice approaches to social life more widely and criminal careers in particular did not last long and this theoretical approach is largely dormant at present.

Another theory which emerged in the late 1980s and early 1990s was that proposed by Gottfredson and Hirschi (1990). Their general theory of crime was intended to account for all crimes, at all times, and extended to include other risky behaviours. Their argument is that those people who are most likely to offend are often found to be impulsive risk-takers who exhibit low levels of self-control. The extent to which an individual is disposed towards committing crimes (i.e. has low self-control) in order to fulfil their own goals and meet their own wants, Gottfredson and Hirschi refer to as their criminality. The origins of low social control, they argue, come from the poor parenting and socialization practices employed (or not employed) by many offenders' parents. The criminal propensity of any one individual (their criminality) is instilled early in their lives, but remains relatively stable across their life course. However, criminality can be eroded over time as socialization is a lifelong process, and as such remains open to influence at any point in an individual's lifetime. Even so, Gottfredson and Hirschi note, even when socialization does make an individual less impulsive and prone to offending, low control individuals remain as *relatively* low control individuals amongst any group of individuals or generation. So, whilst control may increase, everyone's levels of control increase at about the same rate. The logical conclusion of Gottfredson and Hirschi's position is that events later on in life (such as marriage, child-rearing and employment) make little difference to criminality, since criminality is determined by self-control which itself is determined at a very young age (usually before the 10th birthday).

On the face of it, this leaves Gottfredson and Hirschi with little way of explaining why it would appear that so many men and women who become involved in crime would also appear to cease offending. Their argument is that whilst criminality remains relatively stable over the life course, the opportunities to commit crimes become, over time, less and less frequent. Thus reductions over time in a cohort's actual offending do not reflect their propensity to commit crime, merely the opportunities that they have to do so. Gottfredson and Hirschi's arguments caused much debate in criminology, but a recent review of the competing theories of desistance (Ezell and Cohen, 2004: 259) found little to support the key tenets of their theorizing.

One of the most innovative attempts at theorizing desistance in the 1990s came from Moffitt (1993). Drawing heavily upon theories of social mimicry, Moffitt offers a theoretical explanation for differences between two types of offenders. The first type of offenders are those who engage in offending for a brief period of their life. This group of offenders usually start to offend in early adolescence, from around the age of 14, and cease offending relatively quickly afterwards, often by the age of 19 or 20. Their offending is relatively minor and is often absent from their younger days (up to age 14) or their later years. This group Moffitt calls Adolescent-Limited offenders, since their offending in confined in the main to a short period of their lives around adolescence. This group's offending is due to their status within many modern societies, which lies rather uncomfortably between 'child' and 'adult'. Their offending is situationally-specific and ceases as they get older and leave behind their 'troubled-years'.

In contrast to this group is what Moffitt calls Life-Course Persistent offenders. This group start to offend much earlier in their lives, often well before they are teenagers. Their offending also continues well after their teenage years. The causes of their offending are often due to negative experiences early on in their lives (such as troubled births, maternal drug use and factors from the local environment) which erode their life chances. Often, Moffitt says, such children are born into families which are unable to cope well with the challenges experienced by such children, and the already difficult child develops into an unruly adolescent. Such individuals are likely to face fewer and fewer opportunities to desist from crime and other problematic behaviours as they lack the skills, experiences and opportunities that might redirect their lives. However, like Gottfredson and Hirschi's theorizing, reviews of Moffitt's approach have not found unequivocal support. Whilst Ezell and Cohen (2004) found a group of adolescent-limited offenders, they also found *six* groups of persistent offenders, rather than the one Moffitt predicted. These six groups did not offend as persistently as Moffitt's theory predicted. The authors ended by concluding that they had 'failed to validate the empirical expectations' of Moffitt's approach (2004: 259), although her suggestion that there appeared to be a group of people whose offending is confined to their adolescence is supported.

Next we come to Sampson and Laub's (1993) theory of age-graded social control. Key to Sampson and Laub's approach is the notion of the bond between an individual and society. The bond is made up of the extent to which an individual has emotional attachments to societal goals, is committed to achieving them by legitimate means, believes these goals to be worthy and is able to involve themselves in the attainment of such goals. Sampson and Laub's theorizing posits that engagement in offending is more likely when this bond is weakened or broken. In addition to this, they argue that at various points during the life course, various formal and informal social institutions help to cement the bond between the individual and society. For example, school, the family and peer groups influence the nature of the bond between many young people and their wider communities, whilst employment, marriage and parenthood operate in a similar way for adults. These institutions and the relationships between individuals that they encourage help the formation of social bonds, which in turn creates informal social control. Thus avoidance of crime is the result of relationships formed for reasons other than for the control of crime. Changes, Sampson and Laub argue, in the individual's relationship with these various institutions are an inevitable feature of modern life and, as such, are key to understanding engagement in offending over the life course.

Whilst much continuity in an individual's life can be observed, key events can trigger changes in an individual's bond to society and hence pattern of offending. Similarly, because many relationships endure over time, so they can accumulate resources (e.g. emotional support between marriage partners: Laub *et al.*, 1998) which can help sustain conventional goals and conformity. In contrast to Gottfredson and Hirschi, who see low levels of self-control as the end of the matter, Sampson and Laub argue that levels of criminal propensity are open to influence, and that these influences are often the result of informal social control. Furthermore, unlike rational choice theorists who saw desistance as the result of a decision, Sampson and Laub's approach enables one to view desistance as the result of a process which stretches over time.

There is one further theoretical stance towards rehabilitation that we feel deserves mention. Cognitive behaviouralism grew out of psychologists' attempts to understand repeated offending on the part of (mainly) prisoners and those serving community sentences. Their central premise is that many offenders exhibit poor decision-making, problem-solving and general thinking skills (see McGuire and Priestley, 1985, for an introduction to this work). This approach formed the basis of a number of interventions aimed at changing the thinking styles and approaches to problem-solving amongst probationers and prisoners (see, for example, Hollin, 1996). The general family of interventions employed include 'thought stopping' (i.e. challenging erroneous thinking on the part of the offender), problem-solving training (i.e. teaching offenders new ways of approaching the problems they commonly face) and social skills training.

However, some reservations about such approaches ought to be noted. Both Mair (2004) and Kendall (2004) express various concerns about this approach and the claims made for it. Many offenders, it was argued, did not have the educational capacities to benefit from the interventions favoured by cognitive behaviouralists, and the effects of the programmes were quite short-lived (Mair, 2004: 26–8). Further, Farrall (2002: 75) found that few of the probationers in his sample exhibited poor thinking skills; in fact, many seemed extremely conversant with and well-informed of the problems faced by ex-offenders. Others (e.g. Maruna, 2001: 131) have argued that for desisters to fully make the psychological break away from crime, they often contradict one of the central tenets of such programmes: accepting blame for one's past behaviours. One recent review of the effectiveness of a number of interventions (Harper and Chitty, 2005) found mixed empirical support for those programmes which relied most heavily upon cognitive behavioural forms of intervention and which had the most robust research designs.

Recent theoretical developments in desistance research

Our review (above) of desistance and some of the theories developed to account for it specifically left aside a number of studies that we wish to comment upon in more detail. These recent developments in desistance research have impacted upon the ways in which we have approached our subject matter at a conceptual or theoretical level. Four key texts have been published since the completion of the earlier study that we feel deserve special mention in their own right. These are those by Maruna (2001), Giordano *et al.* (2002), Laub and Sampson (2003) and Bottoms *et al.* (2004). Taken together, these have provided a further stimulus to the work which we have undertaken, and have aided our thinking in several important respects.

Maruna's aim was to '... identify the common psychosocial structure underlying [ex-offender's] self-stories, and therefore to outline a phenomenology of desistance' (2001: 8). In this respect, he argued that 'to desist from crime, ex-offenders need to develop a coherent, pro-social identity for themselves' (2001: 7). What he found was that desisters amongst this sample displayed an exaggerated belief that they could control their own futures in some way and, in addition, a zealous sense of purpose to their 'new' lives. The persisters, on the other hand, 'shared a sense of being doomed or fated to their situation' (2001: 11).

Desistance, then, was bound up in a process by which ex-offenders came to see themselves as an essentially 'good' person who, often through little fault of their own (2001: 12), acted in 'bad' ways. These previous 'bad' ways and the former 'bad' identity, rather than being something to be ashamed of, Maruna argues, are employed by desisters as a means for remaking sense of their lives and as the basis for making a contribution to society (2001: 12). From offender, to desister, to 'wounded healer'.

Maruna's focus on the 'internal' changes associated with desistance contrasts with much of the work on desistance, which has outlined 'external' factors in desistance, such as marriage, parenthood, employment and moves of residency. In this respect, Maruna posed something of a challenge to the original data analyses, which tended to focus heavily upon employment and family formation as key driving factors in desistance (see, for example, Farrall, 2002, Chapters 9 and 10). In this book we attempt to explore in greater detail the 'internal' world of the desister. This we accomplish in two ways. First, by a greater consideration of what it 'feels like' to have desisted, we explore the emotional trajectories of desistance and the processes that are associated with it. What does it feel like to have once been an 'offender' but to now see oneself as an 'ex-offender'? Are there any lessons that can be used to help others trying to desist, or are all experiences unique? Do desisters feel a sense of pride or achievement at having desisted, as suggested also by the work of Laub and Sampson (2003: 143)?

Second, via a case study of one desister, we explore the existential aspects of desistance from crime. What are the changes in how an individual sees themselves as they desist from crime? What are the challenges which they have to face (and overcome?) in reconstructing themselves as a 'normal' person in the eyes of those around them? Do they always, as Maruna's sample members seem to suggest, develop into 'desistance-missionaries', spreading the gospel of 'reform', or are some of them just 'ordinary people' now worrying about getting to work on time, paying bills and getting dinner ready?

The second of our key texts is that by Giordano *et al.* (2002), which explores the ways in which females desist from crime as opposed to males. There have been very few studies of female ex-offenders, although work by Pat Carlen, Anne Worrall, Mary Eaton, and Deborah Baskin and Ira Sommers has developed our knowledge in this respect. Giordano *et al.* (2002: 999–1002) outline a four-part 'theory of cognitive transformation', which, they argue, the desistance process involves: a 'general cognitive openness to change'; exposure and reaction to 'hooks for change' or turning points; the envisioning of 'an appealing and conventional "replacement self"'; and a transformation in the way the actor views deviant behaviour.

The first of these involves an awareness on the part of the would-be desister that change is both desirable and needed, together with a willingness to embrace change. Indeed, as noted by several researchers into desistance (e.g. Cusson and Pinsonneault, 1986; Farrall and Bowling, 1999), a period of reflection and reassessment of what is important to the individual would appear to be a common feature of the initial process of desistance. Of course, in itself this is insufficient (Giordano *et al.*, 2002: 1001; Farrall, 2002: 225); what is also needed is the exposure to some opportunity to change, and the individual spotting this change as offering a potential 'way out' and then acting upon this. This leads on to the third stage in Giordano *et al.*'s schema: the individual's ability to imagine or conceive of themselves in a new (and conventional) role doing new things. Finally, the process is completed (they argue, 2002: 1002) when old behaviours are no longer seen as desirable or relevant.

Giordano *et al.*, following work on the relationship between agency and structure (e.g. Farrall and Bowling, 1999), argue that 'the actor creatively and selectively draws upon elements of the environment in order to affect significant life changes' (2002: 1003). In this way, they work towards a model of desistance which draws agency and structure together (see also Maruna and Farrall, 2004) via their notion of a 'blueprint' for a future self, which resonates with Gidden's (1984) work on position practices and Sartre's (1943) notion of the being-for-itself.

Our third key text is that by Laub and Sampson (2003). This book updates their earlier study (Sampson and Laub, 1993) in that they follow members of the Gluecks' original sample through to age 70. Although this book does not substantially alter their earlier theorizing on the relationship between informal social controls and patterns of offending over the life course, they do take the time to respond to various criticisms and observations relating to their earlier work. In a nutshell, they argue that a number of informal social controls (such as employment, marriage, community groups and peers), as well as formal control agencies (such as the police, prisons and probation), greatly influence the nature of many people's criminal careers during their life course (see the previous section and Sampson and Laub, 1993).

In their 2003 contribution, Laub and Sampson address the following criticisms of their earlier work: selection effects in marriage (44–6);[4] selection effects and work (47–8); the role of human agency (54–5); and the situational contexts of crime (55–6). These issues are relevant for our own research and so we summarize Laub and Sampson (2003) on these issues accordingly.

A number of critics have suggested that the relationship between desistance and marriage is spurious, as the men who 'decide' to marry are likely to have had different criminal career trajectories anyway. Work by Laub *et al.* (1998) suggests that many of the classic predictors of onset and frequency of offending do not explain desistance, nor the effects of marriage (Laub and Sampson, 2003: 44–5). Furthermore, Johnson and Booth (1998) suggest that personality and interactional styles in relationships are malleable and, as such, a 'good' marriage can alter the behaviour of 'bad' actors. Similarly, employment and the relationships and attitudes which come with it are malleable (Uggen, 2000), something that the case studies from our earlier study also suggested (Farrall, 2002: 146–52, 177–8).

Laub and Sampson (2003: 54–5) also attempted to develop their work on the relationship between agency and structures in the process of desistance. Their ambitions are grand, in that they attempt to consider human agency, situational contexts and historical contexts. However, we believe, with regard to this issue (and this issue alone), their work does not live up to their ambitions. We feel inclined to agree with an earlier review by Modell of their 1993 book, that their case studies feel like a 'microscopic quantitative test of their hypotheses' (Modell, 1994: 1391). This is not meant to denigrate the general tenor of their work, which we greatly admire. Ultimately, however, we feel that Laub and Sampson essentially reproduce the agency versus structure debate in their case studies of desistance (see 2003: 141–9, for example), rather than trying to transcend these debates. This, we argue, represents something of a missed opportunity, since two notable attempts to transcend the agency/structure divide with regards to desistance have already been made (Farrall and Bowling, 1999; Giordano *et al.*, 2002, referred to above), the former of which was approvingly cited by Laub and Sampson (2001: 47). This, taken with the work of Giordano *et al.* (2002), has suggested to us that we ought to address directly the issues surrounding agency, structure and structuration in the course of our work.

Finally we come to the work of Bottoms *et al.* (2004). The contribution of this work is purely theoretical, since their article is the outlining of a new longitudinal study of desistance. Whilst there is much that we could pick up and run with from their article, one contribution stands out for us: their reference to an 'English Dream'. Referring directly to the fabled 'American Dream', Bottoms *et al.* propose a similar English Dream for working class children and adolescents. Such a dream consists of a safe job as an employee of a stable firm, 'enough' money, consumption of certain desired products and services (clothes, meals out, cars and so on), a steady romantic attachment and the likelihood of parenthood (2004: 384). This, of course, as Bottoms *et al.* acknowledge, is only one form of one dream – doubtless there are other dreams which draw their precise configuration from cultural, ethnic, class and other considerations. The concern expressed by Bottoms *et al.*, and echoed by ourselves, is whether, amongst all the changes experienced by UK society, these dreams are still achievable for any one, and particularly those people with convictions. We shall return to this topic and these concerns throughout the course of this book.

'Rethinking what works with offenders'[5]

The book is a follow-up to the study published as Farrall (2002), which reported on the findings of no less than three waves of interviews with the sample members. The book focused on the motivation for desisting, the impact of probation supervision and the influence of social contexts. One of the most consistent findings of the literature on the termination of criminal careers concerns the successful resolution of obstacles to reform by the would-be desister. The men and women who have successfully made the transition away from crime frequently refer to the stigma of their pasts, problems getting work, giving up alcohol dependency, disassociating from criminal friends, poor financial circumstances and a host of other obstacles which stood between them and 'reform'. For example, Rex's (1999) probation-based sample, Burnett's (1992) prison-based sample, Cusson and Pinsonneault's (1986) and Dale's (1976) samples drawn from outside of the criminal justice system, and Maruna's (1997) sample of published autobiographies of desistance all reported that 'obstacles', 'impediments' or 'road-blocks' were common features of the desistance process.

The 199 probationers interviewed as part of the first three sweeps of fieldwork were no different in this respect. Over 50 per cent (101) stated that they faced at least one such obstacle when they were first interviewed (at the start of their orders). Their probation officers were even more downbeat in their assessments: all but 18 officers said that their probationer faced an obstacle (Table 1.1).

Table 1.1: Identified obstacles to desistance: probationers' and officers' reports*

Category	Probationers		Officers	
	N	%	N	%
No obstacles expected	98	49	18	9
Friends and family	29	15	74	37
Financial reasons	17	9	13	7
Drugs and alcohol	37	19	74	37
Social problems	13	6	54	27
Personal characteristics	18	10	60	30
Other responses	8	4	32	16
Total obstacles	122	100	307	100

* Multiple responses possible.

Of the 101 probationers who said that they faced one or more obstacles, their own use of substances (drugs and alcohol) was the most commonly cited (19 per cent), closely followed by their friends and family (15 per cent). Other obstacles were less frequently mentioned. Overall, few probationers cited social problems (such as their employment and housing situations) as obstacles to desistance, despite the well documented evidence that social factors play a large part in offending careers (e.g. Smith *et al.*, 1991; Farrington, 1997). Only one in 10 probationers regarded any of their own personal attributes as obstacles.

Unlike those whom they supervised, nine out of 10 probation officers said that the probationer faced at least one obstacle (Table 1.1). Several officers thought that friends and/or family along with drugs and alcohol were likely to be obstacles (37 per cent). Officers also reported more obstacles relating to social problems, in particular the probationer's employment situation, than did probationers. Interestingly, there were few citations of cognitive-behavioural obstacles (such as poor thinking skills or anger management), suggesting that these were either not features of the current sample's problems or not features which were readily identified by probation officers.

Operationalizing desistance

Whilst relatively straightforward to define (see above), desistance is harder to operationalize. Operationalizing desistance poses a particular problem as it is essentially an issue of 'absence' rather than of 'presence'. That is to say, that an individual is classified as a desister not on the basis of *having* a particular characteristic, but rather because of the *continued absence* of this characteristic over a period of time. This peculiarity has already been discussed by Shadd Maruna:

> Desistance is an unusual dependent variable for criminologists because it is *not an event that happens*, but rather the sustained

absence of a certain type of event occurring. As such, desistance does not fit neatly into the linear, billiard-ball models of causality found most acceptable to criminologists.

(1998: 10–11, emphasis added)

Maruna was not alone in his recognition that desistance is not usually 'an event' but more akin to a 'process'. Chief amongst the theorists of desistance are Robert Sampson and John Laub, who provided convincing evidence that desistance was not abrupt but rather a 'gradual movement away from criminal offending' (Laub *et al.*, 1998: 226). Initial operationalizations of desistance were based on assumptions which are now felt to have been rather crude approaches to the topic at hand (Bushway *et al.*, 2001). Regardless of these definitional 'skirmishes', desistance is probably best approached as experienced by many as a process. Of course, there will be *some* people for whom desistance is more like an event – see Cusson and Pinsonneault (1986) for examples of 'shocking events' which led some in their sample to the decision to desist.

With this in mind, the operationalization of desistance employed in Farrall's earlier investigation (and indeed in this book) has placed an emphasis on *gradual processes*. Such an operationalization both better captures the true nature of desisting from offending – in which 'lulls' in offending, temporary resumption of offending and the like are common – and provides a schema in which *reductions* in offence severity or the frequency with which offences were admitted to could be interpreted as indications of the *emergence* of desistance. An important feature of this schema is that it allows for changes in offending *trajectories* that indicate a shift in patterns of offending towards desistance to be charted. This entailed careful examinations of each probationer's reports of all of their offending at each interview: the outline of the offence(s) committed, the amount of offences reported and the nature and severity of the offences.

Farrall (2002) found that, relative to those who had not overcome the obstacles that they faced, those who had overcome their obstacles appeared more likely to have at least started to desist from involvement in crime (Table 1.2).

Table 1.2: Desistance or persistence by obstacles (probationers' reports)*

	Faced no obstacles N %	Obstacles were resolved N %	Obstacles not resolved N %	Total N %
Desisters	62 (82)	27 (69)	20 (51)	109 (71)
Persisters	14 (18)	12 (31)	19 (49)	45 (29)
Total	76 (100)	39 (100)	39 (100)	154 (100)

* Virtually identical results were obtained when probation officers' reports of whether obstacles had been resolved or not were cross-tabulated against desistance and persistence.

What were the 'motors' which drove obstacle resolution? Was this the result of the good work of probation officers? Was it due to the motivation of some probationers to avoid further trouble? Or was it due to some other factors, or combination of factors? It was these sorts of questions to which the project sought answers. Because the aim of the project was to develop an understanding of the processes involved in influencing these outcomes, rather than just the correlates of these outcomes (Pawson and Tilley, 1997), it was not enough to employ 'black box' approaches to these sorts of outcomes. The keys used to 'open' the 'black box' of probation required a reliance upon both quantitative and qualitative data sources, together with an emphasis on locating probation supervision in wider social and personal contexts.

Supervision and the work of probation officers

The most logical starting point for the enquiries into what 'drove' the resolution of obstacles was the work of probation officers. During the interviews, both probationers and probation officers were asked, for each of the obstacles originally identified, what each of them had done to address the specific needs of the probationer with regard to the obstacles at hand. These reports, when analysed, suggested that very few of the modes of intervention employed by probation officers were related to whether the obstacle had been resolved. This implied that few particular modes of intervention were any more likely to be effective than any *other mode* and that virtually all modes were ineffective in combating the obstacles. Similarly, none of the reports of the probationers' actions were significantly associated with the 'successful' resolution of obstacles either. However, officers who reported that the probationer had *not* been motivated to address the obstacle were also significantly more likely to report that the obstacles had *not* been resolved ($p< = .000$). In other words, from the officers' and probationers' accounts of their own work and the actions of the other, it would appear that no particular modes of intervention were more effective than any other in helping probationers to overcome the obstacles they faced. Similar analyses were undertaken, this time controlling for the extent to which officers and probationers appeared to have worked together. Again these analyses suggested that the extent to which officers and probationers had worked together was not related to the resolution of obstacles.

Motivation and the orientation of individual probationers

Having the motivation to avoid further offending is perhaps one of the key factors in explaining desistance. Shover (1983), Shover and Thompson (1992), West (1978), Pezzin (1995), Moffitt (1993) and Sommers *et al.* (1994) have all pointed to a range of factors that motivated the offenders in their samples to desist. These included: the desire to avoid negative consequences (such as death or serious injury); realizing that legitimate financial gains outweigh criminal gains; wanting to 'lead a quieter life'; and embarking upon a committed personal relationship. Burnett (1992, 1994) suggested that those ex-prisoners who reported that they *wanted* to stop offending and, importantly, felt they were *able* to stop offending were more likely to desist than those who said they were unsure if they wanted to stop offending:

> ... more of those who desisted stated unequivocally at both the pre-release [from prison] and the post-release [interview] that they wanted to desist.
>
> (Burnett, 1992: 66)

In the original study, both probationers and officers were asked if the probationer wanted to stop offending and if they would be able to do so. The following responses indicated that there were three groups of probationers:

- Some 110 probationers said that they wanted to stop offending and felt that they would be able to stop offending *and* their officers agreed with these assessments (referred to as the 'Confident').
- The second group (n = 46) of probationers said that they wanted to and felt able to stop offending, but their officers did *not* support this assessment – they felt that the probationer did not want to desist, was unable to desist, or both. These cases were referred to as the 'Optimistic'.
- The 'Pessimistic' (the remaining group of probationers, n = 43) said that they did not want to stop, would be unable to stop, or both. In some cases, officers supported their assessments, but in others they did not.

These groups of probationers, on further inspection, were found to have subtly different criminal pasts, as summarized in Table 1.3.

Table 1.3: Criminal histories at commencement of supervision

Average for each group	Confidents	Optimists	Pessimists	All
Age at start of order (years)	25	25	26	25
Age at first conviction (years)	20	19	17	19
Previous convictions (N)	6	11	19	10
Previous prob. orders (N)	0.5	0.6	2.4	0.9
Previous custody (N)	0.6	2.4	2.3	1.3
OGRS (%)	53	61	68	58
Total	110	46	43	199

While there was little difference in their age at the *start* of the orders, the Pessimists were younger when *first convicted* (being on average 17 years old) compared to the Confident (on average 20 years old) or the Optimists (aged on average 19 years when first convicted). Consequently, the average length of their criminal careers varied: Confidents had the shortest careers at five years, Optimists' average career length was six years and the Pessimists had by far the longest, with an average nine-year criminal career. There were substantial differences in the average number of convictions recorded against each group: the Confident were the least frequently convicted (averaging six convictions each), with the Optimistic the next most convicted (averaging 11 convictions each) and the Pessimistic the most convicted (averaging 19 convictions each). Their average number of previous probation orders also differed: the Confident and Optimistic had had little experience of either, whilst the Pessimistic had had more experience. When previous custodial sentences were considered, the Confident can be seen to have had very little experience, unlike either the Optimistic or the Pessimistic.

To what extent was motivation a factor in the frequency with which probationers faced obstacles and overcame them? Analyses like those described immediately above were repeated, this time controlling for motivation. These analyses suggested that there were few differences in the *nature* of the obstacles that probationers faced, but that there were differences in the rates with which each faced obstacles and resolved these. This is represented diagrammatically in Figure 1.1.

A model of desistance started to emerge from the analyses. Solving obstacles *was* related to desistance (Table 1.2), but it would appear that the mode of probation intervention was *not* associated with resolving obstacles (see above). Motivation, however, *does* appear to influence the extent to which obstacles were both faced and overcome. These relationships are presented diagrammatically in Figure 1.1, which charts the progress of each of the three groups of probationers towards desistance.[6]

Fewer of the Confident (40 per cent) faced obstacles than either of the other groups, whilst almost five out of 10 Optimists and eight out of 10 of the Pessimists faced one or more obstacles. Of the few Pessimists who faced no obstacles, 67 per cent desisted. However, 64 per cent of those Pessimists who faced an obstacle but *overcame* it desisted, whilst even fewer – only 31 per cent – of those Pessimists who faced an obstacle but did *not* overcome it desisted. For the Optimists and Pessimists, solving obstacles was particularly strongly related to desistance: of the six Optimists who overcame the obstacle they faced, all but one desisted. On the other hand, of the 11 who did not overcome the obstacle they faced, five desisted and five did not (one was lost during the follow-up). Desistance rates were highest amongst those groups that faced no obstacles and lowest (with one exception – the Confident) amongst those who faced obstacles but did not overcome them. This suggests that overcoming obstacles is successively more important for each group. Most of the Confident desisted regardless of their resolving their obstacles. However, 64 per cent of the Pessimists who resolved their obstacles desisted, compared to 36 per cent of those who did not.

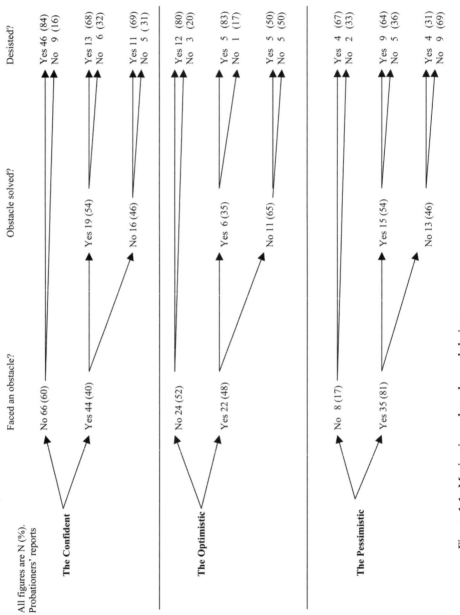

Figure 1.1: Motivation, obstacles and desistance: a summary

Social and personal circumstances

To the above model, a further dimension was introduced – that of social and personal circumstances. Qualitative data suggested that positive life changes were associated with changes in employment and family relationships. As probationers gained work, were reunited with family members or developed attachments to new partners or children, so they refrained from behaviours likely to result in offending – drug use, excessive drinking, 'aimless hanging around' or general aggressiveness. Further quantitative data, again not presented herein, suggested that those probationers who took the lead in addressing the employment and family-related obstacles they faced (itself indicative of possessing the motivation to confront and resolve problems) were also those most likely to have solved such obstacles by the time the order had been completed.

These analyses, taken together, suggest that the outcome of probation supervision (i.e. resolving obstacles to desistance) is the result of a series of interactions between motivation and social and personal contexts. Gaining employment would, from the descriptions of probation officers and probationers, appear to have brought about dramatic changes in the lives of the probationers. Similarly, families of formation appear to have acted as a motivating influence on probationers' desires to desist, whilst families of origin appear to have offered an avenue of support in achieving this change (see Farrall, 2004, for an extended discussion of these points).

When the role of probation supervision in helping probationers to achieve these changes was considered, the themes established earlier re-emerged. That is, while officers would appear to have identified appropriate obstacles and taken what they considered to be appropriate steps to tackle these obstacles, and while most of the obstacles identified *were* indeed resolved by the end of the order, this appears more often to have been the result of the probationer's own actions and their own circumstances rather than a result of the actions of the officer (see also Crow, 1996: 60).

As such, it was possible to develop further the model of desistance outlined in Figure 1.1. Figure 1.2 introduces to the model the issue of social and personal contexts.[7] The introduction of these contexts, especially the extent to which these circumstances remained stable or either improved or worsened, had the unfortunate effect of reducing cell sizes. However, by including change in social circumstances, the study demonstrated the extent to which some probationers started in a more advantageous position and also the extent to which improvements in social circumstances were related to both the presence of obstacles and the resolution of obstacles.

Consider in Figure 1.2, for example, the Confident who faced no obstacles: of those who were living in good contexts at the start, 79 per cent were still living in good social circumstances at the follow-up. Of the Confidents who did face obstacles, more were living in poor rather than

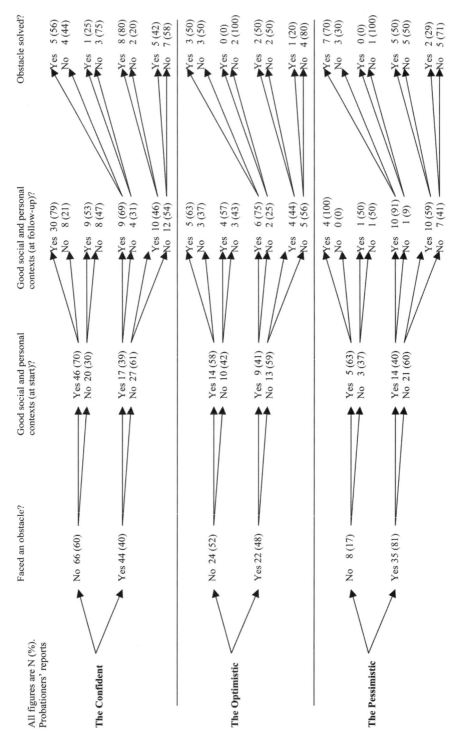

Figure 1.2: Motivation, obstacles and social contexts: probationers' reports

good social circumstances (61 versus 39 per cent). Living in social circumstances which were initially good, but which deteriorated was, irrespective of motivation, more frequently associated with failing to resolve obstacles than with resolving obstacles. For example, of the four Confident probationers who were initially in good social circumstances that worsened, only one resolved the obstacles which he faced. Similarly, of those Confidents who *never* lived in good circumstances, 58 per cent did not overcome the obstacles they faced. However, of the 10 Confidents who were initially in poorer circumstances but which *improved*, eight overcame the obstacles they faced.

The initial starting points (for which motivation is both important and a proxy of other key factors, such as previous criminal histories) are important in understanding both who faced obstacles and who solved their obstacles (see Figure 1.1). Solving obstacles appeared to be especially important for Optimists and Pessimists, whilst for the Confident the resolution of an obstacle was less important. Similarly, changes in social circumstances influenced the extent to which obstacles were resolved. The policy implications which flowed from the earlier study were discussed at length in Farrall (2002). In sum, they were that more attention ought to be given to providing probationers with access to employment and counselling towards becoming better spouses and parents.

Topics for exploration

There are a number of topics that we shall explore during the course of this book. Some of these were 'natural' for any longitudinal study which retraced and reinterviewed previous sample members. As such, we provide an update on various topics, including changes in personal and social circumstances, continued involvement in offending and the longer term impact of probation supervision. Other topics that we shall explore, however, push us into relatively uncharted areas of research. As referred to above, we explore the emotional and existential aspects of desistance in response to the work of Maruna (2001). In addition to this, we explore the relationship between feelings of citizenship and desistance, and the relationship between offending, victimization and desistance.

Changes in personal and social circumstances

The earlier study (Farrall, 2002) made great play of the importance of personal and social circumstances in accounting for desistance. Improvements in circumstances were related to the resolution of obstacles to desistance (see Farrall, 2002: 211). The follow-up therefore explored a number of issues:

- 'Where' were the sample now in terms of their social position and their personal relationships? What role did these have in their desisting or continuing to offend?
- Had previously 'good' circumstances turned sour? If so, why and with what outcome(s)?
- What was the response of sample members to these changes? Did these responses alleviate or exacerbate these issues?

In short, we wished to explore the ways in which our sample's lives had progressed in the four or five years since we had interviewed them previously.

Continuities in involvement in offending and desistance

As one would expect, not all of the probationers managed to avoid offending during the main study (see Table 1.4). Yet even some of those who *did* offend appeared to be desisting. Who has managed to continue to avoid offending? How have they managed this (for example, via the application of insights derived from their supervision)? Similarly, some will have continued to offend. Is this the result of some long term problem (e.g. substance addiction) which was not adequately identified or addressed during probation, or the result of some other set of factors? Whilst official data sources can provide some details, they are unable to get to the heart of the matter and the extent to which 'reform' can be attributed (even in part) to supervision. For example, it could be that desisting probationers have reacted differently to the problems that they have faced.

Table 1.4: Probationers' reports and officers' assessments of desistance

	Probationers		*Officers*	
	No.	%	No.	%
No offending	64	32	105	53
Showing signs of desisting	28	14	33	17
Subtotal: desisting	92	46	138	70
Continued offending (trivial)	20	10	15	8
Continued offending (non-trivial)	18	9	15	8
Continued offending (escalating)	27	14	30	15
Subtotal: continuing	65	33	60	31
Impossible to code*	42	21	1	–
Total	**199**	**100**	**199**	**100**

* Those cases seen only once were deemed impossible to code.

From the initial study, the largest group of probationers were those who, on the basis of their self-reports throughout their orders, were classified as 'showing signs of desisting' or who were reported not to have offended at all whilst on probation. Of all 199 probationers interviewed, 46 per cent fell into these categories on the basis of their self-reports. From the officers' reports, the corresponding figure is even greater: 70 per cent of the sample were classified as either 'showing signs of desisting' or having avoided offending altogether. Amongst other topics, we will explore the extent to which 'showing signs of desisting' equated to later desistance. Since these two topics (social circumstances and offending behaviours) represent an exercise in 'where are they now? studies', we marry them together as Chapter 2.

The longer term impact of probation supervision

As the original study was as much a study of the outcomes of probation supervision as it was of why people desisted, it is important for us to reflect, via the experiences of our sample members, on the longer term impacts on their lives and offending careers. At the time of their previous interviews, few of the probationers felt that they had gained much from their periods of supervision that would be of help in avoiding offending. Is this still the case, or have the probationers now started to see the longer term benefits of probation? Have they been able to apply some of what they learnt in order to avoid further offending? Do they now see their time on probation in a different light? We know precious little about the longer term impacts of probation supervision. What was the role of other sentences, especially imprisonment, in achieving desistance? For example, were particular strategies for achieving desistance successful? For these reasons, we devote Chapter 3 and an Intermezzo on the effects of imprisonment to a consideration of these issues.

The existential aspects of desistance

In addition to the above, we aim to explore the existential aspects of desistance from crime (Chapter 4). In this respect, we will chart the changes in how an individual sees themselves as they desist from crime. Such an exploration will throw further light on the challenges which desisters routinely have to face in reconstructing themselves as 'normal' people in the eyes of those around them.

The emotional aspects of desistance

As noted above, Maruna's focus on the 'internal' changes associated with desistance contrasted with much of the work on desistance, which has outlined 'external' factors in desistance. In this book, we attempt to explore in greater detail the 'internal' world of the desister via a greater consideration of what it 'feels like' to have desisted. For example, does the move towards the cessation of offending entail a different emotional process? We report on our explorations of the emotional aspects of desistance and the processes that are associated with it in Chapter 5.

Citizenship and desistance

In recent years, criminologists have become increasingly interested in the extent to which concepts such as citizenship are able to inform debates about crime and offending. We therefore explore (in Chapter 6) the extent to which the ex-probationers have become 'active' members of society. That is to say, the extent to which they are: working in legitimate fields of employment which allow them to contribute to taxation, national insurance and pension schemes; caring for others (children, other family members, other members of society); and engaged in the processes which will allow them to contribute to important society-wide decisions (e.g. voter registration). More importantly, we argue, we explore the extent to which desisters share the *values* of liberal democracies.

The relationship between offending, victimization and desistance

Building upon Farrall and Maltby (2003), who found high rates of victimization amongst sample members, we again explore the victimization of this group of offenders/desisters. Because the earlier analyses relied upon data gathered during the second sweep of interviewing, it was not possible to analyse victimization in terms of desistance. Chapter 7 specifically considers a number of intriguing questions thrown up by the close relationship between victimization and offending: to what extent does victimization reduce as offending reduces? What is the role of victimization in desistance? (Does it aid desistance, hinder desistance or have no impact upon it?)

We end with one further chapter and a methodological appendix. Chapter 8 considers the wider processes of structuration that underpin much of our previous discussions. It ends with some pointers towards policy matters and future research areas. We close with a discussion of the methodology which we employed to retrace and reinterview sample members.

Notes

1 In the USA these included the Philadelphia Birth Cohort in the late 1950s, the National Survey of Youth and Youth in Transition Survey in the 1960s and the National Youth Survey in the mid-1970s, whilst in the UK the Cambridge Study in Delinquent Development started in the early 1960s.
2 There is also, of course, the issue of domestic violence, which clearly calls into question the observed association between partnership and desistance. For a

discussion of findings relating to desistance from domestic violence, see Fagan (1989); Feld and Straus (1989, 1990); Tolman *et al.*, (1996); Quigley and Leonard (1996).

3 Farrall (2002: 28, fn 6) expands on this point.

4 This refers to the suggestion that the relationship between marriage and desistance might be the result of ex- and non-offenders being more attractive marriage partners than active offenders, thus desistance proceeds marriage, rather than marriage preceding desistance.

5 This section reviews and draws from Farrall (2002), specifically pp. 73–5, 86–7, 99, 102–3, 108–9 and 164–7. Readers already familiar with the study may wish to skip this section.

6 For those who faced more than one obstacle, the overall extent to which all of the obstacles they faced was used to determine whether they were counted as having their 'obstacle solved'. For cases which had equal numbers of obstacles solved or unsolved, the outcome of the main obstacle was used.

7 These measures were summations of the social and personal circumstances which probationers reported were 'problems'. Those with three or more problematic circumstances were classified as not having good contexts.

Further reading

Ezell, M. E. and Cohen, L. E. (2004) *Desisting From Crime*, Oxford University Press, Oxford.

Farrall, S. (2002) *Rethinking What Works With Offenders*, Willan Publishing, Cullompton, Devon.

Graham, J. and Bowling, B. (1995) *Young People and Crime*, HMSO, London.

Maruna, S. (2001) *Making Good: How Ex-Convicts Reform and Rebuild Their Lives*, American Psychological Association Books, Washington DC.

Shover, N. (1985) *Aging Criminals*, Sage, Beverley Hills.

Worrall, A. & Hoy, C. (2005) *Punishment in the Community*, 2nd edn, Willan Publishing, Cullompton, Devon.

chapter two

Life after probation: offending and the development of social and personal contexts

Offending trajectories
Social and personal circumstances
Obstacles to desistance: long term outcomes
Summary

> ...there's a lot changed since then...
>
> (Al, fourth sweep interview)

Whilst several studies have considered the lives of men and women immediately after they have been released from prison, few studies have considered in-depth the social and personal lives of those men and women who have completed probation supervision. Typically, ex-prisoners face numerous problems immediately after release and during the years which follow (e.g. Eaton, 1993) – but what of ex-probationers?

We last interviewed the bulk of our sample members in 1999. Therefore, by the time that we interviewed them again in late 2003 and early to mid-2004, it had been five years since they had last been interviewed. This chapter reviews that period of time and assesses the extent to which in terms of their offending they 'stayed stopped' or continued to offend. In this general overview, we also consider one of the repeated concerns of the earlier phase of the research – obstacles to desistance.

Offending trajectories

One of the key issues to address is the extent to which those people classified as desisters in the earlier phase of the study had remained out of trouble in the five years since. If they had returned to their previous behaviour and re-embarked upon episodes of offending, then the conclusions of the earlier report on this cohort (Farrall, 2002) would need to be carefully re-examined. Similarly, if those previously classified as persisters had started to desist, we would need to account for changes in their patterns of offending. Let us commence by describing the offending trajectories of our sample when interviewed for this book (sweep four, Table 2.1). As noted in Chapter 1, the current study employed a similar operationalization to that used by Farrall (2002), and confirmed as reliable by Farrall (2005). As can be seen from Table 2.1, the vast majority of our sample were showing signs of desisting (57 per cent), with a further 14 per cent reporting no offending since the previous interview.

Table 2.1: Offending trajectories at sweep four

Classification	*Probationers*	
	%	N
No offending	14	7
Showing signs of desisting	57	29
Continued offending (trivial)	4	2
Continued offending (non-trivial)	12	6
Continued offending (escalating)	14	7
Total		51

Two cases had continued trivial offending (such as minor episodes of shoplifting) and a further six had continued non-trivial offending (such as commercial burglaries and robberies). Only seven reported that their offending had escalated in the five years since they were last interviewed. Table 2.2 reports on each sample member's status at the end of the previous phase of research (desister or persister) and their status for the time since that assessment was made.

Table 2.2: Offending trajectories over time

		Status at end of sweep three		
		Desister	*Persister*	
Status at sweep four	Desister	24 (52)	11 (24)	35 (76)
	Persister	5 (10)	6 (13)	11 (24)
	Total	29 (62)	17 (37)	46 (100)

All figures are N (%).

Not everyone interviewed at sweep four was seen sufficiently during sweeps one to three to enable a classification of their offending trajectory to be made during the earlier phase of the research, hence Table 2.2 reports on only 46 cases. Nevertheless, one can see that of the 29 respondents classified as desisters at the end of sweep three, the majority (24, some 83 per cent) were again classified as desisters. However, eleven of the 17 respondents classified as persisters at the end of sweep three had managed to start to desist by the time of the fourth sweep interview. In the main, therefore, respondents' offending trajectories remained consistent between sweeps three and four (some 30, 65 per cent of the sample, did not alter their classification).

Why did those cases that changed their offending trajectories do so? Let us look first at the 11 cases previously assessed as persisters who had stopped offending or at the very least started to show signs of desisting. No less than seven said that they had stopped offending because of the influence of a new partner or the adoption of the role of 'father'. Ben, for example, clearly put his reform down to family life:

AC: So what stopped you [offending]?

Ben: Just, me girlfriend, my little kiddie ... er ... knowing that I just don't want to get back into trouble with a criminal record, I want to rebuild my life. I'm 29 and I need to, you know, grow up.

AC: So you said that your girlfriend and your kiddie helped?

Ben: Yeah.

AC: In what way?

Ben: Well, just to make me a bit happier. Er, you know, I keep out of trouble basically for them as well. You know? So they want to make a go of it, I do want, you know, I want a good job, and I want some qualifications and I want a, ... you know, [to] settle down.

AC: Settle down?

Ben: Yeah. Definitely. But I have changed a lot though. I am a lot better than I used to be. You know? I mean I didn't have feelings for any people, you know, when I were younger, cos [I was] rebelling against everyone and getting into trouble. So I just, you know, didn't have no respect for anyone or owt.

Ben went on to describe how he managed to put his reliance upon heroin behind him:

AC: So can you talk us through how you managed to stop using heroin?

Ben: Well, basically I just broke away from everyone I were getting into trouble with, settled down with me girlfriend. I've been with girlfriend for seven years now. Er ... I just grew up a bit, you know what I mean, [I] thought 'it's not really life, can't keep doing this', you know what I mean? Getting into bother, going to prison, going to court, it's no good. Plus every time I were getting fined and penalties all the time and I couldn't always afford to pay them and I think that's what causes people to go out bloody pinching sometimes.

Other ex-drug users referred to the fact that they had developed a religious faith that had both turned them away from crime and acted as a mechanism for maintaining their motivation when times were difficult. Sally-Anne was one such case; in this extract she discusses the experiences of 'reaching rock bottom':

AC: Why do you think that was this time [that you stopped]?
Sally-Anne: I think I was just ready to sort it out. For me, do you know what I mean? I'd reached rock bottom again and again and again and again. And it was like I was always fighting the drugs, it was, you know, I could get clean but I couldn't stay clean. I could clean up for a season, but I'd always go back to it. I'd always go back to drugs or you know. It was like a magnet to me, do you know what I mean? Yeah, I think maybe this time, I mean I was 27 when I went [to the rehab unit], and I wanted, I just wanted off, I was suicidal at the time. It was just a nightmare, I was a real mess. And I decided, you know, for me that I wanted to do it, you know. And I stayed longer than ... I mean the first time I went to rehab, my parents, my mum put me in there, I was under pressure to be there, I didn't want to be there. It was three months. I mean, you can't change like ... I'd used heroin for eight years by this time when I went there. But I'd been abusing substances since the age of thirteen. There was a progression, do you know what I mean? I didn't just start with heroin. I smoked dope, then took ecstasy, cocaine, speed, just progressed from there. And for me, instead of it being just a social thing, some people can go out to night-clubs, pop pills, smoke some dope, get up and do a regular job. But for me it was always, I was always the potential addict if you see what I mean. I'd use more than everybody else. I'd have to be in control of my intake of drugs; I couldn't rely on anybody else getting it for me. So for me it was always worse than anybody else. Do you know what I mean? And like there was a big progression to getting there. So to think that you can go into a rehab for three months and undo fourteen years of abuse, was crazy and that's what I thought, that's what my mum, that's what my family and that's what everybody thought. 'I'll put her in a rehab for three months, bom, bom, bom. She'll speak with some doctors, get some counselling and then she'll be fine.' But it goes a lot deeper than that.

When discussing her faith, she said:

> It's just having something else to believe in, other than yourself. When you look at how powerless I was over drugs, the fact that I tried to control it and tried to stop it in my own strength time and time again and failed. And then it was when I finally, you know, surrendered it to something else other than myself, was I able to deal with it. Do you know what I mean? It's like you're trying to fight, like you're trying to do it on your own. The first introduction to the programme that you do is surrender, powerless you admit ... and then you surrender. So first for you to admit that you're powerless over your drugs, that you can't control it as much as you try, try to cut it down, try going on Methadone, try to substitute one for another. You know, give up the street drugs, try to take the recreational drugs that have been prescribed off the doctor. No matter how I tried to control it, I was completely powerless over it. And you look at the unmanageability, the fact that your life is a complete mess basically. And then surrender the fact that you need to surrender it to something other than yourself, in order to be able to deal with it. So for me as a, I'm Christian, so there's always been something there, as a little girl I can remember attending like church, from Sunday school, things like that. Yeah, and always believed, always believed in Jesus anyway, but didn't really follow anything through with that. I can remember when I was little, thinking, believing in God and things like that. And then when I went back down there, because it was a Christian centre, it worked for me, because I already had faith, kind of thing, yeah.

For others, the realization – after years of the uncertainty that resulted from unemployment and a lack of a sense of purpose – that they now 'had a future' was enough for them to reorient their lives. Al said:

> Knowing that I've actually got a career for myself and now I know I can get anywhere as a [...]. I can go into any [...] and get a job as a [...]. I can, I've had head [...] jobs or I've had jobs off everyone what I'd die for you know what I mean?

More troubling, of course, were those cases previously rated as desisters but who had not managed to avoid further trouble (n = 5). What did these cases say were the reasons for their return to crime? With only five cases to draw upon, it is hard to make any firm statements. However, they either seemed to deny that they had actually harmed anyone in any way and/or appeared to have unrealistic goals for their futures. For example, Will denied that the Section 18 wounding for which he had been found guilty was anything to worry about:

> AC: So why would you say you haven't been able to stop offending since we saw you last?

Will: Need the money pure and simple. Maybe I'm being a
        hypocrite. I don't know. You need money. You need money.
AC: But the Section 18 wasn't to do with money.
Will: I'm not bothered about that.
AC: How do you feel about that now?
Will: I don't think about it.

Will went on to describe what he thought would help him to stop
offending:

AC: Is there anyone or anything that is going to help you stop
        offending?
Will: Give me a job.
AC: Okay. Any job?
Will: Anything, that pays £500 a week. I won't work for nothing
        less than £500 a week.
AC: You need £500 a week?
Will: Yep.
AC: Why?
Will: Because that's the going rate now, £100–£110 a day labour.
AC: So it would need to be £500 a week?
Will: Which is the normal rate for labouring on a building site.

Others, in this case Bernard – who had assaulted his partner, several police
officers and several other people – said:

AC: You were also asked last time, the last time we interviewed
            you, you were asked, you know, are you able to stop
            offending? And you said yes to that. How would you
            answer that question now?
Bernard: I have, I have.
AC: You already have?
Bernard: What I call offending is not this, I ain't offended. In their
            eyes I broke the law, that's not right mate, you don't know
            the whole … If you was there you wouldn't think I had
            offend because I didn't. If anything I stuck up for myself,
            do you know what I mean, through the police and that …
            Maybe I offended with the other things but on the slightest
            fucking thing it was all blew out of proportion, because it's
            me then they were 'yeah, yeah you've done blah, blah …'
            and they fucking milk it and I get hammered for it. But it
            wasn't all that.

In summary, then, it appeared that recent desisters pointed to the range of
factors already identified by numerous other studies (see Farrall, 2002;
Maruna and Immarigeon, 2004). Meanwhile, those who had recently
offended again appeared to either be unaware of the impact of their
offending (or in denial of it) or were leading lifestyles which did not help

to steer them away from crime. Many of the once-desisting who had started to reoffend appeared either to have problematic relationships with their partners and ex-partners or not to have regular partners. Their employment appeared to be somewhat 'patchy' too (see also Farrall, 2002: 183–92).

And what of the six cases identified at the end of sweep three as being persisters and who had continued to offend? Three of them claimed that they had stopped offending, and they seemed to think little of their offending (which consisted of commercial burglaries, possession of offensive weapons, missing court appearances as well as a range of other offences). Three of the six were also either in prison serving sentences or on licence from prison. Two referred to being either 'addicted' to shoplifting or enjoying burglaries. In short, their claims to have desisted appeared somewhat weak in the light of their actual behaviours. As desistance and the experiences associated with it are the main focus of this book, we reserve further comment on the desisters until future chapters afford the space to discuss these topics in detail. However, we report here that those people with employment (either full time or part time) were more likely to have stopped offending than those without employment (p = .014). Furthermore, of those with employment, a partner and children (15 people in all), 14 (93 per cent) had stopped offending. Of those who did not have all of these aspects of the 'English Dream' (Bottoms *et al.*, 2004), fewer (67 per cent) had desisted. It would appear therefore that the 'package of adulthood' (employment, a stable relationship and children) is associated at some level with desistance.

Social and personal circumstances

The earlier phase of the research suggested that social and personal contexts played a large part in whether people stopped offending or not. It seems fitting, therefore, that we continue our exploration with a consideration of our respondents' lives and an assessment of how these have progressed since they were last interviewed. At each sweep of interviewing, respondents were asked to provide a description of a number of key aspects of their lives (family, accommodation, employment, substance use and so on) and to give an assessment of whether each was or was not 'a problem'. The average number of problems at sweep one was 2.6, falling to 1.9 at sweep two and 1.5 at sweep three. In short, over time problems were resolved (although, as reported in Farrall (2002), this was not often due to the direct intervention of probation officers). The 51 men and women who we interviewed at the fourth sweep appeared to exhibit a similar trend. Their average number of problems at sweep one was 2.8, falling to 1.9 and 1.7 at successive sweeps. However, at sweep four, their average rose dramatically to 2.6. Further analyses suggested (see Table

2.3) that this sudden reversal of fortunes was due largely to the persisters experiencing a high number of such problems. As can be seen from Table 2.3, whilst desisters and persisters interviewed at sweep four did not differ much in terms of the problems at sweeps one, two or three, at sweep four there was a marked divergence.

Table 2.3: Social problems over time

Interview sweep	Group	No.	Mean	Std dev	Sig
One	Desisters	38	2.68	1.802	NS
	Persisters	13	3.31	1.888	
Two	Desisters	32	1.84	1.417	NS
	Persisters	10	2.30	2.263	
Three	Desisters	29	1.72	1.222	NS
	Persisters	7	2.00	2.000	
Four	Desisters	35	1.97	2.007	**
	Persisters	13	4.38	3.176	

NS = not significant. * = $p < .05$, ** = $p = < .01$.

Persisters at sweep four identified on average well over four problems each, whilst for desisters this figure was lower, at just under two problems. This confirms the findings of the earlier phase of the research (in particular, Farrall, 2002: 207–12), highlighting the role of good social contexts in the desistance process. Interestingly (in the light of the finding that the desisters had on average just under two problems), the previous study took the definition of greater than two problematic social contexts as equating to having a 'poor' social context (Farrall, 2002: 228–9). Social factors therefore appear to be key to understanding offending trajectories.

Obstacles to desistance: long term outcomes

Obstacles to desistance – those things which might make it hard for the respondent to stop offending – were a constant theme of the earlier phase of the research. Probationers and their officers were both asked at each interview to nominate up to four obstacles which the former faced and were then asked what they were planning to do to solve these. At each of the follow-up interviews (i.e. sweep two and three interviews), they were then reminded of the obstacles they had identified and were asked about what they had done to address these and what the eventual outcome had been (for a report on the findings of the previous phase of research on this topic, see Farrall, 2002: 73–169). During the sweep four interviews, we followed up *all* of the obstacles that our respondents had identified at any point during their previous interviews. In all, there were 22 respondents who identified between them some 36 obstacles. These ranged from drug addiction to homelessness and getting on badly with one's family. Table 2.4 reports on the relationship between solving obstacles and desisting.

Table 2.4: Obstacles by desistance

	No obstacles faced	Obstacles solved (or improved)	Obstacles unsolved
Desister	19 (68)	14 (88)	4 (67)
Persister	9 (32)	2 (13)	2 (33)
Total	28 (100)	16 (100)	6 (100)

All figures are N (%).

As one can see, those people who had faced no obstacles had, in the main, desisted by the time of the sweep four interviews. Of the 28 people who had not faced any obstacles, 19 (68 per cent) were desisters. Where problems had been faced and solved, again the trend was towards desistance. There were only six cases where obstacles had not been resolved, making trends hard to disentangle with any reliability. In order to breathe more life into these findings, let us examine a few of the individuals who had or had not resolved the obstacles which they had faced. Lucy, a persister who had not resolved the two obstacles that she faced (being addicted to shoplifting and depression), said of the first of these:

> Going into town is still difficult. Still difficult to avoid it. I only go into town if I have to. You know, I can't go into town with my children. When they want clothes, I have to send them on their own. Because I'll pinch everything for them, do you know what I mean? I just avoid it. It is, it's like being, imagine you was a witch and you could perform magic, but you have been told to use it sparingly. It's a bit being like that. If I went into town, I'd use the magic, so it's best to stay away 'cos I have to use it sparingly.

Ben, who we met briefly above, faced two obstacles: returning to heroin use and slipping back into his old lifestyle. He successfully overcame both of them and desisted:

> AC: The last time we asked you if there was anything that might make it hard for you to stay out of trouble. And you said 'drugs, the chance that you'd slip back into using harder drugs', and also 'changing lifestyle', that you would go back to your old lifestyle if you didn't have something to keep you occupied, a job to keep you busy. What's the situation with these two difficulties now? Firstly with the drug use?
>
> Ben: No, I've got no trouble with drugs and I've got no problem with . . ., just employment really, you know? I need to keep in mainstream employment, you know, steady employment. But I've no problem with drugs, I don't feel tempted to use

drugs. I did do a few years back, you know, I were tempted to go back on heroin, but now I just look ..., looking back on it you don't want to go the way I used to be. I used to be scruffy, stupid and I just don't want to go back to where I used to be.

AC: Right.

Ben: Definitely not.

AC: So what's changed from last time?

Ben: As I say, I've got on with my life a bit, grown up a bit. Kept a job down, you know, I've always tried and kept a job down, I mean, then I couldn't work.

AC: Sure, but there's been times when you've been out of work?

Ben: Well yeah, but like I said, I've got my family to support me, you know ... 'cos they know I'm not on drugs. And they're there to help me.

Similarly, Paul, who had faced two obstacles (his friends, who used drugs, and his brother, who also used drugs, which led to his worrying that he may return to drug use himself), talked us through how his life had moved on in the past five years:

AC: At the last interview we asked you, you know, if there might be anything or anyone that might make it hard for you to stay out of trouble, and you said, you gave us two examples, you said, firstly your friends' influence.

Paul: Yeah. A lot, a lot of my friends do commit crimes. I mean it's not through their choice, it's, it's through ... like the drugs they do. I mean ... but I've been careful this time to, like I say, I've took meself out of that situation, so no, there's no way on this earth am I committing crime.

AC: Okay. What's, what's changed you from last time?

Paul: What's changed?

AC: With, with regard to, to the, the previous difficulty of your friends' influence?

Paul: Before, when I first did, the interview with, with that lass, I were young. But now I'm a lot older and a lot wiser. And I tend to think more before I act. In them days I used to act before I thought. It'd be like, I'd do summat and then it'd be like, 'Oh shit, I shouldn't ha' done that.' But now it's, well look, 'I won't do this and then I can't get into trouble.' So I've took, I've ... I've took meself out of that, out of that situation so there's, there's no way am I getting back into trouble. Like I say there's, there's just this possession [charge, of cannabis] and then that's it, it's all done and dusted. I can have a nice quiet life then.

AC: Okay. You also said your brother's influence as well, 'cos your brother was getting into trouble at the time?

> Paul: Yeah.
>
> AC: What's the situation regarding that now?
>
> Paul: Oh I ain't seen him in over five or six years, he lives in [...]. I've seen him once, what it was, before, why I said that is because me brother, he was in a lotta debt and a lot o' bad people were gonna do him in. And basically I did summat that I shouldn't ha' done just to bail him out. I pinched somebody's credit card and after that, no, no more. I did it as a one off, just because he were me brother. Yeah, fair enough, I like see him now and again but, you know, it's, it's one o' those things. But now he's not on the scene, no, there's, probably zero per cent chance of me reoffending.

Regardless of the details of each individual's circumstances, it does seem clear that not facing obstacles or solving those that were encountered was indeed related to desistance.

Summary

This chapter, we hope, has achieved two things. We have given an update – albeit somewhat cursory – on the lives of the 51 people we retraced and interviewed. It appeared that most of those people we identified as desisters at the end of the first phase of the research had gone on to avoid further offending or to continue their travel towards complete desistance. Desistance appeared to be played out in front of a background of more stable social circumstances. Persisters, it appeared, had more social problems than those who we had classified as desisters. Finally, resolving obstacles also appeared to be associated with desistance. The last of these two observations echoes the earlier phase of the research. For the moment, we have not explored in anything more than the most rudimentary manner the processes associated with desistance, nor the wider social contexts in which desistance emerged. This is deliberate and brings us to our second aim. Since this book devotes its remaining chapters to a discussion of desistance and the contexts that surround it, we hope to have whetted the reader's appetite for the rest of our contribution.

Further reading

Burnett, R. (2002) 'To Reoffend or to Not Reoffend? The Ambivalence of Offenders', in S. Maruna and R. Immarigeon (eds) *After Crime and Punishment*, Willan Publishing, Cullumpton, Devon.

Farrall, S. (2002) *Rethinking What Works With Offenders*, Willan Publishing, Cullompton, Devon.

McCulloch, T. (2005) Probation, Social Context and Desistance: Retracing the Relationship, *Probation Journal*, 51(2): 8–22.

Rex, S. (1999) Desistance from Offending: Experiences of Probation, *Howard Journal of Criminal Justice*, 38(4): 366–83.

chapter three

The longer term impact of probation supervision

'Advise, assist, befriend' or 'talk to, chivvy along, raise the consciousness of'?
Probation: leaving good roads open
Offender management or rehabilitating offenders?
Discussion

If I was in a club and I was pissed up I wouldn't think 'ummm, I'd better not get in a fight 'cos I'm on probation and I don't want to go to prison no more'. It wouldn't enter my head.

(Anthony, sweep two interview)

It [anger management] was a load of bollocks. You sit there with eight or nine other kiddies, just discussing stupid things, like I just said. Like stupid questions. Or like, they give you a form, you go there every week, they give you a form, you have to tick the box 'how you feel today' and all that kind of thing, 'what's wound you up that week' and stuff like that. Stupid things really.

(Anthony, sweep three interview)

I wouldn't say anything's [that probation officer said] stuck with me but it chipped away if you know what I mean, it sort of chips away at you. [Right]. They don't stick in your head but occasionally you'll get that little thought of 'maybe I shouldn't do this because I've . . .'. And maybe he told me about this or . . . you know what I mean? It chips away at you I suppose.

(Anthony, sweep four interview)

There have been very few studies of the long term impacts of probation interventions. Furthermore, most of those that have taken a longer term perspective usually involve solely analysing conviction data. For example,

Oldfield's (1996) study of Kent probation orders reported on a five year follow-up of conviction records. Whilst these sorts of studies have undoubtedly helped further knowledge about patterns of offending, they are limited in a number of ways. The most obvious of these is that since the data analyses are almost always purely quantitative investigations of official records (e.g. Smith and Akers, 1993), little insight is gained into the subjective changes experienced by the probationers. Because most studies of this nature deem 'failure' to have occurred following a conviction, often the most one gains from the longer term perspective that such studies allow is a greater percentage of reconvicted sample members. In addition, it is, of course, almost impossible to detect a 'probation effect' after such a long time. We believe that this study, therefore, is able to throw more light upon the longer term impacts of probation.

As others have argued (McNeill, 2003: 160), research on desistance, when viewed from the perspective of those interested in the work of the criminal justice system, 'underlies … a commitment to seeking the views of people involved in offending … as important as … quantifiable indicators of success'. In short, whilst quantitative data sources are helpful (indeed, absolutely required) to trace the *contours* of the impacts of various interventions, it is only from qualitative data sources that we are able to open the 'black box' of such interventions in order to uncover *how* and *why* such interventions work (or do not work). For McNeill, following Farrall (2002), this entails that we learn more from probationers (and ex-probationers) about what helped to persuade them to desist and which forms of support they found most helpful. In this chapter, we seek to throw further light on these processes.

Although there have been few studies of the long term impacts of probation supervision, one such study is that by Leibrich (1993) of 48 men and women who had remained conviction-free for around three years after completing a period of probation supervision. Because Leibrich's sample had all finished their sentences some years previously and because her methodology was qualitative, she provides one of the best examples of an investigation into the long term impacts of probation supervision. Leibrich found that few probationers spontaneously mentioned the impact of probation when describing why they had stopped offending (1993: 172). Of those who did say that they had taken something from probation, most referred to 'the chance to talk things through' as being the main aspect of their supervision which they had valued. Asking difficult questions and painting various scenarios appeared to be what mattered for some of Leibrich's sample (1993: 182–4). These aspects of supervision appeared, at least for some individuals, to result in a 'different outlook' on life (1993: 188). However, even when this did occur, it would appear to be buried underneath a host of other changes in an individual's life and social circumstances (see the case of Marcus in Leibrich, 1993:188–9). Thus, and as found in the previous fieldwork from this study (Farrall, 2002), probation supervision did not help many people directly to stop offending, and even when it did it was often the least significant of a number of factors.

At the time of their previous interviews, few of the probationers in the current sample felt that they had gained much from their periods of supervision that would be of help in avoiding offending (Farrall, 2002). It was therefore with some trepidation that we asked our sample of ex-probationers about what they felt they had gained from probation five years on. During our follow-up interviews, we sought to assess if they still felt that probation had offered them little, or if some of them had started to see the longer term benefits of probation. Had they been able to apply some of what they learnt in order to avoid further offending, for example? Did they now see their time on probation in a different light from their earlier interviews? Have once 'solved' obstacles re-emerged to blight their lives still further, or have they managed to respond to such obstacles in ways that will be of benefit to them? We asked sample members whether they had learnt anything as a result of being on probation, and if so, what; how it had helped them stay out of trouble; whether their officer had done anything that helped them to stay out of trouble; and whether they got helpful advice from their officer.

The overwhelming response from the vast majority of ex-probationers was that probation had been of little help. It was still far from clear that probation had been of assistance in helping very many of our sample to stop offending. Take, for example, Michael, originally sentenced to 24 months' probation for burglary. His first conviction was when he was 13 years old (he was 28 at the start of the previous research project and was approaching his mid-30s when interviewed for this book) and he had several convictions for burglary, violence, theft and handling, and drug offences. When asked if he had learnt anything from his previous time on probation, he said:

> Yeah back in that time I did learn that, you know, I was . . . I thought I learnt a lot of things at that time but I didn't, I didn't use none of it you know? I really had a good probation officer and she was a good probation officer, and that, she was fair but firm. And if I wanted to use, if I would have thought about it and used what they had on offer I could have done a lot. I could have got a lot from it but as I say, it was like, I was trying to play in two different playgrounds. I want to try and be on the straight and narrow, be an honest person and do the best I can, go to work and just lead a . . . what do they say, 'a normal life' sort of thing. And, err, I don't know, you know, as I said I was going to probation talking all the talk with them but going out playing in the drug playground. So it wasn't working, the two of them weren't working for me. So I didn't use what they had on offer. I'd go there just to sit down and say 'yeah I'm okay, this is what I'm doing, that's what I'm doing'. As I got more and more into drug use I had more responsibilities to turn up to. I did learn from there, though,

if you try, if you're willing to try, they're willing to help. I did learn that because my probation officer at the time helped me, you know she did all she could to get me in a treatment place, treatment centre and done a lot for me.

However, the probationer had been in and out of prison ever since and was, at the time of interview, on licence having just served a three year prison sentence for committing a commercial burglary in order to feed his drug habit. Others, and the example below is typical of many respondents' sentiments, implied that there was actually very little that probation could do given the limited contact and the social and economic problems that they faced:

AC: Did you learn anything as a result of being on probation?

Geoff: No, not really no, not at all. It was just an inconvenience going up there. And in the end of it just to sign in and sign out, you just have to do it.

AC: I mean has it helped you to stay out of trouble since?

Geoff: No, not all. It wouldn't matter. Probation's not, it's not a good purpose. I don't know ... I don't know what you think about probation. I really don't know ... Because all you do is just go and speak to them. Alright, they'd listen to what you were saying, there's nothing they can do about it and nothing they really help you about. And it's, after a period of time, after a couple of visits it's 'come in', 'hello', 'goodbye' and 'see you'. And it's just, it's a period you have to do and then you go up for two weeks, every two weeks and then ... It's a waste of time.

In some cases one can surmise that, despite the bellicose rants against probation, it may well have been the probationer themselves who had limited the impact of the supervision by their failure to engage honestly with their officers. Take Jamie, for example:

Well if you were to look on the probation side of things, probation has not helped me at all, has not made me a better person. I've made myself to be the more mature person. Probation couldn't help a stranded cat in an alleyway to be honest with you, if that's what you want, truthful views. Probation is a load of crap as far as I see it. I mean, probation couldn't steer me in no direction, the only reason I've worked and got myself out of trouble is because I wanted to get out of trouble, not because probation has told me to. I mean, you can go like to probation, you can tell them any old, you can tell them any old load of shit, they don't know, they can't tell you how to do your life or they don't even try, they don't, can't help you out. You come into probation you tell them lies, they just accept it, it's on the sheet and off you go, like a big conveyor belt.

All of these quotes resonate with the findings of the earlier phase of the research (see Farrall, 2002, most obviously). These observations are hardly ground breaking then: probation officers do not have much time with which to work and often they face vast impediments in affecting change. However, we also found more encouraging evidence of a longer term impact that was distinctly positive. In the following section, we outline some of these various impacts before examining, in depth and via the use of two case studies, how these longer term impacts emerge and what their effects are.

'Advise, assist, befriend' or 'talk to, chivvy along, raise the consciousness of'?

During its early years as a religious mission in the nineteenth century, and later as a professional institution based on social work values, the phrase 'advice, assist, befriend' was seen as the service's mission statement, encompassing its approach to dealing with those placed under its supervision. The theory was that personalized one-on-one contact could enable officers to build trusting personal relationships with their 'clients'. By using skills such as listening, negotiation, persuasion and motivation, and by leading by example, officers helped to reform offenders into useful citizens. Whether conducted in a framework of evangelism or non-judgemental counselling, the belief was that self-development and transformation using this method was achievable. However, the efficacy of this rehabilitative approach was challenged in the 1970s when research indicated that 'nothing worked'. Studies repeatedly concluded that there was no evidence that any intervention or 'treatment' by the probation service had any significant effect on reducing recidivism (Martinson, 1974; Davies, 1969; Folkard et al., 1976). With its very purpose questioned, probation sought to justify its existence by redefining itself as 'an alternative to custody' and later, following the 1991 Criminal Justice Act, as a punishment in its own right. While the 'What Works' agenda has meant the revival of rehabilitation, the preferred setting has been groupwork rather than one-to-one supervision and has focused specifically on challenging offending behaviour through cognitive-behavioural techniques. As Worrall writes, 'changing the whole personality through insight-giving, or changing the offender's environment through welfare assistance are no longer seen as feasible goals' (1997: 101). Nevertheless, despite probation's 'crisis of confidence' and the increase in groupwork, the break with the past should not be overestimated, as one-to-one work is still the main basis of probation supervision for those sentenced to it (Morgan, 2003). Furthermore, both probation officers and probationers regard the purpose of probation as one of rehabilitation and help (Farrall, 2002; Rex: 1999). Thus the idea that probation officers ought to befriend their caseloads, and that in so doing they might be able to advise and assist them in ways which ultimately prove to be rehabilitative, is presently a deeply unfashionable one. Despite this, we have to admit that all of the examples that we came across of probation having a longer term impact could broadly be grouped under the heading of advising, assisting and befriending. We use slightly different terminology, reflecting what we see as being the important long term impacts. Thus we discuss these impacts in terms of helping with practical issues and raising the consciousness and awareness of probationers.

Practical help, possibly one of the aspects of probation supervision which probationers most want, appeared to revolve around gaining employment (see also Sandra in Chapter 4) or accommodation. The following probationer, Meera, despite her previous experiences of employment, still found contact with her probation office useful when re-establishing her career:

> ...when I applied for this job I actually had to phone up the probation office because I wasn't sure whether I had to declare [my conviction] or not. And even though I couldn't speak to [my officer] I spoke to somebody else there and he was really helpful and advised me what I could do, what I couldn't do and sent me out the relevant information. And I thought to myself never in a million years under normal circumstances would I have ever thought of phoning up a probation office.

The same woman said that she had also found probation supportive in terms of encouraging her and helping her to build up her motivation more generally. She had originally been given a probation order after she had stolen several thousand pounds from her employer in order to pay off debts she had accrued. Although this was her only conviction, it is clear from the four interviews that we have conducted with her that she had been very depressed both in the run-up to her offending and in the months immediately afterwards. The following quotes all come from her fourth interview with us:

> One thing probation period does re-emphasize to you is that you're not on your own and there are people there who are prepared to help you, who are prepared to listen, who are prepared to help you correct your life to make you a better person.

> I learnt a lot about myself. I learnt to open up more, become a stronger person, become more confident within myself. And I realized that I wasn't on my own, that I could handle things on a day-to-day basis and if I needed the help it was there.

> Well with the bankruptcy [my PO] actually got me the Citizens Advice Bureau address, when I wanted to do courses, etc. she actually found out about courses and things that I could go for, places that I

could apply for jobs if I wanted to go out to work. So she did a lot for me.

As well as helping people to tackle legal issues around re-entering the labour market, some of our probationers pointed to the help that they received from their probation officers:

> ...like I say, they went outta their way to get me a bail hostel which did help me. Err, the fact that, err, I had to go and see them every couple of weeks or whatever it was, certainly made me think about why I was going to see them, what I had done. It just started kind of kept things in the air for me, what I was doing, what I had been doing to get myself into that situation. You know?
>
> (Andrew)

For others, like Gary, sometimes the advice given referred directly to avoiding those circumstances in which he might offend again. Gary had been found guilty of arson whilst drunk, his drinking triggered by the death of a close relative. As well as trying to work with him on his drinking, according to Gary, his officer had also imparted strategies for his avoiding further trouble. In the following extract, it appears to be advice that if he does smoke, he ought not to carry only a lighter with him in case he is picked up by the police:

> AC: If you could just reflect for a minute, did your probation officer say anything or do anything for you specifically that has helped you to stay out of trouble in the future?
>
> Gary: Well there is one thing she did say to me was because by the time I'd come out [of prison] I'd started smoking and she said, 'If you're going to start smoking always carry a lighter and a pack of fags with you. So if you're walking around the street on your own and you've got a lighter on you they are going to think, what are you up to?' I mean not being nasty but when I take the dogs for a walk even now I do it, I always leave me fags on the table so when I'm walking down the park and there's something going on in the park I won't have anything on me to do it. That's the first thing I did and then I can't get accused of doing it. So that's what I do.

However, amongst the most interesting responses which we encountered when asking our respondents about what they had taken away from probation were those which suggested that, over time, something which their officer had said had struck a chord with them. In this respect, probation supervision acts as a 'consciousness-raising' exercise in which the feelings and perceptions of other people are made clear to the probationer. Bernard reported that he particularly found the style of his supervision helpful in this respect. When asked why, he said:

Well it just makes you see the bigger picture doesn't it? Do you know what I mean? Even if you take half of what he said and think about it for ten seconds, even if it lasts in your head for ten seconds, you know what I mean, ten seconds later the world's different, innit? Do you know what I mean? If you're fucking angry and someone's given you shit or something, ten seconds, if you took out ten seconds and just relaxed, fucking hell, you'd see it as a different picture wouldn't you? I know I would because for the first ten seconds I want to kill the cunt. Do you know what I mean? And then after that, it's totally different.

In some cases, it would appear, this process might take a long time to unfold. Here is another interviewee describing how he had experienced this:

AC: Talking about probation again, looking back, do you feel that your experience of probation has had any effect on the way that you've approached problems?

Frank: Now I do yeah. I mean what [first officer] and [later officer] taught me, ... basically like how to address problems. Basically, instead of going about it the wrong way.

AC: You said now you do, as in like you *now* recognize that, did you feel the same way when you were on probation?

Frank: Getting there, getting there but it didn't quite register to be honest with you.

AC: Could you just tell us a bit more what you mean?

Frank: Well it's, at first, when I first started going to probation I thought 'oh I've got to go and sit in a room and talk to people I don't know' and towards the end of it ... it's like a ... really, half way through it, I really started to get into it. And from the information, like, what they know, like how to go about things, not like what they know, I mean you should know that yourself but it's like how to be helped to address different situations. Yeah I found that quite helpful.

Whilst Frank had some trouble in fully articulating what it was he had learnt, one certainly gets the feeling that somewhere along the route he started to realize that probation was not just a tax on his time and that there was valuable information to be gained. This even appears to have been the case with the following case, Anthony, who was one of the most ardent critics of probation interviewed as part of the previous study (see Farrall, 2002: 131–41, and the quotes at the start of this chapter). However, when interviewed for a fourth time, even he suggested that over time he had started to see things differently:

Anthony: ... if you've got a problem and that, like you owed some rent and you're going to get kicked out of your lodgings or something, or the council are on your back because you fucking owe them rent or whatever, then [probation] make a phone call for you and get them on, sort it out for you and give you a bit of leeway so you can go and sort it out yourself. Do you know what I mean? And tell you how to sort it out. That's just an example, there's lots of other examples, like, if you tell him you're tempted to go and fucking do something and he'll talk to you about, 'don't do this because of this'. Do you know what I mean? Whether you listen is a different thing, innit?

SF: Yeah sure. That sounds like the kind of practical advice, you know, helping you sort out your rent. I mean was there, kind of, I mean, had there been times in that five years since I saw you last when maybe something that [officer] said or something that he tried to...?

Anthony: Like stuck with me?

SF: Yeah, stuck with you and kind of helped in some kind of way?

Anthony: Err, no not really. I wouldn't say 'no'. I wouldn't say 'yeah'. [Officer's] alright but he's done, like I said he speaks to you down at your level and you know what I mean. Everything he tells you is nothing you haven't heard before really from your parents and everyone else you know. I wouldn't say anything's stuck with me but it chipped away if you know what I mean, it sort of chips away at you.

SF: Right.

Anthony: They don't stick in your head but occasionally you'll get that little thought of 'maybe I shouldn't do this because I've ...'. And maybe he told me about this or ... you know what I mean? It chips away at you I suppose.

SF: How do you mean it sort of chips away at you?

Anthony: Well, you're hard faced ain't you? When you're like, like I was sort of thing. I'm not making out I was some big gangster because I ain't, I ain't a gangster I'm just like millions of other kiddies that go out drinking, or went out drinking a pint and smoking a bit of puff you know or whatever. When I was doing that kind of thing you get hard faced towards people. Do you know what I mean? You're like 'fuck everybody else', you do what you want to do. But when you start getting, when [officer] was chatting to you, after not a first few weeks but after a while you start to think about like your victims in the situation. Because it was that kid he was on about to me, I suppose I had a bit. I acted a bit irrationally there you know what I mean, I fucking head-butted him when I shouldn't have done.[1] I should have probably just given

> him a bit of verbal. And he's sort of like saying to me what
> if you didn't head-butt him, what if you didn't do that?
> And when you're in a pub and you're about to have a fight
> with someone suddenly you get that 'what if?', like that
> 'what if?' comes into your head. And I don't think that
> would have been there if I didn't, if someone wouldn't
> have put it there.
>
> SF: Right.
> Anthony: I'd say [officer] put it there, probation put it there because
>   they make you think a bit which chips away at your sort
>   of like hard-face exterior if you know what I mean.
> SF: Right, yeah.
> Anthony: It does eventually, it does. Because obviously once some-
>   one talks to you it goes in but it stays in but do you choose
>   to remember it when you feel like it or not.

Anthony and his progress on probation have already been described several times (see Farrall, 2002: 131–41; Farrall and Maltby, 2003: 43–6; Farrall, 2003: 258–66, Gadd and Farrall, 2004: 136–9). In short, Anthony had been on probation for 12 months and failed to successfully complete his probation order, ending it in breach for failure to attend an anger management programme. He had had problems with his accommodation and had discussed his hostile feelings towards his ex-wife. During his period on probation, he continued to become involved in fights with other men in and around the pubs in the town in which he lived. These fights were often the result of drunken 'spats' on weekend nights. While the issues surrounding his accommodation and his feelings about his ex-wife formed some of the 'practical' issues which he and his officer had discussed, it is clear that some of what he discussed with his officer also affected the way in which he approached violence (witness his statement, 'when you're in a pub and you're about to have a fight with someone suddenly you get that "what if?", like that "what if?" comes into your head. And I don't think that would have been there if I didn't, if someone wouldn't have put it there'). True, in his other accounts Anthony emphasized the role of his current partner in this withdrawal from violent behaviour (see Farrall, 2002, especially).

However, it would appear that, several years down the line, Anthony was prepared to admit that as well as gaining practical help from his officer, he also found that his 'hard facedness' was 'chipped away' by some of what his officer had said to him. This 'consciousness-raising', at least in the cases where we have observed it to have occurred, appeared to take several years to unfold fully. Empathy, introspection and self-awareness do not occur overnight. These issues we now take up, in order to explore them in more detail, via the first of our two cases studies.

Mark

Mark was 24 years old when he started his 12 month probation order after being found guilty of burglary. He had to attend a group programme called 'A Fresh Beginning' as part of his order. This was not his first offence; his previous convictions included one for burglary, one for theft and handling, one other indictable offence and three summary offences. For all of his previous convictions, he had been given community service and, as such, he had no direct experience of either probation or prison.

Mark's offence had been committed after he had been out clubbing with some friends. He and another friend left early. On their way home, they walked past a shop with a hole in the window. They knew that the alarm would have been shut off and so they smashed the glass and climbed in (at which point Mark's friend ran off). Mark picked up shirts and hid them further along the road, then he went back to meet his mates and told them about it. They persuaded him to go back and pick up the goods. When he did so the police were waiting and he was arrested.

At the time of his offence, Mark was living with his parents and at the first interview presented the picture of a 'normal lad' who liked to go out clubbing and drinking. During this first interview he also said that he was impulsive and 'easily tempted', and therefore was unsure if he would be able to avoid committing the same or a similar type of offence again. However, he did say that he wanted to stop offending and felt that he was able to do so. As events turned out, Mark did not report any further offences, something corroborated by his officer, the Offenders Index and Police National Computer. Mark also said that he found probation 'boring' and that he 'switched off' during meetings with his officer. He also said that he felt that his officer was trying to 'brainwash' him as she had told him that he was racist. His officer did, in fact, mention his views and described him as 'deeply racist', attributing this to the views of his parents. She also said that he drank a lot at the weekends and was regularly taking speed, ecstasy and cocaine. She added that very little work with him seemed to have any impact and that he did not like being challenged.

Six months later, at the second wave of interviewing, we caught up with Mark again. He had been breached for failing to attend three appointments and described the order as being a 'pain in the arse'. When asked if he had learnt anything on probation he said, 'I know I haven't got any more chances,' adding that he was fed up with offending as he did not want to go to prison and that 'looking over your shoulder' was too much 'aggro'. He also reported that he was using drugs far less than he had done previously and had given up smoking cannabis completely. When asked who or what would help stop him offending he said 'me' – previously he had said 'nothing'. When asked how likely he felt it was that he would offend again he chose the 'high unlikely' category of responses offered to him. Previously he had said that he was 'easily tempted'. At this stage his officer was also interviewed. She confirmed that he had been breached and added that he was not engaging with the order and that he 'hadn't got much out of it'. However, she felt the breach had scared him and he was now attending as required. During their sessions they had discussed decision-making and Mark's officer reported that she had continued to challenge his racism. She said that Mark was open to looking at his views and was starting to question some of them. At around this time he started to become friends with someone who was black, but this aspect of his life is never referred to again. During this time he continued to live with his parents and to work for the same company, gaining promotion to a more senior position in the firm where he worked.

Around six months later, after the end of his order, Mark was interviewed again. He reported that the group programme he had been on was 'crap' as they 'just kept trying to make you feel guilty'. He added that the group had only served to teach him new ways of offending. Mark was around 26 years old now and reported that he was less into music and clubbing than he had been previously and that this had had the effect of reducing his alcohol intake. He also reported that he had not taken any drugs since the previous interview. When asked why he had stopped offending he said that he was frightened of a further court sentence and that he had 'grown out' of that phase of his life. When asked how likely he felt it was that he would offend again he chose the 'extremely unlikely' category of responses offered to him. He continued to live with his parents and was still working for the same employer. He had also started to see more of his girlfriend. His officer said that, looking back on the order as a whole, Mark had found it useful and developed more confidence, but, she felt, had not taken a lot of it in. The group programme he had been on, 'A Fresh Beginning', had helped Mark learn about victim awareness, she said. Overall, she felt that he had settled down a bit more and was not going out as much as he used to. She also added that he was not as racist as he used to be. She added that probation had acted as a turning point for Mark and that he had learnt that he had too much to lose by offending.

We saw Mark again in early 2004, some five or so years after he had finished his probation order. By this time Mark's life had moved on considerably. He was the father of two children (one aged four years and the other six months) and was planning to marry their mother later in the year. Mark had met his partner-to-be whilst out one night and her subsequent pregnancy was unplanned. At this point they decided to 'settle down' and buy a house together. These changes had come as a shock, as Mark got used to having to provide for his family (he was the only earner when we interviewed him). At around this time, Mark also decided to 'knock on the head' clubbing, 'binge drinking' and taking drugs. He saw far less of his friends than he used to and now spent most of his time looking after his children. Mark had continued to work, but had changed jobs in order to help look after his growing family and was now, although employed, very much his 'own boss'. Mark also said that he had 'got a bit older, a bit wiser'.

These changes are not all that different from the sorts of changes which many other members of this sample reported at around the same points in their lives (see Farrall, 2002, Chapter 9), or indeed which other studies of why people stop offending have found (see Chapter 1 above). Our aim in this case study, however, is to highlight probation work, and especially those aspects of it that Mark appears to have gained from. We are not arguing that all of the above counts for nil when accounting for Mark's desistance; rather we are trying to learn more about what he took from probation and why this might have been the case. One of our initial questions asked respondents to think about whether (and how) they are different to when they started probation:

AC: Would you say you're any different from when you started that probation order?

Mark: I would. From when I started to when I finished the probation?

AC: Yeah.

Mark: Err yes, yes. It's quite interesting some of the things that they sort of talk to you about. You don't always think you know everything you do there is always someone on the receiving end. You know there's always a victim. No matter what it is, there is always a victim and like you don't think about that. You know what I mean? From the slightest little thing to what people do, you know from like stealing the wheel off their car to like you know someone being murdered, there's always a victim you know.

AC: Yeah.

Mark: And it's like you don't think about things like that.

AC: Was that something you talked to your probation officer about?

Mark: Yeah, yeah and the Fresh Beginning thing.

So Mark would appear to have gained an insight into the effects of his offending on other people, namely 'victims'. Initially, as his comments during the first of our interviews with him attest, he was less than enthusiastic about probation. During our fourth interview with him, he reflected on this:

Probably think 'oh yeah, yeah, I'll just do this probation and you know get it out of the way and . . .'. But the more, the longer you have to dwell over things, you know, the more you sort of think 'oh well, yeah, you know, there's victims and all this, they're all suffering for what you've done and . . .'. You know, you sort of cause a lot of damage and then when you get to court you know you may get a little fine, a little bit of commentation [sic] but they, the people you've done, whatever, to they've still suffered, you know.

So, like Anthony and several of the cases we refer to above, Mark initially viewed probation supervision, and especially group programmes, as a bit of an 'easy ride'. A strong sense of his feeling that 'if I can hide at the back of the group and keep my head down it'll all be over' comes across from Mark's interviews. However, like Anthony and Frank (above), Mark slowly started to realize that there was more to his supervision than just attending and speaking nicely to his officer – a fact probably underlined by his being breached. How does all of this relate to Mark's wider life? Again, his final interview sheds more light on this:

AC: And all the changes [fatherhood, impending marriage, home-making and employment], what was the role of probation in helping you with that?

Mark: Err, I think it does get you started. You know sort of, you know you only sort of spend an hour, I think it's about an hour a week it was to start with. It sort of definitely, it starts you thinking you know?

AC: Yeah.

Mark: That sort of made you sort of start thinking, you know, what you should be doing and, you know, what, how things should be working for you. Obviously if you don't, if you don't do it you sort of, you know, you say you're going to do your community service and you won't, you know, you might still have a laugh there, you think that you have to muck about here and . . .

AC: Yeah.

Mark: With going to probation and you start mucking around or whatever, you know you're going to be straight back in court before you know it.

Despite his claims that probation 'started me thinking', it is hard to get a sense from Mark which things probation helped him with. Although nothing *very* tangible comes forth initially, further questioning suggests some of the ways in which this thinking emerged for Mark:

AC: Can you just describe that process of starting thinking for me? What types of things do you start thinking about?

Mark: Err, the thing is because it's, because you just sit down and it's like one-to-one you just, you do actually sit down and properly think about things, you know? And then, err, then they just sort of start going on to, you know, they sort of give you a few options, you know, just draw out a few options as to where you could be going from there.

AC: Yeah.

Mark: You can either go in a straight line or off [on] the prison one or you know just end up doing nothing at all and ... They're sort of trying to help you sort of a little map, you know sort of try and map your life out. Sort of, you know, say 'start here, we can try and do this from now on'. Yeah, I suppose it does, it does help, yeah.

So the time and space in which to start thinking about the rest of his life and what he wanted from it helped Mark to gain a sense of the things he ought to be doing and provided him with some underlying rationale for making these choices. This all sounds rather vague – and perhaps this is because such processes *are* rather vague. As academics, government officials and so on, we are accustomed to career reviews, appraisals and such like. When these processes work well they offer people a chance to reflect on what they have achieved so far, why they chose the courses of action they have done and what they might wish to do in the future. Goal setting, planning and developing a 'map' (to use Mark's term) are common practice in many firms and a part of middle class life. Mark, on the other hand, having worked in a semi-skilled manual occupation and at the age of 24 and 25 when he was on probation, would probably never previously have encountered a process like this. As vague as appraisals and probation supervision are, on the evidence of the widespread use of the former and Mark's comments on the latter, they appear to 'work'. For Mark, simply the idea of *planning* was probably a novelty, which might explain why so much of what he reports as having learnt from probation is about 'options', the consequences of choices and so on. In some respects the following serves only to confirm this:

AC: Would you say your probation officer helped you to stay out of trouble?

Mark: Yeah, she was ... she was good actually. Yeah she was very good.

AC: Okay, how?

Mark: Err, I suppose at the time, you know what she was going on about was, well it just seemed as though that it weren't much interest. But everyone, the more you think about it, what she was actually just getting to the point, you know. Sort of saying 'right we can either take that road, that road, or that road', you know. Yeah, just sort of try and point, give you a few options, you know. 'At the end of the day you know, it's your choice. I can't, you know, I can't tell you which way to go but it's up to you, you know when you leave here and what you do, it's entirely up to you sort of thing, you know?'

AC: Yeah. And what do you think about that now?

Mark: I suppose, yeah, they're right ain't they? It is up to us, up to individuals what they do.

AC: Okay.

Mark: It just opens your eyes to, err, you know, where you could

go, what you could be doing and, you know make something
... You know, if you say, you know, you've been to college
for five years and it's stupid to waste it, you know, ending up
in prison and things like that, you know.

Earlier, we reported Mark's claim that the only thing he had learnt from
the group programme was how to commit further offences. When seen
during the fourth interview, Mark provided some evidence that this too
had been of rather more help.

Mark: You know, it's surprising once you get older you just think
         about things more, don't you? Not so much you've got more
         time to think about things but you just, before you do any-
         thing you just think, think a bit more about it. Well I suppose
         when you're a bit younger you're a bit 'yeah, yeah, yeah',
         you know, everything's in the fast lane and all in a hurry, you
         know.
AC: Yeah.
Mark: It's like 'oh yeah, do that', 'oh yeah, do this, do that, do this'
         and, you know, you just can't do it anymore.
AC: Why not?
Mark: [Laughs] Well Yeah ... Dunno it's so hard you just, just
         think, you know, just think first. Don't just jump in, think
         first.
AC: So where did this approach come from?
Mark: Probably find it does stem back from the probation. You
         know and this Fresh Beginning thing, just sort of, you know,
         you just think about, you know, as I say the victims and the
         different ways you can go, you know.
AC: Yeah.
Mark: All of that and, yeah, just that at A Fresh Beginning we used
         to sit down there must have been about ten of us and we all
         used to discuss, well, what we've done, or why we was there
         or what we've done and our backgrounds and ... Yeah, you
         just sort of think 'blimey'. Well some of them had been to
         prison two or three times before and then talked about it and
         you think 'oh God, don't fancy none of that'.

The image we now have of Mark's period of supervision is rather different
from the one that he initially painted for us five or so years earlier. Rather
than being the 'boring' one-to-one sessions aimed at brainwashing him, or
the group programme which taught him only further ways to offend, we
now find a rather more thoughtful and relaxed report of a period of his life
which, in many ways, helped to make Mark who he was when interviewed for the most recent time.

George

With George, what we wish to do is to explore how some of what happens in supervision plays out in the 'real world' as desistance is achieved. Previously, with Mark and the snippets of other cases we have cited, we have very much tried to 'hold constant' the probationers' social and personal lives. With George, we wish both to draw upon changes in his life *and* relate this to some of the things which he and his officer discussed. Our basic contention is that George's desistance was greatly aided by the work of his officer, but, like many personal achievements, owed as much to various other factors and downright 'good luck'.

George was 19 years old when he was given probation for 18 months after being found guilty of burglary. He had broken into a school and stole about £20 so that he could buy food (at the time he had no permanent address, but was living in a hostel). He was arrested sometime later by the police who arrived to search his hostel room. During this search they also found cannabis, ecstasy and a stolen mobile phone. At this time he said the following were problems for him: accommodation (he was living in a hostel); employment (he was unemployed); finances (he was living on reduced social security); and his relationship with his family (his mum kicked him out of home when he was 16 years old). He also said that he was finding life a bit boring (due to having nothing to do).

At the time of the first interview he said the following were problems for him: employment (unemployed still); finances (he owed £400 in court fines, £100 to the water company and £100 in rent); and drugs (he admitted that he needed to cut down on his cannabis smoking). He also said that he had a gambling problem, again due to boredom. He went on to describe himself as an impulsive person but said that he valued probation and did not want to 'ruin it'. He identified his debts as something which might make it hard for him to stop offending but said that his officer had helped him sort this out, by phoning his creditors and arranging monthly payments for him. His officer confirmed many of these details and said that the purpose of probation was to 'get him to look at his life'.

The second interviews with George and his officer took place about 11 months later. By this time George had found himself a job. According to his officer, this was as a result of their discussions about how his life needed to change and about how he needed to mature. George painted a slightly different picture, saying that although his Employment, Training and Education (ETE) officer had taken him to the job centre, it was George himself who had found this particular job. He said he had actually wanted (and enjoyed) this job, whereas the previous jobs he had looked at or taken had been only to keep his ETE officer 'off my back'. Whatever the case, George said that he had learnt to respect money and was now in his own flat. This gave him something to work for and was enjoyable as it was a regular income flow (crime, of course, is less reliable in this respect).[2] He had also been able to pay off some of his debts. George also acknowledged that his officer had given him advice about budgeting. He was still smoking dope, but less so now he was working. His officer said that George had tried to engage with their work together and had made progress. She felt that the order had reinforced in George's mind his situation and acted as a reminder to him to stay out of trouble. He was, in her opinion, more aware of his gambling problem. Her work appears to have been aimed at helping George to take responsibility for himself.

At the third interview, things seemed to have turned full circle. George had given up his job, but was planning to look for another. Whilst he said he still enjoyed talking to his officer, he said that it had all become a bit 'obsolete' as time had worn on. His debts were mounting up again and he said that he felt 'like [his] mind is going to blow up just thinking about' his arrears. However, with only a few months of probation left, George could not see much of a role for probation in helping him with his debts. His officer painted a similar picture, saying that George 'couldn't hack working' and adding that he had started to gamble again. However, George had at least managed not to offend during this period.

It was four and half years before we next interviewed George. It was fairly easy to locate George, a trawl of sample members currently on probation with the probation area that had previously supervised him turned up both a new offence (of common assault) and a new contact point. George's offence appeared to have been the result of defending his girlfriend against someone who was trying to attack her. He was on a 200 hours community punishment order with fines and costs of around £1,000. Despite this, George saw himself very much as a non-criminal and portrayed his offence as a one-off which had emerged out of circumstances which were unlikely to reoccur and which stood in isolation from his previous offending. Other than this conviction, his only other offences (committed some years ago it would appear) were smoking cannabis and stealing the occasional car radio.

Since previously interviewed, George had started work (doing jobs he 'enjoyed') and had been in work constantly thereafter. He had also met his partner (Sally) during that time and they had recently had their first child. In words that echo so many men on this subject, when asked to describe the biggest change in his life since previously interviewed, he said:

> ... having a child, meeting my girlfriend, having a child because I've always just been myself. You know, the repercussions on yourself, you, I think a lot of people just go out and don't mind. You know, if you do something wrong and you get punished, well, you've done it to yourself, you know. Now obviously I've got responsibilities with my child and my girlfriend.

This development had come after a period during which George had become 'very annoyed' with his life and during which it sounded as if he had wondered why he was alive. Meeting Sally had also helped George find the motivation which he had previously had to sort out his debts:

> Yeah, [I] started to get in debt again, you know. And it started to become a problem again where I would owe that £300, then £500 owed [to] this and obviously when you're working and that you've got all the bills to pay, council tax, the rent, the electric, and again it was all starting to get a bit hectic. But then when I got with my girlfriend the drive to sort it all out was there, you know, because obviously I needed my flat, needed my child somewhere to live. Got that job, the ability with the money is again dramatic and I paid all my bills off, done up my house. And I couldn't be sitting in a better position.

Thus George had, as suggested by Ford (1996), needed to develop both a sense of meaning and a purpose to his life before he was able to achieve a sense of happiness with his life. What was it amongst all of this that George had learnt from probation? Let us return to the period of his life immediately after he had finished his previous order:

> After probation again it all started to go down hill, you know. I started spending it on fruit-machines and just living life, I weren't thieving, weren't doing anything wrong, certainly weren't in any trouble with the old bill. But it was just cascading down with my flat to the point where I couldn't even be bothered to tidy it up sort of thing. And again as I say before I met my girlfriend and I just had enough of it all, you know, I'd had enough of this life. And I knew that I was sick of this life until I'd meet someone that I care about because that's the only other thing in life. Three things really, get a job, get a place and have a family, you know. They're the three keys in this world, you know, and if you don't go with that then all you're ever going to be is a criminal, drug-user and a bum you know.

However, upon meeting Sally, George refound his enthusiasm for life and started to work at improving his lot.[3] When asked directly whether probation had helped him, George was dismissive of its impact:

> AC: Looking back would you say you've learnt anything as a result of being on that probation order?
>
> George: I have to say 'no' but I don't think that's a fair answer, you know. For me it was just ... I just took the benefit that it was nice to go and see someone and have a chat, you know. I never went to probation and thought 'oh they're going to sort my life out, they're going to take all my troubles and make them go away'. I'd never had any disillusions [sic] to myself that that was going to be the case.

So the 'impact' according to George was that he enjoyed chatting to his officer, but got no real help from her at all. However, from other passages in his interview, one feels that this is somewhat illusory, and that, in fact, he actually had gained rather a lot more from probation:

> But, again, having just meet a nice person and having somewhere different to go on a Saturday, you know, helped took me out of them circles. It did have a positive impact in my life in the way it would take, even for an hour, take me out of my circle, you know, but that would be no good if I didn't have the attitude in myself to get on in life, you know. Even if I didn't have the attitude in myself to get on in life, I would have still enjoyed going and talking to the bird [his officer] but I wouldn't have done anything about it, you know. Whereas if I'd never had received that probation order I'd still be here today, not meaning on this particular order, but I'd still be standing where I'm at in my level position, the job, girlfriend, child, still got my ... you know. I'd still be here because that's the kind of person that I am. I would have got on with it and I would have still ended up here. But everything either makes the journey easier or harder, you know. And I think for having probation two years did make my journey that little bit more easier for numerous reasons, i.e. taking me out of my circle, for like, you know, bits of encouragement, you know, to drive where I was already driving to, you know.

This process of 'making the journey easier' takes on a slightly different light when one thinks back to some of the advice that his officer had tried to instil in him. Advice on budgeting, taking responsibility and the reminder that he needed to address various problems head-on (such as his gambling and his bills) appear to have seeped into George's thinking without him ever realizing it. Take the following, for example:

> AC: The last time we interviewed you, you were asked what aspects of your life might make it harder for you to stay out of trouble. And you said 'financial problems' because you owed a lot of money, and 'accommodation' in case you lost that. And also, you were feeling anxious as well, you were feeling anxious and down because of your financial situation. What's the situation regarding these now?
>
> George: The situation regarding these now that they're no longer a problem. As I've explained earlier on, I managed to, through luck, Lady Luck she always pays some parts of somebody's life, and that was the demolishment [sic] of [his previous home] and the £1,500 [council relocation grant]. That was the very first breather for me, that was when I actually felt the strength inside myself to say, 'Right, you've got this opportunity now to get on top of it all, this is what's getting you down, this is what your problems are, this £1,500 will sort you out.'

These sentiments echo the observations made by Athens (1995: 575; see also Denzin, 1989, and Shibutani, 1961, both cited in Athens, 1995), when discussing how counselling advice assists in processes of change, who writes that 'the solution finally arrived at is transformed through a circuitous process into a personal revelation'. Moreover, and in line with current thinking on why and how people stop offending (see Giordano *et al.*, 2002: 999–1003), George not only wanted to stop but also saw the opportunity to turn chance events (the demolition of the flats he was living in) to his advantage. In this respect, George's current approach to his finances sounds remarkably like some of his earlier statements about what he and his officer used to talk about during supervision (namely respecting money, having something to work for, changing his life, becoming more mature and budgeting):

> So I only look forward you know, and I can only see things forwardly. I can't look back in that sort of way and thinking of myself going back. Now I can see things coming in life, you know, debts and worries and stress, but I feel a hell of a lot more confident about myself to deal with these sort of debts.

And again:

> It was helpful to be able to talk to somebody and sort of get some opinions back and some help back. The lady at probation was very helpful when it come down to my water bills and other types of bills. But I wasn't mentally ready in my head at them times to deal with them sort of problems. Even though I knew they were great problems and I had to deal with them and that, I didn't want to face up to dealing with paying water rates and rent and bills like that.

In short, probation led to George getting a job, which in turn led to him taking greater control of his finances and being able to plan and prepare for bills and so on. In amongst this, as others have argued (Willis, 2003), getting work provided George with the chance to meet and then 'care for' his partner and their child, which appears to have motivated him, along with the residual memories of the advice from his officer, to deal with the responsibilities demanded of him by various other social institutions (creditors and employers being the two most obvious examples). Work also helped him address his gambling:

> I had a fruit-machine addiction, which cost me that's why I was in so much debt. The reason why I had a fruit-machine addiction is boredom, plain and simple.

Working and meeting Sally, along with the eventual additional task of raising a small child, would have put paid to any time during which boredom could set in. In addition, by being able to afford his own place, George was able to avoid some of the people with whom he previously used to offend:

Back in probation times I'd hang around with a lot people my own age, a lot of people older, in big groups or big numbers, which means a lot of people off doing lots of different kind of things. So you can get drawn in to doing other types of stuff if, you know what I mean, say if someone makes their mind, gets a bit rowdy, they're likely to go out and fight, whereas I would go out and steal you know. Back them days I used to hang around with them people. I stopped hanging around with them people, really, when I got my own place you know. It started to pull me out of that circle. Obviously, I'd have my own front door to shut myself in which to me has been the most important thing in my life that I've got, you know. If I didn't have that then I wouldn't know where I'd be today. Because I've got me own place and something to concentrate on – I had my own home, you know, my own front door – I didn't have to go [out]. Before I got my own place I would stay around friends' houses, you know. And they might want to go out thieving, they might to do this, they might want to do that, and because I'm staying there you've got to go with the flow because that's where your head will rest that night. So everything's sort of changed for me is, I've got my own place.

To this extent, George would appear to have gone a long away towards having stopped offending. He was on probation when seen, but both his own testimony and his criminal record suggest that, by and large, his offending career is behind him and that he is moving away from that period of his life both in terms of his attitudes and his own personal circumstances. Bottoms *et al.* (2004: 384) refer to the sorts of goals which many young adults in England call the 'English Dream'. This 'dream', which they see as analogous to the 'American Dream', includes 'a not-too-onerous but safe job as an employee of a stable company, enough money, some consumer luxuries, a steady girlfriend and (possibly) kids'. Indeed, as noted above, George seems to echo these desires:

Three things [in life] really, get a job, get a place and have a family you know. They're the three keys in this world you know and if you don't go with that then all you're ever going to be is a criminal, drug-user and a bum you know.

We hope that we have demonstrated that in achieving these goals, George (and for that matter Mark and Anthony also) has benefited from being on probation. True, this period of probation supervision has not operated outside of the influence of other factors, but it has in some way 'helped them along the road'.

Probation: leaving good roads open

AC: What's the role of probation in helping you with...?

Barry: Keeping me out of prison and keeping me from going down the wrong sort of roads. Leaving the good roads still open instead of just bad roads. Because I find that prison don't do nothing but opens up other doors to other bad ways of life, if that makes sense.

That engagement in crime 'closes down' certain future opportunities is not a new idea (Moffitt, 1993). That probation might leave some future avenues open, and that these might in turn aid desistance, is an obvious but unacknowledged one. We would like to reiterate the observations from the earlier phase of this research (Farrall, 2002): that in and of itself, probation is *not* the main explanatory factor in why people stop offending. Employment and family formation seem much more important motivating factors in this respect. However, probation was able to provide some support to them in helping them to address various problems that they faced and, in so doing, assisted them in their passage of travel towards desistance (by leaving 'good roads open'). We therefore wish to develop one of the original suggestions made by Farrall (2002: 220–2, 2004) and developed by McNeill (2003), namely that of making probation work desistance-focused. As non-practitioners, we find McNeill's proposals more than persuasive. He argues that desistance-focused work needs to be thoroughly *individualized*, as various factors (age, gender, previous offending history, previous personal history and current social circumstances) all blend together in such a way as to make abstract generalized messages inappropriate as the basis of interventions. This is not to say that there is nothing to learn from generalizing from research findings on desistance, but rather than when moving from this body of knowledge to practice, one must move carefully.

Personal maturity, social circumstances and attitudes and motivation are the three features of an offender which McNeill highlights as the basis of desistance-focused interventions (2003: 157, figure 9.1). Working together (cf. Bottoms and McWilliams, 1979: 172–3), McNeill suggests that officers and probationers identify which aspects of the latter's life can be utilized to foster desistance and which might need work to ensure that they do not hinder it. In some cases, all of these factors will be 'pulling together' to steer the probationer towards desistance (i.e. they have the motivation to avoid trouble, they are sufficiently mature and they have an appropriate social network to support law-abiding behaviour). However, such cases will be the minority, and McNeill writes:

...an offender might have secured work and shown some signs of seeking to reconstruct his or her identity through that work, but may seem to lack the personal maturity required to sustain the employment in the meantime. In such a case, the focus of support might be on strategies aimed at accelerating the maturing process [...]. Similarly, an offender might have formed a positive relationship with a supportive partner who discourages offending, but remain wedded to aspects of his or her identity as an offender [...]. In such a case the worker might work with both partners to build on the strengths of the relationship...

(2003: 158)

In this way, probation work would be in a position to work with individuals and, importantly, address their individual needs and problems, whilst not losing sight of wider social and community influences upon individuals' behaviours and actions. Such work would, of course, ideally be prospective and tuned to the contexts in which the individual concerned was located. These ideas are not new – in July 1910 Winston Churchill, during a debate in the House of Commons, called for interventions to be individualized (Churchill, 1910). In many aspects, this individualized programme resonates with the 'strengths-based' approach promoted by (amongst others) Maruna and LeBel (2002). This approach focuses on the positive contribution to society that an individual can make in an attempt to re- or de-label them as a 'bad person'. Encouraging family responsibilities and socially productive work (volunteering and work with and for 'worthy causes') are the cornerstones of such an approach.

Offender management or rehabilitating offenders?

Finally, we wish to comment on the implications that stem from our research for future efforts at evaluating the impacts of probation supervision. The processes by which probation aids desistance are, or at least appear to be, vague. The issue of 'what caused' or even encouraged an individual to behave in a particular way at a particular time has never been easy to ascertain. Trying to achieve an understanding of how a probation officer influenced a probationer to desist is even harder. Key phrases, key moments from supervision and so on somehow get 'lodged' in the minds of probationers and are recalled sometimes long after supervision has ended, creating a slow 'chipping away' of attitudes (see Anthony above). Doubtless maturation is at work here too, but were it not for the key phrase having been delivered, then it would not have been there to have been remembered. The processes of reform are vague and slippery when encountered at an individual level, and these aspects ought to be more widely recognized by both those designing interventions and those evaluating them.

The management of offenders, if it is executed poorly, *could* lead to the outright abandonment of one-to-one supervision. This, it appears from the above, is the source of the 'seeds' which start the process of 'chipping away' at offenders' anti-social beliefs and attitudes. If probationers are seen by numerous individuals, the chances of such seeds being planted and later maturing may be lost for ever. The 'seeds' will probably only be sown in one-to-one supervision and, we feel, are most likely to grow when trust is developed between individual officers and probationers. Advice is more likely to be inwardly digested when it has been tailored to the needs of a specific individual. One-to-one work still seems – to us at any rate – the best way to do this.

This brings us on to another issue regarding the management of offenders: the use of cognitive-behavioural groupwork programmes. Such programmes, designed at a distance by academics and policy-makers, do not leave much room for variations designed to be individualized and hence desistance-focused. Even if they were to be designed to allow for greater flexibility, this still might not provide enough room for intensive desistance-focused work to be undertaken given current resourcing con-straints. Groupwork programmes may offer 'quick fixes', but as others have found (Brown *et al.*, 2004), quick fixes may not be so quick and may only lead to a heightened sense of failure for some. If the feelings reported above by Jamie (who likened probation supervision to 'a big conveyor belt') are anything to go by, groupwork programmes may be hindering the chances for effective supervision work to be undertaken. In addition to the critical voices questioning the use of cognitive behaviouralism (Kendall, 2004; Mair, 2004), it is far from clear that such schemes actually 'work' (see Harper and Chitty, 2005: 77, who report that the evidence in the UK is 'mixed').

It also follows, we feel, that the assessment of probation impacts needs longer term evaluations, allowing for a longer time for probationers to put any learning and so on to use. Follow-ups of short periods of time (by which we mean two years or less) appear to us to be insufficient. Proba-tioners may not have had the time to fully digest and reflect upon what has been said to them; some people need to encounter particular episodes in order for what their officer said to them to become meaningful (e.g. marriage, child-rearing, employment and so on). For this reason, we suggest that longitudinal qualitative research become a key tool in the investigation of probation supervision and that it work alongside cross-sectional and longitudinal quantitative research in this area. There is an assumption that interventions have a shelf-life and that after a certain period of time little impact will be detectable. Our research has suggested that this may be incorrect – in fact, the process may be inverted for some: over time, impacts become stronger.

Notes

1 This refers to the assault which Anthony committed to receive probation in the first place.
2 On this George said, 'I got pissed off walking around early morning in the rain looking for places to burgle and coming home empty-handed.'
3 See Goffman (1963: 119–20) on the practical help partners can provide those individuals coping with stigmas.

Further reading

Burnett, R. (2002) 'To Reoffend or to Not Reoffend? The Ambivalence of Offenders', in S. Maruna and R. Immarigeon (eds) *After Crime and Punishment*, Willan Publishing, Cullumpton, Devon.

Farrall, S. (2002) *Rethinking What Works With Offenders*, Willan Publishing, Cullompton, Devon.

Rex, S. (1999) Desistance from Offending: Experiences of Probation, *Howard Journal of Criminal Justice*, 38(4): 366–83.

McNeill, F. (2003) 'Desistance-Focussed Probation Practice', in W. H. Chui and M. Nellis (eds) *Moving Probation Forward*, Pearson Education, London.

McNeill, F. (2004) Desistance, Rehabilitation and Correctionalism: Developments and Prospects in Scotland, *Howard Journal of Criminal Justice*, 43(4): 420–36.

Intermezzo

The impact of imprisonment

I know not whether laws be right,
Or whether laws be wrong;
All that we know who lie in gaol
Is that the wall is strong;
And that each day like a year,
A year whose days are long.
                    (Oscar Wilde, *The Ballad of Reading Gaol*, 1898)

AC: What was the effect of prison on you?
Jimmy: It fucking devastated me.

Although our study was of probation supervision, many of our sample members served some time in prison for further offences. In this brief sojourn from the main topic of our enquiries, we explore the impact of imprisonment on this sample of men and women and their offending careers.

Prison as a time and place to think?

Some of our sample members reported that being in prison acted as a 'wake up call' and allowed them the time to reflect on their lives and make new plans for the future. Michael, for example, when interviewed for the fourth time, said:

I end up doing another prison sentence, I'd done another, err, what did I do? I'd done a twelve month prison sentence after that twelve month prison sentence. I was out there I think for eighteen months and I was committing offences because I was still using [heroin] but I was unhappy with what I was doing. And then this [current] sentence I got this three years two months I think that was the wake up call that I needed. I think it was at the time where I landed in there, I realized what I was doing to myself. Realized that, err, I was just getting the same results out of drug use and all the results were negative. It was like I was punishing myself and then I took it upon myself to find the support in prison. I thought if I don't change nothing, nothing ain't gonna change. And, I've got older so like as I'm getting older I'm thinking, 'I ain't living no life here, I'm not seeing nothing out there and it's time for me to start doing something about it myself.'

He went on:

That twelve month prison sentence I think that was like it had an impact on my life. It had a sort of positive impact really because I went in there, I got clean in the prison. I got my fitness back up to scratch, you know, it sort of give me a breathing space from all the madness that I was doing and that and it give me somewhere I could really think. Also the impact it had is, where I spent the six month I'd done half of the twelve month and spent the six month on a drug free wing in there. It sort of like made me realize that I am clean and what I've been doing, what I have been doing. It was the start of like the process I'm going through now really because I did get out from there and, err ... I did after, I think a week or so, I started slipping back into using and around the same thing, the same people that I'd left behind and, err ... But the level of using, the level of offending have gone really down and I think that twelve month sentence, the change it had on me is that it brought me to a stage where I would now realize that what I was doing was wrong. I didn't want to be doing it and I'd no need to be doing it but I was sort of still walking that, walking that road.

Whilst this initially sounds like 'good news' and the desires of a man who now wishes to put his past behind him, he had already spent much of his life in prison anyway, as the interview with his former probation officer from the second sweep of interviewing testifies:

I can't [say what has been the biggest change in his life]. I remember seeing him. I saw him once in prison and he asked me this question but from what we were talking about it doesn't look like much has changed. He seems to be going the same way as he has been going before because I know that he has been so many times in prison and he has got so many convictions for burglaries and this [was] his first probation order so the change *should* have been that. But there was no sign of very significant [change] in his personal life.

So, despite his optimistic outlook, on the basis of past events, the time to reflect provided to him by prison will probably be of little or no use. For some, even when prison did act as a 'wake up call', the effects soon wore off, as Tim found:

Tim: You learn to cope. Like when you interviewed me in jail [previously], that were the first time I'd been to prison, that.

> That were a bolt out of ... A real awakening call that one, a real awakening call. I didn't like it at all.

AC: And how did ...?

Tim: But you just get used to it, you ... And now, you know, I quite like jail. I know it's a sad thing to say, but I mean not, I mean, I'm giving you the bare facts about it.

And, in fact, for Tim, over time prison became easier and easier (see also Meisenhelder, 1985):

> You see the more you go to prison, this is how I work it out, the more you go to prison, they're all the same sort of lads that go, if you know what I mean, all the same sort of people that go to prison. So the more you go, the more you get to know 'em. It's like going to school, you know what I mean. The next time you go, you know 'em and get to know their friends. And then next time you go you know them and get to know *their* friends.

This slow accumulation of friends and the habituation to prison life which comes with it means that, for some, prison actually takes on the status of 'a laugh'. Here is a short extract from the fourth interview with Bernard:

AC: So how did you feel about the prison sentence?

Bernard: It didn't bother me. I knew it was coming so I just got it out of the way.

AC: And what was the impact of that on your life?

Bernard: It was a big impact really, pissed me off. [Laughs] I missed my little girl's first birthday by a day. Do you know what I mean?

AC: You didn't get out 'til the day afterwards?

Bernard: The day after yeah. Apart from missing my little girl and my missus, that was it, there was no impact. It didn't bother me being in prison, it was quite funny at some times, do you know what I mean? I enjoyed it sometimes.

AC: In what way did you enjoy it sometimes?

Bernard: Just like when the boys, do you know what I mean? If you're with your friends once you start living with people and you see them everyday, every morning, and every dinner time, every whatever, do you know what I mean? You start having a laugh and that, funny things happen.

As Jose-Kampfner (1995: 120) notes, the acceptance associated with imprisonment (and in the case above, the attempts to extract something positive from the experience – 'a laugh') does not mean that the inmate has become content with prison. Rather they have become *numbed* to it. She writes:

> When the women reach acceptance, they become disinterested in the outside world, even what is happening with their families. An inmate

says: 'There is nothing I can do about this. They forget about you, and you need to do the same in order to go on.'

(Jose-Kampfner, 1995: 119)

The slow existential death described by Jose-Kampfner in her study of women serving over 10 years was not as apparent amongst our sample, many of whom were serving far shorter periods of imprisonment (although one, case 232, did say that being in prison made him 'feel like I was dead'). However, their comments – some of which we reported above – lead us to question the notion that somehow prison time leads to a period of reflection which encourages desistance. Prisons are not monasteries, tucked away on sunny hills in Tuscany or the Pyrenees. Prisons are places were crime is common (O'Donnell and Edgar, 1996a, 1996b) and where people are far from being in a situation in which they can 'kick back' and reflect on their lives so far. They are noisy, 'bustlely' places that many people find 'dehumanizing'. Boredom, not reflection, characterizes many peoples' experiences of imprisonment. We can find only two studies which provide evidence to the claim (Cusson and Pinsonneault, 1986; Cromwell *et al.*, 1991) that prisons are places where offenders reflect on their lives and decide to desist, and both were heavily influenced by the rational choice perspective on offending careers. Far more frequent is the evidence that far from acting as a period during which they consider the crimes they have perpetrated against 'good decent society', prison serves only to increase the likelihood of further offending. As O'Brien (2001: 2) reminds us, imprisonment achieves all of the following for women who are imprisoned – and, we feel, many of these could be extended to include men:

- A loss of custody or access to children, or at best having relationships severed or damaged.
- A loss of the 'web of connections' which reinforces non-criminal values and encourages the adoption of values and knowledge which make offending easier and more likely (see below).
- The loss of accommodation.
- The loss of employment and, therefore, the income which may be used to support a partner and children.
- The acquiring of the stigma of 'ex-prisoner' and the attendant implications which this has for employment.

In the light of these observations, we find it hard to find either the evidence that somehow prison helps people stop offending by giving them 'time out' or why it is that criminologists have done so little to bring an end to this myth. As Meisenhelder reminds us:

... prison is structured, and the staff come to act, on the basis of the inmates past (that is, as one who has committed a crime) or his present (as a prison convict). His future is not granted much significance by the prison's organization.

(1985: 47)

In this respect, prison serves only to *hinder* desistance as it fails to provide a structure in which desistance-focused work is possible.

The lived reality of the impacts of imprisonment

If prison could not provide a 'place to think', what then did it do to those members of our sample unfortunate enough to experience it? Here we focus on four aspects of imprisonment, all of which, we ought to stress, the literature on desistance suggests very much will *not* help people to stop offending.

Loss of partners and families

Although we have to be careful when considering the effects of partnership on those who marry or co-habit with ex-offenders (see Gadd and Farrall, 2004), as a general rule most of the literature on desistance supports the idea that marriage and family formation is associated with desistance. Whether this is due to selection effects or not is the subject of some debate (see Chapter 1 for our position on this, which broadly follows Laub and Sampson (2003) in rejecting the selection argument). Certainly for men, there is no evidence that depriving them of their partners and families will help them to cease offending.[1] Jose-Kampfner (1995: 119) describes the sense of mourning for loved ones which accompanies many women's time in prison. Similar experiences were reported by many of our sample:

> Because since, I mean, when I come into prison, obviously, I was still with Jenny, still living with her. After a couple of months of visits and letters of support she eventually trailed off, wouldn't answer me letters, wouldn't answer the phone.
>
> (Andrew)

> I miss my kid. I wanted a family. I've always wanted – 'cos I have never had a mum and dad there for me – I always wanted to be the dad to my son that my dad wouldn't be to me [...]. As she sees it, she'd rather me not be there at all, than be going in and out of prison every time. My son [is] getting used to me being there, then me not being there, then getting used to seeing me then me not being there. I thought she had a point. He knows who I am now – I talk to him on the phone all the time. Went down there – past few times I got out of prison I just get a travel warrant off the jail.
>
> (Al)

As Shover (1985: 139) notes, for young men time may feel like it is dragging since so much of their prison reverie is devoted to girlfriends, wives and families. O'Brien (2001: 119) reports how the women in her study found the remaking and rebuilding of relationships, especially with mothers or with significant others who they believed could help them move on from their time in prison, particularly frustrating. Andrew again:

> So I've had a lot of trouble dealing with that. My family don't really want to, even still now, I can't really talk to my brothers because obviously even though, even though I knew, err [...], with Jenny maybe that I was, the relationship formed made on, err, drugs, yeah? I was still very much attached to her and, err, I still, I found it quite difficult first of all to deal with the fact that, I was on my own now, you know, no support.

So, for Andrew, the loss of Jenny was compounded by the fact that he was unable to talk to his family about how much he missed her and how 'alone' he felt. Others reported similar problems:

> Because when I was away from like my mum and my girlfriend like, it hurt a lot and then my brother as well like. I didn't really want him to know that I'd gone inside. Like before I went ... when I went in I was telling my mum ... I was still lying and that. I don't know what happened, but when I went in I told my mum that I hadn't gone in. I said that I've gone to do something with [his probation officer], that I had to finish off my community service. I didn't really want her knowing until I came back that I was in jail.
>
> (Case number 026)

Again, following Jose-Kampfner (1995: 118), we note how prisons are not conducive places in which to talk about your emotions. This, coupled with the deprived nature of any contact with family members (which typically takes place in semi-public spaces cramped with other prisoners meeting their visitors), perhaps goes a long way to explaining both why so many families do not survive the imprisonment of one or other of their members and why so many people contemplate suicide in prison:

> Prison, do you know what I mean? If I come back to prison basically I have had that much of it, they could hit me with a heavy sentence if I get nicked for say burglary or ... because that's what my normal trade is. I know I am going to get a big stretch and I don't want to go into it and I'll just top myself.[2] Because I have already contemplated [killing] myself already, do you know what I mean? But I thought, 'It's not worth it.' [...] Took you away from my kid and my missus and it's [the victim's] fault not mine, do you know what I mean? At the end of the day the judge can give me, that's, oh well, if he does give me time, he can't punish me that much, do you know what I mean. He can't give me no more than a three year sentence or something stupid like that, do you know what I mean, because, like, the facts confronting. I was trying for an hour to stop [the victim]

from [becoming involved in a fight with me] because he was throwing pebbles at me, do you know what I mean?

(Jimmy)

Loss of employment

Of course, family relationships are not the only aspect of imprisonment to come under strain. One of the probationers interviewed during the fourth sweep (Frank) reflected on his experiences of employment after coming out of prison:

> AC: How's employment been over the last four, five years?
> Frank: Err, up and down. I find it hard, like, to get a job when I went to prison, like, when I come out. Couldn't, like, really hold, like, a job down to be honest with you so, that's why I decided, like, just to start up on my own.
> AC: Okay. What problems did you have holding down a job?
> Frank: Err ... it was, like, if you get close to people you tell them, like, certain things and things would just get back to other people, like, the bosses and err ...
> AC: Are we talking about your record specifically here?
> Frank: Yeah, yeah. Or people who've known me have, like, basically said 'oh all right I'll like watch out for him' [i.e. keep an eye on the probationer], do you know what I mean? Just keep your eye on him or ... Yeah it's happened quite a few times.
> AC: Okay.
> Frank: And which is quite annoying to be honest.
> AC: Are we talking about work gossip?
> Frank: Yeah, really quite annoying.
> AC: Okay. So on average how long did you usually hold a job for?
> Frank: Six months.

For those facing the possibility of going to prison (usually those on bail but awaiting trial), life is put on hold until the outcome of the trial is known. One probationer, case 042, reported how he had completed his NVQ1 in welding, but was unsure if he would continue his studies as he was awaiting a trial at which he expected to be given a custodial sentence. At the fourth sweep, another case, Andrew, said:

> There's a lot people coming into prison, especially younger people, who come to prison for a couple of years and they go home, they've still got no chance of getting a job, you know. But at least this here is supposed to be a training prison,[3] but I don't really see a lot of training going on.

Prison, therefore, interrupts or disrupts entirely two of the processes which we know are most frequently associated with desistance, namely family formation and employment. Thus prison often robs people of the means by which they can take responsibility for both themselves and their families, making it increasingly likely that they will not be able to make the break from crime.

Feelings of being 'held' or 'put' back

As Meisenhelder (1985), writing about the phenomenology of time in prison notes, every inmate knows that whilst he is on the 'inside', the rest of the world marches onwards. Just as 'time and tide' waits for no man, so the lives of others move on too. These observations were also made by some of those in our sample:

> I feel ... Okay ... I feel good but I just, I feel, like, I'm thirty-six in two weeks time, I think I've wasted an awful lot of time not knowing what I was doing. I think basically, I really feel as if the years from when I was twenty-nine, when my missus and me kids left me, 'til this moment in time now have been really wasted. *Hmmm*. You know? I've achieved nothing. And I'm back to, from when I leave prison now, I'll be in a worse, the same position than I was when I was twenty-nine, still without a home, no money.
>
> Andrew

When asked to discuss his feelings about prison, the same prisoner explained how it made him feel:

> Absolutely devastated. It just tears your whole life up. I didn't have that much of a life but everything I did have ... Obviously I think I committed a crime, I think prison is justified, that's the penalty you pay. But I also think what it has done to, err, it's put me back, it's basically put me back two and a half years. And it's made me miss out on me kid's life, I feel a bit bitter about it to be honest with you.

Prison as a 'breeding ground'

One of the most common responses we encountered, however, referred to prison as a 'breeding ground' for further crimes:

> Well, what I think is, they see someone like me in with things like, you've got a combination order which is twenty-four months' community service, twenty-four months' probation and X amount of community service. But between them, what are you going to achieve? What's the right [sentence], send me to prison? I've been to prison, I'd be out in two months' time, free as a bird, mixing with the harder criminals, people that's just gonna, you just don't care. Prison is just a ... all prison is to me was a joke, it was a breeding ground of,

you could still smoke blow in there, it was fighting, [it] was a breeding ground for criminals. [...] Prison don't work for no one as far as I'm concerned, I've been to prison about eight or nine times in my life and not once did it learn me a lesson, not once. All prison to me was okay, it was few months away from your problems, it weren't hard, it was nothing, it was rough, there's a few tough nuts in there that wanted to do you but that was about it. Prison was nothing to worry about, its just a breeding ground, you come out knowing more than you went in with.

(Jamie)

066:    Yeah, because I've learnt a couple of things in here of what I didn't know outside.
SF: What, things that you could use outside in terms of offending?
066:    Yeah.

The fact is prison won't, what is it the word, 'reform' or whatever or 'rehabilitate you', that won't do nothing like that to me, it'll just make me worse.

(John)

One possible explanation for this comes from the following ex-probationer/ex-prisoner:

You go in there and they go 'oh, you know you'll get caught doing that again, you'll go back to prison for a long time'. That is no deterrent if you have just come out of prison. Especially if you can ride it [cope with it] anyway. Just come out of prison – you think 'fuck it'. 'Cos when you come out of prison, you are used to prison, so them first weeks with no job and no money is when you usually go back, 'cos you are still used to prison and you think 'fucking hell – I'll go back – still know everyone there ...', so then you think 'no money – I'll go hit something'. That is it – they should sort you out some money.

(Jamie)

Discussion

Regardless of whether one thinks that prisons ought to provide ex-inmates with greater resources or not, it is clear that the experience of imprisonment is far from being the Benthamite desire for reflection upon one's sins and the acquiring of a determination to cease offending. Prison, in our view – and supported by research evidence and the lived realities reported to us during our fieldwork – is *not* a sensible way of encouraging desistance. Imprisonment, even quite short periods, has the potential to disrupt family relationships and employment patterns and opportunities, creates feelings of being 'held back' and can act as a breeding ground for future criminality. Upon release, many prisoners will experience a reduction in their resources and, depending on the length of time they have been incarcerated, may have few memory traces of social rules and norms (Richards and Jones, 2004; Jamieson and Grounds, 2003). In processes associated with the structuring of rules and resources, they may carry with them 'prison rules' which make adjustment to life outside even harder (Richards and Jones, 2004). We return to these topics in our concluding chapter, where we discuss the processes of structuration which influence offending careers.

Notes

[1] With the caveat that those who regularly offend against their families will cease to do so if prevented from contacting them. However, they might well victimize others or offend in other ways, of course.
[2] 'Top myself' meaning to take one's own life.
[3] Andrew is referring to the fact that the prison was one where inmates were given training aimed at helping them gain employment.

Further reading

Eaton, M (1993) *Women After Prison*, Open University Press, Buckingham.
Goulden, C. (2004) Beyond a Drug Trafficking Offence: No Way Forward?, *Probation Journal*, 51(2): 155–63.
Meisenhelder, T. (1985) An Essay on Time and the Phenomenology of Imprisonment, *Deviant Behaviour*, 6: 39–56.
O'Brien, P. (2001) *Making It in the 'Free World'*, SUNY, New York.
Shover, N. (1985) *Aging Criminals*, Sage, Beverley Hills.

chapter four

The existential aspects of desistance

Existential sociology
Existentialist thought within criminology
Becoming anew: human development and desistance from crime
Struggling to 'become'
Discussion and conclusion

> I nodded, sinking into new levels of misery as it began to dawn on me
> that I had let down not just my family but also a huge army of friends,
> supporters, lawyers, constituents, well-wishers and prayer-givers.
> (Jonathan Aitken, 2003: 226)

This chapter will chart and theorize – via the experiences of one woman –
the key existential processes and moments in the transition from being an
'offender' to being an 'ex-offender'. Existentialism, as we shall come to
illustrate, we feel captures both the 'internal' changes in self-identity and
the processes which foster such changes, but yet does not lose sight of the
wider social world and the problems which it can create for those wishing
to change important aspects of their lives.

In the following section, we outline the key tenets of existentialism,
relying as we do most heavily upon its usage in sociology since the late
1970s. We then pause briefly in order to assess the (somewhat limited) use
made of this perspective by criminologists. Following this, we draw
insights from the desistance literature, skewing our focus heavily towards
those studies which (albeit implicitly) contribute to our understanding of
the existential processes associated with the termination of the criminal
career. We then embark upon a detailed case study of one desister that
demonstrates the power of the existential perspective for illuminating the
issues surrounding change from a 'criminal' to a 'non-criminal' social
identity.

Existential sociology

In a number of edited volumes (Douglas and Johnson, 1977; Kotarba and Fontana, 1984; Kotarba and Johnson, 2002), a loosely affiliated research group has charted what it has referred to as existential sociology.[1] This existential sociology they have variously defined (or just described) as being concerned with the following issues:

> Existential sociology is defined descriptively as the study of human experience-in-the-world (or existence) in all its forms. [...] The goal is to construct both practical and theoretical truths about that experience, to understand how we live, how we feel, think, act.
>
> (Douglas and Johnson, 1977: vii)

> Existential sociology is the sociology that attempts to study human beings in their natural setting – the everyday world in which they live – and to examine as many as possible of the complex facets of the human experience.
>
> (Fontana, 1984: 4)

These definitions, as one would expect, draw heavily upon philosophical existentialism, defined by Manning thus:

> Existentialism is [...] a philosophy arguing that through his life, man makes decisions and builds up meanings in line with them (if possible), and is in fact forced to act, to accept freedom.
>
> (1973: 209)

More specifically, existential sociology is an attempt to understand the above via a detailed concern with the following tenets.

The search for a meaningful identity

As well as importing the existential preoccupation with the 'futility of existence' (Fontana, 1984), existential philosophers and sociologists have highlighted the individual's search for a meaningful identity (e.g. Sartre, 1943 [1958]; Manning, 1973) and the feelings and angst that this entails. Many of the existentialists whose work is reviewed herein are deeply engaged in exploring how a meaningful identity – often following part of a period of change and executed over varying periods of time – is sought out, adapted to and maintained (e.g. Sartre, 1943 [1958]; Ebaugh, 1984; Douglas, 1984; Kotarba, 2002; Johnson and Ferraro, 1984). Of course, and as hinted at above, these processes of change are not simply linear, nor are they without their moments of self-doubt or angst, as vividly recorded by Ebaugh:

> The application [to leave the convent] came, I [Ebaugh] put it away in my desk drawer, and for three weeks was unable to look at it. It was

not so much a process of intellectually weighing the pros and cons but of becoming comfortable with the idea of no longer being a nun.

(1984: 167)

...feelings of a void just before [the nuns] made a final decision to leave [the convent], feeling like a stranger at the point of leaving...

(1984: 159)

For one year I [Ebaugh] lived in the order again as a nun. That entire year was a kind of vacuum for me.

(1984: 168)

As these quotes suggest, the search for a meaningful identity – be it a 'new' identity or the ongoing project of 'self' – presents certain threats to an individual at an existential level. As such, these quotes echo Sartre's work on 'being in itself' and 'being for itself' (1958: 73–84). The being in itself is a 'non-conscious being' (1958: 630) which simply exists without very much critical awareness of itself. Being for itself is in many ways 'opposed' to being in itself, since being for itself seeks to transcend the in itself in order to become 'the particular being which it would be' (1958: 89). Being for itself is concerned with establishing what it is not (1958: 77, 180). As time progresses, the 'for itself' becomes the 'in itself' as the individual develops a new consciousness of who they 'are' (1958: 208). Sartre goes on to write that 'it is necessary to see the denied qualities as a constitutive factor of the being for itself', since the being for itself partly defines itself against what it once *was*. Hence the above threats to the individual's sense of self are partly the *cause* of periods of reassessment of 'who' one is and partly the *result* of such periods. The extent to which these threats create intense feelings of ontological insecurity (the feeling that one's very being is at risk) is a core focus of existential philosophy and hence also of existential sociology (see, for example, Douglas, 1984: 76–83).

Applied to the study of reforming alcoholics, Denzin (1987: 158–9) writes that an individual 'comes to define herself in terms of who she no longer wants to be', adding that, over time, 'the self that is moving forward judges the momentum of this movement in terms of where it used to be'. Thus the 'for itself' becomes an ongoing project, continually striving to understand and improve itself in some way. In this respect, as others have observed (e.g. Meisenhelder, 1985), the self is continually being projected forward into the future, as this becomes the temporal space in which the for itself is realized.

'Self' and 'other'

It ought to be clear from the foregoing discussion that one of the core *foci* of existential interest surrounds changes in the self and definitions of 'oneself' (Fontana, 1984: 11; Douglas, 1984: 69; Ebaugh, 1984: 156; and more recently Giddens, 1991: 125). As MacQuarrie (1972: 202–3) in his overview of existentialism writes, 'To exist is to project oneself in to the future. But there is always a lack or disproportion between the self as projected and the self where it actually stands.' In this respect, one of the chief concerns of, and in, existential sociology has been the 'slowly evolving sense of inner self' (Douglas, 1984: 69) and transformations in self-identity which occur as individuals move from one social setting or institution to another (e.g. Ebaugh, 1984) or adapt to new social roles (e.g. Fontana, 2002). As Kotarba summarizes:

> The existential self refers to an individual's unique experience of the being within the context of contemporary social conditions, an experience most notably marked by an incessant sense of becoming and an active participation in social change.
>
> (1984: 225)

Of course, as an individual's sense of who they are develops, or as they leave one social institution and/or join another, so their relationships with other individuals may also change (Douglas, 1977: 14). This is another central preoccupation of existential sociology. It refers not just to specific individuals, but also to social groups or types of relationships. For example, Ebaugh's study of ex-nuns describes how ex-nuns found themselves forging new relationships with not just specific others, but with certain social groups and types of 'role occupants' (for example, landlords, classmates, work colleagues and male friends). These then were not just changes in specific relationships, but changes in terms of who one could and needed to associate with.

As Goffman (1963: 64, 137–8) observed, the character of any individual is inferred from who they are seen spending time with – the assumption being that 'he is what others are' (1963: 64). Similarly, part and parcel of 'who' one 'is' is 'where' one is (Goffman, 1963: 102–4). That is to say, the social spaces which an individual routinely inhabits are 'read-off' by both themselves and others as providing some indication of 'who' they are and what they do. The importance of situated places in the ongoing production of a meaningful self is another of the key concerns of existential sociology (Douglas, 1977: 70; Clark, 2002: 172). Who one 'is', therefore, is not just about one's own feelings, actions or identity, but also partly inferred from the places which surround oneself and the sorts of activities which are commonly held to occur in those social spaces (a point we expand upon in Chapter 8).

Feelings and emotions

Almost all of the existential sociologists writing at the core of the school place a heavy emphasis on understanding the role of feelings and emotions in the human experience (e.g. Fontana, 1984: 159; Lester, 1984: 53–7; Ebaugh, 1984: 159; Johnson and Kotarba, 2002: 3; Clark, 2002: 157, Douglas and Johnson, 1977: xii; Douglas, 1977: 10; Manning, 1973:

209). One author (Fontana) even goes as far as to suggest that, in this respect, existential sociology is defined by its focus on the 'forgotten elements of the social sciences' (1984: 4).[2] Of particular importance is the experience of conflicting emotions and how these are resolved (or not), and the impact that this has on the subject's self-identity (Lester, 1984: 58). In this respect, as Ebaugh highlighted in her account of how ex-nuns find a new social identity after they have left the convent, existential sociology charts the peculiar mix of rational and non-rational elements that imbue many human experiences, and especially those periods characterized by processes of change and transition. In this respect, existential sociology provides a welcome break from the 'rational'/'non-rational' dichotomy which haunts much criminological thinking, as Lester notes, 'a central orientation of this perspective is the fusion of rational thought, action and feeling' (1984: 53).

The fusing together of thoughts and feelings brings us to one of the other core foci of existential sociology, namely a focus on an individual's values. Beliefs about what is 'right' or 'wrong' and how (and when) these beliefs are translated into feelings is another preoccupation of existential sociologists. As Douglas writes, 'basic values, supported by strong feelings of pride when we live by them and shame and guilt when we do not, orient us towards our social world' (1984: 83). In this respect, beliefs and the feelings associated with them at various points are key to helping the individual to make sense of the wider world and particular activities within it. The extent to which and the ways in which the sense of oneself and of one's behaviour are uniquely linked is summarized by Douglas in the following passage:

> It is our sense of self that gives us the feeling that 'that is not like me', 'but I'm not like that', 'but I'm not the sort of person who would do such a thing', 'but I could never', 'but I feel violated', 'I would not feel right', 'I just sense that it's wrong for me', and so on, all the time. We cannot generally say exactly why 'it is not like me'. We do not know in words, but we know immediately.
>
> (1984: 97)

This in turn brings us to a consideration of two recurring themes in existentialism and the sociology that it has inspired: guilt and shame (Douglas, 1977: 45; MacQuarrie, 1972). These powerful emotions help the individual to understand 'who' they are and 'what' they believe to be 'right' and 'wrong'. Of course, there is almost certainly a feedback loop between such feelings and the ongoing production of a sense of self: feeling shame at one's past actions or deeds helps to engender a sense of 'who' one is, which in turn may influence what things one thinks to be right or wrong, which in turn may find expression in new actions which reinforce the emerging self-identity, and so on. In many respects, it is these sorts of issues that get to the heart of one of the other central concerns of existentialism: problems of freedom and choice (Johnson and Kotarba,

2002: 3). This concern with freedom and choice is most obviously articulated in the writings of Sartre (Fontana, 1984: 5) and is a key organizing principle in Ebaugh's study of ex-nuns (1984: 165–6). For the ex-nuns in Ebaugh's study, leaving the convent was finally initiated when the nun realized that she had the freedom to decide whether she stayed a nun or not. Ebaugh reports that this moment was often associated with a strong feeling of elation (1984: 166).

The existential methodological stance

Although, as Fontana (1980: 156) notes, existential sociologists have not devoted much of their energies to outlining a uniquely existential methodology, a number of principles which partly suggest research strategies do emerge from a reading of the literature in this field. The first principle is a focus on 'natural settings' (Fontana, 1980: 156, 1984: 4; Lester, 1984: 57; Douglas and Johnson, 1977: ix; Douglas, 1977: 22; Arrigo, 1998: 74–5; Quinney, 2002: 206). This commitment to study humans in their 'natural' habitat comes partly from a desire to gain a deep understanding of the individual in question's everyday life (Lester, 1984: 56–7). This has most commonly meant existential sociologists engaging in in-depth interviews, ethnographies, participant observation and introspection. For example, Ebaugh relied upon interviews with ex-nuns, ex-doctors, ex-teachers and a range of other 'ex's' for her study of changing identities (Ebaugh, 1988). Similarly, Fontana (2002) relied upon his own experiences to discuss how he was able to adopt a new role of racing enthusiast at the Bonneville Salt Flats, whilst Warren and Ponse (1977) relied upon participant observation and interviews for their study of gay communities. By and large, the research techniques employed are drawn from the methodological toolbox of the qualitative investigator: in-depth interviews, observations, documentary sources and introspection.

   The second principle embodied within existential sociology is a concern with capturing the 'total person' (Fontana, 1984: 5). Quite exactly what is meant by the focus on the 'total person' is never fully spelt out in existential sociology. However, it is not unreasonable to assume that this refers to a desire to capture in detail all of the nuances of individual human lives. The fusion of the rational and the irrational, the heady mix of emotional states (sometimes intense, sometimes mundane), the specific locating of individuals in particular times and spaces and the uniqueness of this experience, and the desire to combine both 'the human' and 'the social' in one account best represent what is meant by the attempt to capture the 'total person'.

Existentialist thought within criminology

Whilst it is true that criminologists have not exactly been falling over themselves in recent years to employ existentialist concepts in their research (Morrison: 1995: 351), there have been a few notable studies which have either drawn directly from existentialist thinking, or which have employed very closely related concepts. Amongst these is the study of 'upper-level' drug dealers and smugglers by Adler (1985). Adler's ethnography demonstrates how these individuals, being disenchanted with the modern world (1985: 152) have retreated into 'heavy end' drug smuggling in order to avoid pain, achieve pleasure and to satisfy their brute inner drives (1985: 151–2). The lifestyle which these individuals chose for themselves allowed them to feel excitement, glamour and spontaneity and to attend to their inner drives for impulsive self-expression. As Adler writes, 'they ceased to think of their selves as something to be "attained, created and achieved", and focused instead on discovering and satisfying their deep, unsocialised inner impulses' (1985: 154).

As Morrison himself notes (1995: 358), the work of Jack Katz (1988), whilst not directly referring to existentialist thought in any depth, resonates with many of the concerns of existential sociologists. Katz, via a number of sharply focused studies of specific types of crime or criminal, draws our attention to the experiential aspects of offending. The thrill of breaking and entering a neighbour's house, the attempts to avoid degrading or humiliating situations or the desires to create an extreme, deviant identity can all be read (as Morrison does) as attempts to create new meanings, new identities or to experience exciting emotional states which echo many of the existentialist agenda outlined above. Using notes from interviews which he had conducted himself, delightfully interweaved with examples from the work of Katz, Gottfredson and Hirschi and various others, Morrison demonstrates how by emphasizing the sensuality of crime one is provided with a new perspective on both crime and criminals. It is a perspective which encourages one to reconsider not just why people offend, but also what may be done to discourage such behaviour (1995: 378). Other criminologists (such as Ferrell, 1998; Quinney, 2002) have devoted some of their efforts to a discussion of existential concerns to the study of crime. However, as noted above, few have explicitly tied existentialist concerns directly to the issues confronting contemporary criminological enquiry.

Just as the study of deviancy can help to illuminate the basic contours of social order and the ways in which fundamental desires clash head-on with social conventions, creating possibilities for social change (Kotarba, 1979: 359–60), so an existentially inspired understanding of crime and criminals can help to illuminate current criminological preoccupations. In particular, it is contended here, the existential perspective is especially insightful when applied to the concept of changes in the criminal career.

When people try to stop offending, try to make amends for past behaviour and (when some of them) succeed in doing so, they are not merely 'no longer offending', but in some instances have gone through quite lengthy periods of rebuilding, remodelling or remaking their own social identities.

How these processes of desistance are best conceptualized and operationalized has been the subject of some debate (e.g. Maruna, 2001) and looks unlikely to be resolved in the immediate future. However, by understanding these processes of change (sometimes self-initiated, sometimes supported by criminal justice agencies, and almost always 'propped up' by the likes of partners, parents and offspring), we are able to understand how people 'remake' themselves. This is not an insight without possible usage: with prison figures topping the 70,000 level in England and Wales, with around 70,000 community rehabilitation orders and community punishment and rehabilitation orders being made in England and Wales (Home Office, 2002: 4, Table A) and with around half of these people being reconvicted within two years, we are in serious need of not just 'smart' policies which 'work', but also the knowledge base from which to develop new insights into change.

It must be said that some of the very best work in the desistance and reintegration field has started (like Katz) to echo some of the core interests of existentialism. For example, in their study of why females desist, Giordano *et al.* (2002) rely heavily upon the concept of a 'blue print' for a replacement self. Their four-part 'theory of cognitive transformation' involves the following four stages: 'general cognitive openness to change'; exposure and reaction to 'hooks for change' or turning points; the envisioning of 'an appealing and conventional "replacement self"';[3] and the transformation in the way the actor views deviant behaviour. Additionally, they focus on emotional aspects of the desistance process (e.g. 2002: 1042).

Other 'classic' studies of ex-offenders suggest other moments of resonance with existentialism: for example, Cusson and Pinsonneault (1986) on shocking experiences which force the individual to embark upon a period of renegotiation of 'who' they are and 'what' they do; Shover (1983) on changes in goals, 'tiredness' and the impact which these processes have on self-identity; Bull (1972, cited in Shover, 1983) on feelings of despair and the motivation to change; or Meisenhelder (1977, 1982) on an individual's use of social locales to reinforce the projection of a new personal identity. More recently, Maruna (2001) demonstrated that whilst catalysts for change were external to the individual, desistance was reported as an internal process which enabled the 'real me' to emerge. Without explicitly referring to it, many of these commentators have been following a research agenda that mirrors many (but not all) of the concerns associated with existential sociology.

Becoming anew: human development and desistance from crime

This section seeks to introduce some of the core *foci* of existential thought and existentially inspired sociology to the study of why people stop offending. This perspective adds a new school of terminology to the study of desistance, which helps us to describe the processes associated with desistance and internal change and which can contribute to our theoretical understanding about desistance and reform.

Accordingly, we relate the experiences of one individual: a young woman who we shall refer to as Sandra. Sandra was chosen for examination in this instance because, in total, we had access to seven interviews with or about her. The first six of these interviews were all conducted by the same individual (although neither of the authors) and the seventh was conducted by Stephen Farrall four and a half years after the main period of fieldwork. Sandra and her supervising probation officer were each seen three times during the main fieldwork stage, and there appeared to be a very good level of rapport between the interviewer and both Sandra and her officer. This is witnessed by Sandra disclosing to the interviewer during the very first interview the fact that she had been raped as a child and was unsure if she was not a lesbian. The tape-recorded interviews also testify to the good level of rapport between interviewer and both interviewees. Sandra and the interviewer were both female, of a similar age and lived in the same city. The follow-up interview was also characterized by good rapport and disclosure of material of a sensitive nature.

A number of issues suggest that we can be reasonably sure of the veracity of the accounts elicited during the interviews: a common set of themes emerged from the interviews with both Sandra and her officer, suggesting a successful triangulation of perspectives (see also Farrall, 2004). In addition, we undertook extensive searches of both the Police National Computer (PNC) and the Offenders Index (OI). Both of these successfully 'located' Sandra and suggested that the offence for which she received her original order had been the last for which she had been convicted. In addition, she reported only occasional cannabis use during the first set of interviews, and at the later follow-up reported that she no longer smoked. All of this suggests – as well as any such assessment can – that she has indeed desisted.

Sandra was aged 22 when she commenced her 12 month probation order and represented a 'fairly typical' female probationer. Like many women starting probation orders she had no previous convictions (Worrall, 1990: 36). Sandra had been found guilty of theft from her employer (as a cocktail waitress she voided the bar's till and pocketed the cash during some of the transactions she made whilst serving customers). In many important respects (honesty with interviewer, openness, certainty that desistance was achieved, data triangulation and typicality), Sandra represents an extremely good start point from which to commence an existentially focused exploration of the process of desistance.

Struggling to 'become'

When seen for the first time, Sandra said that she had stolen from her employers to find the money to spend on drugs (chiefly cannabis, cocaine and amphetamines) and alcohol. While working in the bar ('CJ's') she had rung through bills on the till, but if the customer paid in cash, she voided the transaction and took the cash. 'Officially' this lasted for around six months, during which time she made around £2,500. However, during the seventh interview, when probed in more detail about this, Sandra said that this represented a considerable underestimation of the amount she had taken. When asked at the time by her employer how much she had taken and for how long she had been taking money, she said she had stolen about £100 a week for about six months. However, she felt that the true figure was nearer double this. This was the second time she had done something like this. Previously, while working in a similar establishment, she had also stolen money in this fashion, again over a period of several months, although not as much. On that occasion, however, when caught, she had simply been sacked.

Sandra had disliked working in 'CJ's' and 'wasn't happy there'. This partly accounted for her drug and alcohol usage ('[I was] drinking every day, five or six cans of lager and half a bottle of vodka or whiskey during the week, more at the weekends'[4]). When asked how she had been feeling in the period leading up to her offending, she said that she'd been feeling down and depressed due to a culmination of problems with her family, growing doubts over her sexuality, the rape and sexual abuse she had experienced during her childhood and a sense of confusion over where she was heading in life. It would appear that Sandra was leading a life that felt devoid of any positive meanings for her self.

Starting on probation and finding a job

Sandra said that when she found out that she had been given probation she felt that she had deserved worse and 'should have gotten a prison sentence'.[5] At the time of her offending, Sandra had been living in the same city as her parents, but had moved away from them. She reported that she felt as if they had never loved her and she found it hard to get on with them. Her probation officer confirmed most of these points. Shortly after the start of the second interviews (about six months into Sandra's order), the topic of the 'single biggest change' in Sandra's life since the previous interview was broached. Her probation officer said:

Well, in that time she got a job. I think she thought that nobody would want to employ her again[6] because the offence was actually for dishonesty – which was against her employer. So the fact that it was a breach of trust, in employment … so that did present some difficulties … when she went for this job, but in the end they decided to give her the job because they got a fairly favourable report from the [alcohol] project that she was attending. And she hasn't relapsed for months now. But it was basically the offence in itself why they were a little bit reluctant to employ her.

Sandra revealed how even getting the job had initially been stress inducing. Sandra had asked someone she knew who was working whether there were any vacancies at her place of work. This friend said that she would ask for her. In a panic, Sandra later telephoned this woman to tell her about her conviction, something she felt compelled to do as it involved dishonesty to her former employer. In this respect, and again following Goffman (1963: 95, 124), Sandra had to choose her timing for an 'appropriate disclosure' carefully. To disclose this information too early may have prevented her from feeling that she would be able to ask her friend for help. However, failing to disclose it, or failing to do so quickly, may have reinforced the perception that she was dishonest (assuming, which was likely, that her previous conviction would come to light). By asking her friend for help, receiving an agreement to help and *then* alerting her friend to her status, Sandra was able to achieve the status of a 'help-needing' and 'help-able' friend who was also honest about her past dishonesty. Sandra was invited for interview after her friend had asked about vacancies on her behalf. When asked about the biggest single change since she had started probation, Sandra referred to distinctly 'internal' changes:

Now I don't blame myself for everything. I have also accepted that I am allowed to be happy. I think they are the two major things – not anything physical.

However, when the interviewer probed further in the precursors of these changes, Sandra said:

I'm a lot more chilled with my parents. I don't snap back at every little thing that they say anymore. Work is a blessing. When I first got the job, I thought 'five days? Monday to Friday? Urrrrgh!' Now it is nice, 'cause I know where I am going every day, and even there, I don't let it stress me out.

This acquisition of a job was associated with Sandra's desistance, not just because it acted as a simple outlet for her energies during the day, or because it provided a legitimate income for her to spend on alcohol. Rather, the job acted as a way of Sandra 'rebuilding' who she was and who she could *become*.[7] In this respect, Sandra's experiences echo that of the participants in Kotarba and Bentley's (1988) study of workplace wellness programmes, in that this has allowed her the chance to create a new set of meanings for her self. Sandra's probation officer again:

> She is more positive about life and everything. She saw that that wasn't the end of her life really. 'Cos before, as far as she was concerned, she was never going to be able to get a job. She never thought that she would be able to control the drinking. [...] She has seen that things have happened, things have changed.

Her same officer also said, 'When I last spoke to her she was enjoying it [work]. It has lifted her confidence a bit.' When asked to elaborate on the changes which employment had initiated, Sandra's probation officer said:

> I think it has done her the world of good. She's ... well I hope ... The first time she came in she had really made an effort – she had done her hair up, dressed a lot smarter, her whole attitude and ... what's the word I am looking for ...? When she comes in she doesn't look so down about things ... she's really happy. She is really pleased about it.

Without wishing to completely challenge this glowing account of Sandra's new job, it is prudent to remind ourselves that even exciting and beneficial episodes in human lives can still leave one feeling anxious. Whilst initially feeling elated (see Ebaugh, 1984: 166), Sandra needed to impose some rules upon herself:

> The very first Friday I worked it was, 'Yeeerrrse! Down the pub! Down the pub!' I got absolutely rat-arsed, and felt so really ashamed of myself on the Saturday. I thought, 'Okay – that is allowed, that is your first Friday, first full week at work. Okay, it is not going to happen next week.' And it didn't and it's been cool. I'm going away on holiday on Thursday ... When I first started work, one of the things that worried me was having money again would just be a ticket to going down the pub every night. But it hasn't been. I want to learn to drive, I want to get out of home, I want these things. So I am just going to have to save up and do it like everybody else. It is all early days again.

In this respect, Sandra's experiences were akin to those of people 'passing' in the company of a new social group (Goffman, 1963: 109). Like any new employee, Sandra felt anxious about how she was fitting into her new workplace and how she was being perceived as getting on by her new bosses:

> It's getting better – the longer I spend time there, it's getting better. The first week I was there I was thinking, 'Urrrrggggghhh – what am I doing here?' I was ready to [quit], but I stuck at it and it is going good.

I am generally pretty happy. I still get anxious – I was very anxious at work. It really was the case of . . . the last week, they've told me that they are happy with my work – which has given me a boost. Up 'til then I was just getting along with it and I didn't know if they were happy with what I was doing. So that was good – they've reassured me. 'We're really happy with you – keep it up.' And just so many people – it is a big office – I'd never done anything like that before. And I found myself getting pretty paranoid in the staff room and that, but it's getting better.

These new experiences, and not least of all Sandra's coming to see herself as someone who *could* hold down a job and who was a valued employee, occasioned changes in her relationships with others in her personal life (see also Kotarba and Bentley, 1988, on the role of feelings of competence in willingness to participate in work-based health programmes).

Becoming 'a normal'

When she initially started working, Sandra found it difficult to 'fit in'. She 'did not know what to talk about' and, having been out of work for about a year during a time of relatively high employment, had no 'recent past' which she felt happy to disclose to others. Wishing neither to lie nor to tell the truth, she said that she had been working in a restaurant, a story which her new colleagues found sufficiently plausible to believe but not so interesting that they would ask about it in detail. In this respect, Sandra was learning about how she would need to control the flow of information stemming from her presence in the office (see also Goffman, 1963: 57–128).

Over time, her 'phantom normalcy' (Goffman, 1963: 148) slowly became an *actual* normalcy. As mentioned, Sandra was a lot more 'chilled' (i.e. calm) with her parents. This manifested itself in terms of changing how well they got on and also occasioned a further change in Sandra's view of herself. Her probation officer again:

In terms of relationship with her parents – that has obviously moved on a lot. I suppose from talking through some of the issues, her trying to understand where they are coming from, trying to meet them half way really, rather than expecting them to make the first move, which I think is what she was waiting for. And has realized that somebody has to make the first step. And she did. I remember one day she came in and said, 'Oh, I'm going shopping with my mum next week . . .' Which some people take for granted, but for her it was a really big step! It was something she had never had to do.

In this way, the social institutions that Sandra was becoming socialized towards and into (i.e. work) were affecting the ways in which she was able to remodel her personal relationships.[8] The magnitude of these changes is not hard to grasp, and especially when one considers 'where' Sandra started from:

> I was very sure that I wasn't going to get a job, I was convinced that I was damned for the rest of my life, and I'd got a criminal record, I'm not going to get a job, nobody is going to want me – and she [her probation officer] kept saying 'no, it might be difficult, and you might not get one straight away, but to keep trying'. And there *are* people out there who are prepared to give you a chance.

Sandra's probation officer echoed many of these sentiments when she said:

> I think she just felt that 'that was it', her life was over. And that nobody would want to know. I suppose even though … until it actually happened she didn't believe that – that somebody there was prepared to give her a second chance.

Sandra had also been volunteering at an alcohol project she had previously been referred to by her probation officer. This, it would appear, had helped her to take stock of how much her life had changed since she had started to attend the project:

> I'm still involved with – I've been doing some voluntary work done at [the alcohol project] – I've been helping them with the administration, and keeping in touch with those places, keeping in touch with the people that I met there. I went there a few weeks ago. I went in there in a bit of a bad mood. And I came out thinking 'my life is brilliant'. I was sitting there listening to their stories thinking 'no, no, I've really moved on from here',[9] but I need to keep that in touch. I need to keep that in mind – that I can go back there very easily. And as long as I keep those reminders there, I'll be okay.

This insight into Sandra's feelings about 'who' she was, 'who' she is and 'who' she wants to become echoes Denzin's (1987: 158–9; see above) and Goffman's (1963: 130–1) observations. The past, the present and the future help to structure the individual's understanding of who they are and how far they have progressed towards who they want to become (Sartre, 1943; Meisenhelder, 1985). When asked during her second interview if she had offended since she started probation, Sandra said;

Sandra: No. I've been too busy. No, I haven't. My life has changed an awful lot – *I've* changed an awful lot. I've calmed down. I've got a lot of the past sorted out. I'm a lot more focused on the present. And there hasn't been any need. I haven't wanted to.

Interviewer: You mentioned that you changed an awful lot, in what ways would you say you were different now to how you were when you started probation?

Sandra: When I started probation? I was a nutter when I started

> probation! I've calmed down a lot, with myself – I'm
> not as nervous. I was nervous and scared of everything
> and everyone when I came here first of all. And now, I
> feel a lot more confident. I drink an awful lot less. Just
> my outlook on the future is a lot brighter. It feels like a
> whole change, just everything ... from black to white.
> ... Well not completely! [Jokingly]

When asked to discuss her future ambitions, Sandra pointed to what could
be considered medium to long term goals:

Sandra: [Keep] my job, and just keep going really. After I get
             back from my holiday, I want to start taking driving
             lessons.
Interviewer: And after that?
Sandra: I suppose to save up for a place on my own. To keep
             going, to keep going the way I am at the moment.

This stood in stark contrast to the person she had been when she first
attended her probation appointments. Sandra's probation officer again:

> She deeply regretted what she did. I think for the first three months
> she never stopped crying when she came in here. Sometimes I couldn't
> ... before I even said anything, she just started pouring her heart out.
> She just used to cry so much. For the first three months. Even the [pre-
> sentence report], which I did, that took ages 'cos she was crying so
> much, in the end I gave her a whole box of tissues. So she was really,
> really ashamed [of what she had done].[10]

Being settled but 'moving on'

At the fourth interview, Sandra talked openly about how her life had
moved on and reflected upon the important changes in her life more
generally. Sandra's job, as one might expect, formed a large part of these
discussions. Some people, of course, knew more about Sandra's recent
past. As well as the personnel department, two of Sandra's immediate line
managers knew of her conviction. However, following a series of pro-
motions and changes in personnel, Sandra found herself in the situation
where no one at work knew about her previous conviction. This 'felt
good' as 'now no one knew at all' and Sandra's previously 'still recovering' identity was 'fully recuperated'. In all, Sandra had been promoted
four times during the five years she had been at work, and now worked in
a prestigious section of the firm – a position which she had had to apply
for on several occasions before she was appointed.

In following this route, Sandra, albeit inadvertently, produced a fourth
type of disclosure strategy (Goffman, 1963; Harding, 2003). Unlike those
who disclose nothing, disclose everything or who disclose conditionally
(see Harding, 2003, for examples of these strategies as employed by ex-

offenders seeking employment), Sandra disclosed *selectively*, and in such a way that her 'deviancy' was eroded over time as the social institution in which she operated changed staff (and with this personal knowledge). In this respect, she was able to avoid doing what many people managing spoiled identities are thought to do, namely staying in one job for a limited time in order to build a character reference before moving on to another (Goffman, 1963: 116–17).

Away from work, Sandra said that her life now felt 'more stable'. She said that she was better able to cope with personal conflicts. Although Sandra had not told her parents that she was a lesbian, she had introduced her girlfriend to them. Her parents responded by inviting them both to their house for the Easter weekend, something that Sandra was looking forward to. Thus Sandra appeared to have created for herself a more meaningful identity. Part and parcel of this appeared to be an ability to plan for and 'look forward to' the future, which, for Sandra, was now more certain. In terms of her alcohol use, Sandra said that she 'only drank on a Friday' and 'not during the week', and said at this point that 'sometimes it is nice to stay in and cuddle up on the sofa and watch TV'. When asked how it felt to have put her previous experience behind her, Sandra said it felt good and that she felt 'proud' of herself for having accomplished this change. We wish now to reflect upon the periods of Sandra's life as recounted above and to provide an analysis of Sandra's transformation of herself.

Discussion and conclusion

Let us be quite straight from the outset: Sandra did *not* become a completely different person. She did not undergo some radical change of personality. She was still working in a fairly low paid sector of the economy and was still not living completely independently. Her new job had initially been working in an office in a junior role (although she had been promoted several times) and she had moved from living in a bedsit to living back with her parents. However, she had nevertheless found a new way of 'being Sandra'. Faced with completely understandable anxieties about her past and about her future, Sandra took refuge in drugs and alcohol (see Walters, 1999: 66 and Kandel, 1980, cited in Walters, 1999: 67). She sounds like someone who did not much like 'being Sandra' and sought to obliterate that experience as much as she could. Not knowing 'who' she was, feeling uncertain about her own sexuality, she could not imagine a future for herself. Being incapable of seeing a 'future Sandra' (cf. Sartre, 1943: 204–16), she cared little for the present Sandra and sought out something akin to the 'life as party' mentality as described by Shover and Honaker (1992). Her conviction and subsequent probation order evoked mixed emotions within Sandra: on the one hand, this was a chance to review some of what had happened during her life, whilst on the other, she clearly felt 'that her life was over' – no one would want to employ her now. Had this been the case, and Sandra had not got a job, perhaps her life would have followed a by now familiar course of increasing drug use and increasing unemployability.

On epiphanies

In his studies of the processes of change involved in, for example, recovery from alcoholism, Denzin (1987; see also 1989: 15–18, 129–31) introduces the notion of an epiphany – a moment or point in time when clarity is observed for the first time or a sudden realization is made by the individual in question. Similar processes are reported by Ebaugh (1984: 160) in the decision to leave a nun's convent. Could a similar process be observed in Sandra's case? It is our belief that Sandra did not experience a specific moment or period of intense insight which helped or encouraged her to desist. As Bottoms *et al.* (2004: 383), in discussing desistance processes write, 'Damascene conversions may happen for a few, but we suspect that, for many people, the progression is faltering, hesitant and oscillating.' Similarly, Sandra appears to have experienced a number of staging posts, but no clear epiphany. Her second offence, starting probation, gaining work, being promoted and the revolving nature of modern commercial institutions appear to have been more salient features of her desistance.

However, by getting a job Sandra realized that there were others who could and would offer her a second chance. This is an especially important point, because, as Lee (1987) demonstrates, the single most powerful deterrent to continued involvement in self-destructive behaviour is the belief that one could refrain from the behaviour in the future (cited in Walters, 1999: 71). Starting work was nerve-racking, let us be clear about that also. However, slowly Sandra started to see that she did have a future, and in seeing that there was a 'future Sandra' there was now a reason to take care of her appearance, her health and her relationships with those people that most of us, whether we like it or not, rely most heavily upon at moments of change – our parents. Sandra's understanding of who she was, and of who she was *becoming*, was aided not just by her rebuilding of her relationships with her parents, but also by her realization that she had once been like the new recruits to the alcohol project and had moved on from that point (Denzin, 1987). Sandra, as noted above, is not a 'super-desister' set upon a path of righteousness (and this makes her account all the more compelling for us). She was still prone to bouts of nervousness about her work (indicating that she cared about her employment and about what others thought of her) and she was still 'smoking dope'. Searching for a new, meaningful identity created angst, described as nervousness by Sandra. This was dealt with partly by an initial night in the pub at the end of her first week and at times, but increasingly infrequently, by a reliance upon soft drugs.

On competencies and values

As Sandra saw that there was a new way of 'being Sandra', and that she could become a new person, so her relationships with important people around her (her parents and her employers are chief in her account) changed too. In short, Sandra was looking for both a sense of 'who' she was and a way of being that person. This search took place over the course of a year or so just to be initiated. Sandra is still, in many ways and like many others, actively and continually finding out and asserting 'who' she is and who she will become. However, the longer she remained in the same job and was promoted within the same company, the greater her sense of her own competencies grew (see also Kotarba and Bentley, 1988: 558). Sandra's employment enabled her to create a series of new meanings for her self. Tied up in amongst this process of change, although quite where is hard to pinpoint exactly, are changes in Sandra's values. The once 'criminally carefree' Sandra, happily voiding receipts and pocketing the cash to spend on 'thrills, pills and spills' as a way of avoiding existential fear (Walters, 1999: 65), was now so ashamed of her behaviour that she cried throughout her pre-sentence report meeting and on and off for the first three months of her supervision.

One of the findings which emerged from the earlier study, and confirmed in Chapter 3, was that there was little evidence of probation helping very many of these people to stop offending. One respondent, Mickey (see Farrall, 2002: 227), offered this insight into probation work when he was asked what would have helped him stop offending:

Mickey: Something to do with self-progression. Something to show people what they are capable of doing. I thought that that was what [my officer] should be about. It's finding people's abilities and nourishing and making them work for those things. Not very consistent with going back on what they have done wrong and trying to work out why – 'cause it's all going around on what's *happened* – what you've already been punished for – why not go forward into something … For instance, you might be good at writing – push that forward, progress that, rather than saying, 'Well look, why did you kick that bloke's head in? Do you think we should go back into anger management courses?' when all you want to be is a writer. Does that make any sense to you at all?

SF: Yeah, yeah. To sum it up, you're saying you should look forwards not back.

Mickey: Yeah. I know that you do have to look back to a certain extent to make sure that you don't end up like that [again]. The whole order seems to be about going back and back and back. There doesn't seem to be much 'forward'.

What Mickey wanted (but did not get) and what Sandra wanted (and got, although not directly from probation) was someone to show them that there *was* a future for them, some idea of what this could be like and how to move towards that future. As others have noted, interventions in many people's lives are either shaped by their pasts to the exclusion of many other considerations (Meisenhelder, 1985), or do not provide many opportunities for confronting existential issues when struggling with the possibility to change (Ford, 1996), or often are not well suited to dealing with clients who have experienced similar interventions but done poorly at them before (Kotarba and Bentley, 1988). Perhaps the tone of our interventions needs a rethink. Once recent review by Maruna and Farrall in this field ended by arguing that:

> Much of what is done in the name of 'corrections' can be counter-productive – provoking defiance or creating dependence rather than strengthening the person's ability to go straight. As such, desistance-enhancing efforts to promote employment can be and often are coupled with desistance-degrading interactions (e.g., stigmatization and degradation rituals). Such odd coupling can leave promising efforts looking ineffective in formal evaluations when in fact babies are being thrown out with the bath water. At the very least, then, developing a coherent account of how and why former offenders go straight can help those of us in the research world make sense out of our null findings in corrections research.
>
> (2004: 188–9)

However, without a willingness to at least consider in depth the experiences of individuals who have successfully negotiated the transitions from 'offender' to 'convict' to 'ex-convict' to 'normal person', it is hard to see how sustained efforts to encourage desistance (e.g. the What Works movement: McGuire, 1995; Mair, 2004) will produce the sorts of results so desperately craved for.

Notes

---

[1] This should not, however, be taken as an indication that either existentialism or existential sociology represents a unified or agreed upon position. See Manning (1973); Fontana (1980); and Copleston (1972: 125).

[2] However, it ought to be recognized that this is becoming 'less forgotten', and this is certainly the case in criminology following de Haan and Loader's (2002) edited volume of *Theoretical Criminology*.

[3] See also Carlen (1992: 212) on female desisters' beliefs that an alternative way in life might be possible; and Eaton (1993, Chapter 4) on the practical and emotional impediments to such alternative ways of being.

[4] Again, symbolic perhaps of Sandra's status as a 'typical' female probationer, see

Worrall (1990: 46) on 'Jean'. Sandra's drug usage consisted of half an ounce of cannabis a day and using speed and cocaine 'every weekend'.

5   See Worrall (1990: 75) on the guilt felt by female offenders.

6   A common feeling amongst female offenders: see Carlen (1992: 208), who reported that 27 of the 39 women she interviewed expressed similar sentiments.

7   Seemingly a common phenomenon: see the case of 'Mickey' in Farrall (2003).

8   Again, see the case of 'Mickey' in Farrall (2003: 256).

9   Again, a seemingly common experience: at the end of one interview Stephen Farrall conducted in 1994, the young man he had interviewed expressed thanks for the opportunity to reflect during the interview on how much he had changed since his earlier involvement in offending.

10 See Eaton (1993: 88) for similar experiences as recounted by 'Cara'.

Further reading

Ebaugh, H. (1988) *Becoming an Ex*, Chicago University Press, London.

Goffman, E. (1963) *Stigma*, Penguin Books, Harmondsworth, England.

Katz, J. (1988) *The Seductions of Crime*, Basic Books.

Kotarba, J. and Fontana, A. (1984) (eds) *The Existential Self in Society*, Chicago University Press, Chicago.

chapter five

The emotional trajectories of desistance

Getting emotional
The emotional trajectories of desistance
The first phase: early hopes
The intermediate phase
The penultimate phase
The final phase: 'normalcy'

It's been emotional

(Vinnie Jones as Big Chris, *Lock, Stock and Two Smoking Barrels*, 1998, Guy Ritchie)

Crime and emotions are closely associated with each other. This is evident through only the briefest of exposure to discussions on the subject that take place daily in the media and other forums of public debate. Typically, you can expect to hear of the 'anger', 'disgust' and 'pain' of the victims involved or the 'remorse', 'shame', 'bitterness' or 'contempt' of offenders, along with the 'resentment', 'fear' and 'mistrust' of the public or the 'pleasure', 'sorrow', 'sympathy' or 'regret' of the authorities.

These emotions are more than just adjectives used to punctuate the script of the unfolding 'drama'. They are intrinsic to crime and the processes of the sanctions that deal with it. For example, a person may commit an 'expressive' crime because they feel angry at their relative disadvantage or inability to escape an aversive situation (Agnew, 1985), or because they seek the associated feelings of excitement (Katz, 1988); once convicted they may feel shame (Braithwaite, 1989). The offender has to deal with the emotions of others too. The justice process takes place within an environment where 'emotions ... are an important structuring dynamic of criminal justice and punishment' (de Haan and Loader, 2002: 250), affecting the formulation and execution of penal policy, social control and the general social censure of crime. It is unlikely that perpetrators of crime are unaware of such emotional and moral overtones.

What effect does this have on their future criminal behaviour? If strong feelings are responsible for motivating behaviour, as well as helping to shape the identity of the actors involved, and in turn affect the meanings they give to crime and the behaviour of others, what is their role – if any – in enabling desistance from crime? If emotions are an important 'structuring dynamic' for the commission and punishment of crime, what role do they play in its eventual termination? It is such questions that this chapter addresses.

Getting emotional

According to Stanko (2002: 367), 'criminology, as a discipline, is seeped in the emotionality of its subject matter and the emotions of its subjects'. Emotions are found everywhere when studying crime. This is essentially because people view and experience crime *emotionally*. Furthermore, as Stanko points out, academic criminologists are not exempt from similar subjective forces themselves. It is, therefore, surprising that despite this ubiquity the study of emotions has remained largely absent from criminology. This was highlighted by de Haan and Loader (2002) in a recent special issue of *Theoretical Criminology* that sought to address some of the gaps in the literature and provoke debate on the subject. Whilst the contributors focused their attention on the emotions concerned with the social censure of crime, such as those underpinning the law (Barbarlet, 2002) and the criminal justice system (Karstedt, 2002; van Stokkom, 2002), little further light is shed on the emotions surrounding those who have once been involved in crime and have since ceased, or are (at least) beginning to cease from doing so.

This is the case too for other studies that have specifically focused on the roles played by emotions and crime. Katz argues that in order to address seriously the tricky question of 'why individuals who for the most part of their life are not committing crime suddenly feel driven and propelled to do so', we need 'to understand the emergence of distinctive sensual dynamics' (1988: 4) that take place in that moment. Through his study of largely second-hand sources, he draws attention to the foreground of action – i.e. the personal attractions of crime for its participants, what they expect to gain and how they actually feel when doing it – rather than the background 'reasons' favoured by traditional theories of crime, such as strain theory or Marxist theories. Through a phenomenological approach, Katz highlights the symbolic meanings criminals give their actions and the actions of others. He argues how their emotions construct and justify these meanings – 'the sensual dynamics' he observes – need to be respected and taken as authentic. Emotions are not just the byproducts of criminality but are in fact causal factors that drive and sustain crime: the sneaky thrill of the petty thief, the kudos of the 'walk' for members of male gangs, the power of the 'badass' stick-up, the thrill of carrying out more and more audacious crimes and getting away with it.

As welcome as this explanation of the role that emotions play in explaining how individuals are 'seduced' into crime is, it leaves one major question unanswered: how are they 'seduced out'? Why do almost all criminals over their lifetime eventually find that the incentives of dangers and thrills cease to be sufficiently desirable to keep them involved in crime? If they were so irresistible, surely more people would never stop. However, this is patently not the case. Neither is it simply the consequence of a series of rational choices, whereby the increased experience of punishment means that more individuals make a pleasure/pain calculation that favours stopping crime. This would mean that the incentive pleasures provided by crime remained constant, yet for many individuals in our sample – as we shall see – this was not the case. The emotional pleasures which were once so alluring are no longer seen as such.

The 'positive' emotions associated with desistance

People's lives develop and undergo changes as part of the process of desistance. This introduces them to new positive emotional experiences.[1] For many of those who had desisted, positive emotions were associated with new relationships with their family. This was the case for Richard who had got married and become a father. He reported feeling 'brilliant' as a result of marriage and partnership. For others, like Dominic, ceasing to take drugs and the involvement in crime associated with it had allowed him the opportunity to rebuild previously fractured relationships with his wife and children. Whereas he had previously found family life stressful, he now enjoyed seeing his family:

> Oh that's for better, I know that. I mean it's like before, I mean, I've said this to [partner] before, like I used to think myself, 'right I'm married and I got kids', and that, and like you think yourself in ten years' time. I couldn't imagine, you know, being [partner] and kids around there, [I] expected being in a bedsit somewhere on my own, it's now I can imagine still being with [partner] being with kids. Enjoying it ... I couldn't just work my head around it, I thought no it's not going to happen because I've got this and I've got that. You know what I mean? 'She's not going to be happy, she's not going want to go, kids aren't going to be pleased with me because letting down all the time,' you know what I mean? Never see 'em, you know what I mean? And like now it's total different. Total different outlook on everything really.

This re-engagement with his family had opened the door to pleasures involved in being a father, like taking the kids fishing and buying them presents. When asked the question, 'Looking back over your life when were you happiest?,' he said:

...just being at home with kids and that. Doing things, buying them things. I never used to appreciate, you know like, buying them summat and then giving them it, then just walk off and not like getting no response. But like now, I think, 'Oh I bought that toy, proper chuffed with me.' They don't come and tell me that, just go off on their own, I can see they're happy with it where ever they're doing. [...] As long as they're happy, I'm happy enough. That's the way I see them now.

For others, particularly those whose offending had been related to their problems with alcohol and drug use, their previous behaviour had eroded the trust between themselves and their family. For this group, desisting from their previously stigmatized behaviour had allowed them to feel trusted again and this produced feelings of self-worth and happiness that gave them motivation to continue desistance:

AC: And why would you say you've been able to stop?
Bill: 'Cos I want people to trust me. I want me family to trust me.
AC: Why is that important?
Bill: Why, isn't trust important to everyone? If you go ... to have dinner at your mother's or your grandmother's or whatever, they need to be looking round every time you've gone out of t'door, is something going to be missing with him being here? Now they can say, 'Oh, he's trustworthy now.'

When asked to describe how he felt about having stopped offending, he went on:

As I say, people trust me now. If you've got trust round people then you feel happier in yourself and you suddenly lose that trust 'cos you do something then it's going to take you a long time to build that trust back up again.

For others, the new experience of being trusted was dispersed among more diffuse groups and meant a changing relationship with 'the authorities'. In the second wave of interviewing, Mickey described how gaining work had changed the nature of his interaction with the police, which would have previously been antagonistic:

I got pulled over by the police at one o'clock in the morning, and normally, throughout my life I've had hassle from the police, ... just an attitude off the police. As soon as the police pulled me over, I actually got my wallet out and I said, 'I've finished work late and this is the reason why I'm out late,' and they said, 'Who do you work for?' And I said, 'Shufflebottoms,' and I pulled out an ID card and that was it they were fine. Totally different. Black and white they were like white. And I had bald tyres on the front of my car, and they said, 'No problems – can you sort it out within 14 days?' whereas before it had been 'Here's six points.' It's just little things like my bank manager –

he treated me so much differently when he knew I was working full
stop.

Like many people, offenders who have desisted had a desire to feel good
about themselves. This could be achieved by taking pride in their new
roles. When they found themselves praised and trusted by others, it led to
increases in their self-esteem (Miller *et al.*, 1975, cited in Maruna and
Farrall, 2004: 188). Clive had not overcome either his problems as an
alcoholic or found paid employment in the five years since he was previously interviewed. However, he had recast himself in the role of local
'do-gooder', offering advice and help. The feedback he received from
doing this was extremely important to him and he consequently took pride
in his new reputation:

Clive: I'm now passing that on, that information on to
                younger generations and they're dealing with it and
                that's...
Interviewer: And how do you feel when you do that?
Clive: Brilliant. It's an achievement isn't it, know what I
                mean? When you've achieved something. Compared to
                feeling guilty for the damage I've caused not only to me
                parents, but to numerous other people throughout me
                life, when you help somebody and you get praise for it,
                it means everything, you know what I mean? You've
                got a purpose in life. It's really nice when someone
                thanks you for something, and you don't know what
                you've done, know what I mean, you don't feel like
                you've done anything, so when they say, 'Oh cheers for
                that,' that makes all the difference.

He was later asked his feelings about having stopped committing crime:

Well, like I say, it's the achievement, the feedback you get from other
people telling you that you've done well or that ... The praise you get
is different from getting a bad feedback like this, that and the other. If
someone's calling you, you're looking over your shoulder every five
minutes, it's a big change. Big difference. I don't ... Like before when
I was up the shops hanging about, or wherever it was, in a crowd of
people, I didn't have any shame, I didn't feel, you know, I didn't care
about anyone. Whereas now, I don't stand around them places just
doing nothing. There's a lot of people come over and say, 'Can you
help me do this?' 'Do you know this much?' or 'I've got a problem,'
or whatever, and it's good for them. It helps me, but it's good for
them as well. It's not that I'm not doing anything, it's not that I'm just
there drinking. There's a lot more to it. Been there a long time. I do
that all the time.

Pursuing desistance successfully means that individuals must overcome the temptations and attractions which had previously led them towards crime. This requires them to 'learn' new rewards and ways of gaining them. Matthew felt proud of his ability to exercise restraint:

> I can give you an example of when I first come to [the hostel he was living in]. I just started being able to book out [i.e. come and go as he pleased], because the programme down there is very structured. I was walking, I was booked out to go out that day and I was walking through the city centre and seeing a guy walking down these little side streets and he had a big wad of money hanging out of his pockets. Because of the stage that I was at then, I'd seen this money, do you know what I mean, sort of like started sweating, and the adrenaline goes. I found myself starting to follow him and as I got sort of closer I thought, 'What the fuck are you doing?' and basically changed my course and went to the sauna, do you know what I mean? I recognized what was happening, stopped it and didn't act on it or anything. Within time that's, you know, that's one incident that I can think about. But because the drug use is no longer there, basically I've not, I don't need the funds for anything really ... After it was over I felt quite proud of myself for actually not acting on my first thoughts. Didn't act impulsively, stopped it and felt quite proud. Whereas before if I'd been back on the streets [...] on drugs, I'd have probably walked up there and taken it. But I didn't. I'd say proud.

For many others, new positive emotions emerged in their lives because of their involvement in work (for example, see Sandra in Chapter 4). Through long term employment, others, like Rajeev, have found themselves spending much of their time with people who share society's 'conventional' goals and values and the accepted means to achieving these. The effect of this has meant that they have become resocialized towards these values (see also Chapter 6 on socialization and resocialization). Their previous goals and values are seen as impractical, given the time spent at work, as well as undesirable:

AC:	Okay, and how do you feel about having stopped?
Rajeev:	I feel a lot better in myself.
AC:	Right how, in a few words, how would you describe yourself back then and yourself now? How would you compare the 'two' yous?
Rajeev:	Oh gosh, totally different, total opposite. I've gone from one extreme to another.
AC:	Describe them for me.
Rajeev:	Well, back then I didn't have much focus in life. I just wanted to doss about and go out with friends, go clubbing. But now, I'm working, I'm trying to save up money, err. I'm giving myself five years to actually save enough money

> to put a deposit down on a house. Okay. And that's my main aim now, is to save up some money to buy a house.

For Meera, a white-collar offender, the act of successfully finding employment was seen as an emotional watershed that marked the end of a traumatic chapter in her life. Meera feared she would never get another job and would be stigmatized as an offender for ever. She was proud of her own role in achieving this because it confirmed her own ability and competence and ultimately marked the rebirth of her 'respectable' self.

> It was a very big achievement because I'd gone out, I'd made enquires, things I wouldn't, I didn't want to acknowledge that that situation was there. Oh it will go away, it will go away but it wasn't, it was there and I had to face it and the only way of doing that was by acknowledging it and making the enquiries that only I could make, not my husband or [probation officer] or anyone else, I had to do it. And that's, I think that was the first hurdle that I'd overcome. And once I'd done that it was, it was really a very big relief. My daughter was about seven months at the time and it was a big thing that I'd gone out and done this and I'd done it in the sense of I didn't ask my husband to take me or I didn't ask friends to take me, I'd gone out and done this myself.

When asked how she felt about having stayed out of trouble, Meera said:

> Really good because if I didn't do it there's no . . . Not 'no reason', but if I can do it then I've shown to myself that I can do it. There's no reason or there is hope for other people to try and correct their lives as well.

For some, a new identity itself allowed for the emergence of happiness:

> AC: What would you say has been the biggest change in your life since, well since we last interviewed you five years ago?
> Jules: Stopped taking drugs, working the programme and just being *happy*. And just being happy. Well I've got another partner that I love and that's it really just, you know, just grown up really, I think ... and change and change in everything. There's so many things that have changed, I mean the major thing I suppose is stopped taking drugs ... Yeah [inner changes] in myself, inside myself because I'm me today, I'm not anyone else, I'm just me and I don't need to put on a front to this person or a front to that person, I'm just me.

So, desistance, at an emotional level, is as much about changes in feelings as it is about changes in behaviour, family formation, employment and so on. Whilst these feelings help to reinforce the desires to stay out of trouble, desistance also brings to light a different set of emotions – the negative ones associated with one's previous lifestyle.

The negative emotions associated with past offending

One of the advantages recognized by offenders as they moved away from offending and its consequences was that they were no longer subject to the unwelcome and uncomfortable emotions that accompanied it. The consequences of offenders' behaviour had often had a negative impact on those close to them, such as their family, creating feelings of shame and guilt[2] in the offender. Peter, when he was using heroin, felt that he was unable to avoid acting selfishly and with disregard for the feelings of his family. However, by desisting, he was able to exercise control and therefore could start to rebuild previously damaged relationships:

> I mean I, I've done things in the past, like for instance, I might've owed me grandma £20 and rather than give the £20 to ma grandma I've gone out and bought drugs. And me grandma's always said well, you know, 'You don't care, you only care about yourself,' and that kinda thing. And, for a while, me family were of, of the impression that I didn't care, you know, I were only interested in meself but that wasn't true, it wasn't like I didn't care, I would go out and spend that £20 and get the drugs and then once I'd actually had the drugs then I'd sit and I'd feel so guilty for not giving me grandma the money. But at the time it, I, I had little choice, you know, it were either that or be ill. Whereas now, because I don't have that over me, I don't have that cloud hanging over me, I can think more clearly and I can consider other people. And as I say, I have put a lot of work into it and I think I've built bridges [with my family] ... definitely.

He later explained how having stopped using heroin now meant that he was no longer exposed to the fearful uncertainty that his offending may yet bring further upsetting implications to his grandmother:

> I feel a lot better 'cos I don't have to worry about getting a knock on door, you know. 'Cos as I say, me family were of the view that I didn't care, you know, but, but I do, I care a lot more than they might imagine. And I were always worried about knock on door, not so much for meself ... But it's me grandma's flat, you know, and I don't want them coming bashing me grandma's door down, things like that. So that's another good reason why I don't get involved any more, 'cos I don't want the attention for me grandma. Because she's put up with it, 'cos it has happened. I wouldn't say it's happened regularly but, I would say over the, over the duration of the time I were on drugs I bet police have been at door maybe six, seven times. And twice they've bashed door down, so enough's enough. I mean when me grandfather died, the last thing he said to me before he died were, he said 'Oh I'm, I'm not too worried where I'm going,' he said, ''Cos I know you'll look after your grandma.' And that plays on me mind 'cos pretty much all I did since he died is take drugs and abuse me grandma basically, one way and another. You know, taking drugs

in her house and things like that. So that always played on me mind, so that's another incentive, you know, she looked after me for years and I think it's about time she got a bit back. Which is what I do now.

One of the consequences of avoiding crime is, obviously, that individuals no longer need to fear being arrested as much as they once did. This means they are less likely to be subject to states of apprehension and anxiety. Because of their actions, they were once anxious that they may be arrested at any time. As they had no control as to when this may happen, they were powerless over when these feelings of fear may return. After desisting they found themselves free of this overshadowing concern and this brought with it feelings of relief. This process is illustrated by Niall:

> AC: How do you feel about having stopped offending?
> Niall: I love it because I don't look over my shoulder. I'm happy, free. I don't have to ... yeah, I mean I remember when I used to drive round while I was drinking, I used to drive around and think ... every time I see a cop car I'd start ruddy ... my heart'd start going, sweat on the brow, I'd be like nervous. Now I don't do anything wrong so I've no ... I've nothing eating away at me anymore, if you know what I mean. You know, nothing. I've gone through two years of being eaten away about my dad and my mum, you know, and before that all the crimes and looking over my shoulder and wondering whether I'm gonna get nicked or this, that and the other. I don't have any of that. And you just feel like, yeah, a weight ... it's a weight gone out of life, isn't it? You're just happy, you feel ... you're not happy all the time, but you just feel a little bit more relaxed and comfortable about living your life. And you can turn round, in all fairness, and say to anybody, you know, 'Well at least I've earned what I've got,' you know, or, 'At least I've made the effort to change things.' Whether I've failed or not is a different matter. You know, even if you try and you fail, at least you tried.

Practising and achieving success through conventional goals meant that desisters found themselves in a favourable position when compared to others. As the above example shows, this can generate feelings of pride and self-worth. It also removes the differences that they felt previously existed between themselves and others in 'respectable' society. Without these differences they are no longer open to humiliation and anger by being judged as 'criminals'. Here George describes his experiences:

> AC: How do you feel about having stopped offending?
> George: I feel good about myself. It's more of a conscience clear, one is that you know that no one is going to come to you and say 'excuse me can you come down the nick please I want an interview about this ...?' because, you know, you

haven't done anything. Secondly I think it is important when you meet people that ain't criminals, you know. When you are a criminal and you meet people that ain't criminals there's always something inside you saying 'they're not like you, they're not like you, they look down upon you', you know. And then you start getting angry towards them because 'you can't look at me that way, I did what I did for my reasons', you know. And being not a criminal now I feel that I'm on an equal level to everybody else, you know. There's nobody out there that's better or worser than me. I get up, I go to work, I pay my taxes, I pay my National Insurance, I've got just as much right to hold my head up high as anybody else and feel good about myself in that way.

This theme of the unwelcome stigma of being labelled a criminal is highlighted by Mark's comments on how he feels about having stopped offending:

AC: How do you feel about having stopped offending?

Mark: Yeah, feel better, yeah, because I'm an honest hard-working citizen ... You know, it can't be nothing worse than the bill[3] pointing the finger saying, you know, 'that's the thieving git at the town' or ...

AC: Yeah.

Mark: You know, 'don't trust him he'll nick it', 'don't let him know what you've got he'll nick it'. You know sort of like in a community area ...

AC: Did that ever happen to you?

Mark: Err, I think we was always known in the area for like, you know, it's always started sort of things that go on, it's like, you know, it must be one of them lot. One of them lot must know who's done it and ...

AC: Yeah?

Mark: You know things like that and ... Even at night, you know, when it's getting dark people sort of like cross the road to walk by and start, you know ...

AC: Yeah?

Mark: It's horrible really because they feel we're going to mug them or attack them you know. Yeah, it's stupid things like that and it's just like when I go out now I think oh I've got to stay away from that area, trouble in there and, you know, I just don't want to go on none of it.

AC: No. So you're doing ...

Mark: I'm doing what other people used to do to us, yeah. You know, stay away from certain areas and ... Yes, you know, it's surprising once you get older you just think about things more, don't you? Not so much you've got more time to think about things but you just, before you do anything you just think, think a bit more about it. Well I suppose when you're a bit younger you're a bit 'yeah, yeah, yeah', you know, everything's in the fast lane and all in a hurry, you know.

The emotional trajectories of desistance

In this section we outline a schema of the emotional trajectories of desistance. This is our attempt to classify the sorts of emotions that our respondents reported having felt and the approximate point in the process of desisting that they experienced such emotions. This entailed ranking each of our desisters along a continuum, with the most recently desisted (i.e. those who had only recently embarked upon the road to desistance) at one end and those who had ceased offending several years previously at the other. We then coded each respondent's description of the desistance in terms of the emotions that they said they had felt (see Figure 5.1). From our schema, four rough 'phases' emerged. We are not suggesting that there are four emotional phases which any desister 'needs' to go through in order to desist successfully (for each process has its own unique facets). Rather, our use of the term 'phases' is as much an aid to analysis as it is the result of any analysis.

The first phase: early hopes

Compared with other phases of the trajectory towards desistance, those respondents who were identified as having embarked recently on their desistance journeys, and consequently placed in the early phase, were found to express a narrower range of emotions. The most commonly expressed emotions were that they were now 'happier' than they used to be and they frequently described themselves as feeling 'better in myself'. These positive feelings were largely seen as the result of no longer having to endure the unwelcome negative emotions that were associated with a criminal career, such as the fear of impending arrest, the inconvenience and trepidation associated with further court appearances and the general requirement of continually 'having to look over your shoulder'. The following examples illustrate this point:

AC: How do you feel about having stopped offending?
Frank: A lot better in myself.
AC: Why?
Frank: Just to wake up to know that I haven't got nothing, do you

Phase One: Early Hopes — case numbers: 121, 013, 077, 165, 073, 172, 092

Phase Two: Intermediate — case numbers: 158, 180, 227, 076, 095, 108, 127

Phase Three: Penultimate — case numbers: 146, 115, 094, 081, 059, 110, 114, 223, 105, 051, 198

Phase Four: 'Normalcy' — case numbers: 120, 025, 043, 122, 202, 080, 064, 199

Emotion
- Happier
- Feeling better in themselves
- Hopes and aspirations
- Previous -ve feelings
- Regrets about past
- Rewards and self-esteem
- Guilt, shame and disgust
- Pride and achievement
- Trust and belonging

Broad direction of travel: from crime towards desistance

Figure 5.1: Emotional trajectory of desistance

> know what I mean, to panic myself about, to worry about, looking over my shoulder about. Err [...] Yes it's sort of like a relief, you know what I mean?

In describing how he currently felt compared to before he had started to desist, Matthew said:

> Matthew: How am I different? I don't take drugs and I don't commit crime anymore.
>
> AC: How do you feel about this change?
>
> Matthew: I feel good about it. As I say, I don't have to look over my shoulder, I don't have to appear in court, I don't have to ... The only person I've got to answer to is me really.

He later went on to echo these comments in his description of the alleviation of the disadvantages associated with the chaotic and haphazard lifestyle he had endured when immersed in the lifestyle of petty crime. This lifestyle was required to support his longstanding addictions to crack cocaine and heroin. The disadvantages included fear of apprehension and arrest and the consequences of convictions, as well as the unpleasant, but ultimately inconvenient and mundane, rituals of being 'processed' by the court and criminal justice system. His move away from this towards desistance had meant the following:

> Matthew: Not having to worry about getting arrested or the police coming after you or going to prison.
>
> AC: That was a big worry before?
>
> Matthew: Yeah, yeah it was. It's the lifestyle that you lead, you know, always looking over your shoulder and missing bail appointments and court appearances and one thing or another, so you're constantly on the run, aren't you? If you chance to see a police officer you dodge them. But there's only so much running you can do.

After identifying working 'instead of going out and pinching whatever I could get my hands on' as the biggest change in his life since the last interview, another case, Tom, went on to describe the impact of this change:

> It's a lot better, yeah. It's a lot better. I don't have to look over my shoulder. I were only thinking half an hour ago when I was stood over there at court [the arranged meeting place before interview], I could see people going in and out and I just knew what they were feeling. 'Am I going to go to jail or aren't I gonna go to jail?' and it's a horrible feeling, it really is.

Feeling happier was reported by every one of the eight respondents we placed in this phase (see Figure 5.1) and five of them used the exact phrase that they 'felt better' in themselves. In fact, feeling good and happier than before is reported by almost our entire desisting sample, regardless of the phase they were in, and 'feeling better in myself', although not quite as universal, repeatedly emerged throughout the schema. Thus they may be viewed as two of the most common emotions associated with desisting. The reason for their consistency appears to be that many of those who begin to desist from crime – for example, by reducing the intensity and severity of their offending – automatically reduced, and in many cases removed, the unpleasant aspects and emotions associated with their lives as criminals.[4] This experience appeared to be applicable to everyone who desisted. Compared to the worst times of their criminal past, no matter how far along the process of desisting that they were, the fact that they always felt happier perhaps explains this emotion's ubiquity as a permanent rather than temporary feature of the desistance process.

Several of the desisters in the early phase experienced the emotion of hope. Often this was the hope that from now on they would successfully avoid future offending. This is strongly felt by the cases in this early phase of the schema and would appear to be the most noteworthy emotion in this phase. Like other offenders, 'recent desisters' have an aspiration towards 'normal life,' in line with society's goals such as family, job and place to live (Bottoms et al., 2004; see George in Chapter 3). These desires were regularly encountered in their descriptions of their future ambitions:

> Err, just keep going the way I'm going. Err, and hopefully to get back with [ex-partner] who's like the mother of my son and live a proper, proper family life. And carry on the way I'm going and build on everything I've got already.
>
> (Frank)

> Long term, I don't know. I'll face that when it comes to it. I just want, you know, to settle down and have a couple of kids. Just like everyone else basically. I just want a happy life.
>
> (Ben)

This journey towards 'normality' is not an automatic but rather a gradual process of adjustment and change and probably one that is never fully completed (see Douglas, 1984). At this initial stage, the experience of actually moving in this direction appears to be a conscious one (Maruna and Farrall, 2004). Desisters are reminded that desistance is a worthwhile goal and of the progress they have made, by the fact that the features associated with their lifestyle as offenders often linger. For example, Matthew described the impact on his life of not having used drugs for the previous six months:

> I feel a lot more positive. Getting into what you see as 'normal' society and not be[ing] judged by anyone because I don't have to disclose [my criminality]. Just when we walk through there, the barman says, 'What's in the bag?' I says, 'I don't know. It's not mine.' He says, 'Have you got anything for sale?' I says, 'No, I don't do that

any more.' Do you know what I mean? And before [when using drugs] I *would have had* something to sell, you know what I mean ... That's why people in pubs, you know, ask them kind of things. Yeah, just being able to fit into every day life really.

Furthermore, the respondents in this early phase are more likely still to need to overcome many of the same obstacles to going straight, such as heavy drug and alcohol use or problems with employment, that they faced when they were engaged in offending. It is this precarious position of respondents at the start of the desistance process that means there is a greater degree of uncertainty that this desire for normality can be achieved. These cases not only have travelled a shorter distance away from the circumstances of their offending, but also have a greater distance still to cover until they have completed the process. There is a feeling that they are still *moving* towards, rather than having achieved, a 'normal life' (Goffman, 1963). It is this uncertainty that qualifies the aspiration as 'a hope' to continue the journey towards normality and to avoid future offending. Ben was aware of this himself, as his response to the question 'what have been the major changes in your life since the last interview?' shows:

Ben: Well, I've settled down with me girlfriend. Although some-
       times we do have [our] ups and downs ... erm, my financial
       situation's a bit better 'cos I've been working on and off. I'm
       not always in a steady job though. Er. I just think, you know,
       I'm getting on a bit better with my life, you know, I've grown
       up a little bit but I'm still not there you know.
AC: What do you mean by that?
Ben: I've got a long way to go, you know, before I think, you know,
       I'm settled.

He went on to say that he still 'had a long way to go' to overcome his problem with drugs (he was still on a daily methadone prescription) and find regular full time employment. Being regularly out of work led to times with no money when he felt depressed (which he also attributed to his use of methadone) and which resulted in uncertainty, as seen in the times when he said he had been tempted 'to turn back to crime' and that 'it's always in the back of me head'. Despite owing its existence to uncertainty, the emotion of hope provides an important resource for those at the *beginning* of the desistance process to draw on. It provides them with the vision that an alternative, more 'settled' future *is* possible; it provides them with both a plan and a motivation to continue further in the direction of desistance.

Let us now embark upon a short detour in order to disucss the role of hope in the early phase of the desistance process. As Burnett and Maruna (2004) have demonstrated, hope is an important factor amongst ex-prisoners. However, as our schema (Figure 5.1) suggests, hopes and other feelings ebb and flow throughout the desistance process. In throwing further light on hope in this process, we rely upon the work of Christy Simpson.

A hope-filled parenthesis

Although she was writing in a healthcare context, and was referring to the desire to recover from illness, Simpson (2004) provides a comprehensive description of hope and one which can easily be adapted for the context of desistance and the desire to go straight. Her definition of hope is as follows:

> Hope is an emotional attitude whereby the person who hopes for p (where p is the event or state of affairs hoped for): a) desires/wants p; b) believes p is in accordance with her values and/or goals; c) imagines p is a realisable possibility for her, even though it is uncertain whether p or not-p will occur; and, d) acts in such a way as to support her hope (i.e., where it is possible to affect whether p will occur, she will try to bring p about; minimally, she will not act to foreclose the possibility that p will occur) – this may include making use of available opportunities and resources (personal, material) and/or relying on other individuals.
>
> (2004: 431–2)

Using a brief case study, Jimmy, we wish to illustrate why hope is particularly important to his desires to desist. Jimmy was in his early 30s when he started a 24 month probation order after being convicted of dangerous driving and driving whilst disqualified. He had a long and prolific offending history. Probation records at the time of the first interview in 1997 listed this offence as his 36th formal conviction; his previous convictions mainly comprised burglary and theft offences, but also violence, fraud and summary offences. He also reported committing many more crimes for which he had received no conviction, such as class A drug use, drink driving, dealing drugs and driving whilst disqualified more than 20 times, as well as shoplifting and burglary offences. Unsurprisingly, he was very familiar with both community and custodial sentences and said that he had 'just done seven of the last ten years in jail' on a revolving door basis. At the time of the first interview, he said he wanted to stop offending because he was getting too old, did not want to spend any more time in prison and did not want his son going through 'what I've been through'. He was uncertain whether he would be able to do it but would 'give it a fucking good go'. He talked of owning his own business and a house that would allow him 'to get a different life' away from crime. However, he had no specific plans on how to achieve this other than by moving away from the town he was living in, which he identified as an obstacle to his desistance because of the corrupting influence of his friends involved in crime and his bad reputation with the police.

Despite wanting to stop offending and having a vague plan of how to achieve this, Jimmy was not successful and continued to offend whilst on probation. Both the second and third interviews were conducted in prison whilst Jimmy was on remand for further offences. During the six month period between the first and second interviews, he had succeeded in moving to a new town well away from his home town, found work and had been attending college and was in the process of submitting a business plan to refurbish derelict houses. At the second interview, following his arrest for GBH, he repeatedly spoke about his hopes, saying, '... if I get found not guilty on this, there's hope that I will, I can go straight back to [my business plan]'. He added, 'hopefully, touch wood, have the house sorted' and 'hopefully I will be back in [the new area he moved to]'. However, when he was interviewed for the third time, 11 months later, his bail had been revoked following his arrest for theft and during his interview he no longer expressed such hopes. His hope that he would avoid future offending had been extinguished by his assessment that there was a '70 per cent chance of me committing further offences', and he felt if he stayed in his home town this would increase to '100 per cent'. At the end of the third interview, Jimmy was feeling all but convinced that he would offend again, pessimistic that his previous vision of a life away from crime could be realized, unsure how he would achieve it and not hopeful about the prospects of his desisting.

When we interviewed Jimmy for a fourth time (at the end of 2003), he had been out of prison for six months and was resident in a drug rehab centre. He had not offended since coming out of prison and told us that he had not used drink or drugs for 15 months. As during the earlier interviews, he said he wanted to avoid further offending and said, 'I'm not going back to all the bollocks, you know, criminal shit.' However, whereas these statements had been accompanied in previous interviews with qualifications that buying stolen goods was not 'real offending' but 'just doing a mate a favour', and beliefs that the solution to avoiding crime was to be found in 'escaping' to another town that would bring anonymity, his desire to avoid crime was now from the outlook of a new identity – Jimmy had found God. Jimmy referred to himself as an 'ex-fucking criminal' and emphasized that there would be 'no more' crime. In order to transform his identity, Jimmy had needed to adopt a new set of beliefs and values that would also be goals in themselves. For example, he said that the biggest change in his life since the last interview was that he now 'doesn't do crime' and 'doesn't do drugs'. When asked what he meant by this, he said:

> Doing good and not doing bad. 'Cos I'm a firm Believer now of course ... um, that if you do good, you feel good. If you do bad, you feel bad. Simple as that. Well, it's worked up to now for me so why not? Do you know what I mean? Certainly working for me.

Here we can see how his new values act as a new system of incentives and rewards to encourage him to continue to maintain his desistance. Furthermore, adopting these new values has been something of a necessity in that he has had to replace the previous system of rewards provided by his pursuit of crime. This process is not an easy one: the existential realization that your life is 'worthless' and 'no good' is a painful experience, but hope enabled Jimmy to imagine that there was an alternative future for him and that this was a realizable possibility. This meant that it was worth pursuing, as seen when prompted to explain how he felt about his change of values:

> Very hopeful for the future. Very hopeful. And hopefully I can work with other people who've been, or who was in my situation. And show them that they can ... there is another life out there. 'Cos when you're mixed up in this kind of life, er, it's rotten, you know, um. To take that on board once you're in the middle of it, well the next question is, 'Well what am I going to do about it?' So you can't admit that to yourself. You know? So it's good to do crime, it's good to do drink, it's good to do drugs. But if you say 'no, it's bad' you're fucked, because you've got to change it. And it's a massive, I don't whether you know anything about addiction and alcohol and stuff, even crime, crime is an addiction, um, it's a fucking massive problem. 'Cos it's all, well more or less every fucking behaviour in the book you've got to change. And the force, well. [Sighs] It'll blow you away, you know what I mean? But, erm, it's doable, it is doable, if you want.

For a deep-rooted 'career criminal' like Jimmy an important element of the emotion of hope involves possessing not only the belief but also the imagination that this difficult change from criminal to 'good person' is, ultimately, 'doable'. What makes this 'desire' hope is the fact that it is still subject to uncertainties. Jimmy felt that his friends still posed a threat to his chances of staying straight and he may be forced to 'use violence' in order to persuade them that 'this life is not for me no more' but 'I hope not. I certainly hope not', he says. The idea that his continued desistance is still uncertain, and that there are no guarantees, is illustrated by the following extract where he talks about how he will deal with the difficulties of drugs, alcohol and the problems they might pose for his future desistance:

> Yeah, let me just explain, um, here, um, we've got an AA twelve step programme. Er and we go to regular AA groups every week. Four a week we go to. And the mad thing, I don't know if you know anything about this stuff, but the mad thing is, every time you go to these meetings, you are basically reminded where you come from. That's the whole idea of it. And because you're reminded constantly along the way, where you come from, you don't go back there. Can you see what I'm trying to say? So if I keep going to meetings, um, and

surrender myself . . . recovering alcoholics, drug addicts, I go to NA as well, then basically, um, I'll be alright. I hope. Because there's no guarantees.

Jimmy here uses the resources and opportunities provided to him by the new networks of Narcotics Anonymous (NA) and Alcoholics Anonymous (AA) to support his hope. Jimmy was aware of the hard work ahead of him, however in a passage reminiscent of Maruna's (2001) generative script, he says:

Well, it's worth it. It's worth it because, um, again once I've been out of jail a year I can start helping people again and that's got to give me a good purpose in life. I know about people, 'cos I've been there, done it. And I can pass it back, my experiences, onto trying to help the next one, who are all going through the same shit as me, or went through the same shit as me. You know what I mean? And I think that's what it's all about really. Obviously I'll do other stuff as well. What yet I don't know. I don't know yet, I don't know. But um, we'll get through this, and then we're going to have to look at it seriously. And I'd love to become a counsellor. And I can't see no reason why not. But um, and obviously, again, that's passing my, see 'cos, I don't know whether you can understand the last twenty years, I've had a fucking lot of experience, and um, like you, you go to college to do a degree, can you see what I'm trying to say here? And now, I'm a fucking criminal, it's not the ideal occupation to have, but if you can pass that back to the next robber and try and say to him 'look, I you know you're going to end up there, there, there, there and there, right, and you're fucking, you know it's not a very nice place', surely that's got to be worthwhile? Same fucking bollocks I've wasted the last twenty years. If I try and use that twenty years to somebody else's advantage, does that make any sense? Yeah. Well that's what I'm hoping to do. You know what I mean?

Some level of hope, it would appear, is required at the onset of desistance in order to maintain the belief that one's goals are in line with one's values and are a feasible possibility for the individual concerned.

The intermediate phase

As we move into the next phase of the trajectory, we find ourselves with offenders who have by and large left offending behind for longer periods of time, sometimes around two or three years. However, in many cases they had experienced setbacks and either relapsed and used drugs again or committed one-off, isolated offences. These offences were often comparable in seriousness to the ones they were originally convicted for.

However, despite this, their identity as would-be non-offenders appeared as a result of their 'backsliding' to have become much stronger, as was their resolve that they will not offend again. As these desisters begin to put more distance between themselves in the present and themselves as more frequent offenders, we begin to witness a pattern where they refer back to their experience of previously negative emotions. The emotional experience of this phase was characterized by a growing sense of internal disquiet when they remembered their previous actions and lifestyles. Regrets about the past started to emerge for many. For some, however, merely realizing that they were no longer (or increasingly less) dependent on drugs and alcohol provided new feelings of self-esteem.

For example, at the time of the first interview, Clive reported his use of alcohol as an obstacle to desistance (Farrall, 2002). His proposed solution to overcoming this problem was to isolate himself from 'people who are a bad influence', referring to other alcoholics who drank on the streets. However, he was pessimistic about the possibility of achieving this because, as he saw it, 'it would be an offence to be with them and not to drink. It would mean you are not one of them'. By the time of the fourth interview this sense of obligation had gone. Although he had not solved his drinking problem (he was still drinking daily and had been arrested for being drunk and disorderly), he now felt capable of avoiding peer pressure. Whereas previously he put down the reasons for submitting to this pressure to feeling a debt to his 'community' and not wishing to lose the 'sense of belonging' and support that they offered, he now acknowledged that it, in fact, owed a lot to wishing to avoid unwanted feelings of being degraded and humiliated if he refused to go along with what they wanted. Awareness of these feelings can be seen in his explanation as to how he is different currently compared to the time of the offence:

> Well I wouldn't put myself in that position. I wouldn't do it. Where I had light fingers before, when I was drinking that sort ... don't tend to do it anymore. I don't put myself in that type of company. I used to drink with a lot of lads and, know what I mean, a lot of it was coached ... You felt degraded if you. .. or they made you feel degraded if you didn't do what they wanted you to do. You know what I mean, you just want to be one of the lads, one of the group, and I don't get involved in that any more. That's not, [I] don't have a problem with any of that. If I do drink, it's me own choice now, you know what I mean. It's not ... I mean people don't force you to. I feel like I've changed such as I don't mix with it. I don't set meself up to fail. I don't put meself in that position.

George described how not offending was not only good because it removed the stigma of being labelled as an 'offender', but also that it meant that he no longer had to handle feelings of anger generated by what he saw as the presumptuous judgements of others (see above). Dominic, a previous long term heroin user, referred to the embarrassment he used to feel about his physical appearance. Stopping heroin had led to an improvement in this and the bonus of improving his interaction with his family:

AC: How do you feel about having stopped [offending]?
Dominic: Feel a lot better, in myself alone and for my family. Like I say, kids have noticed it more, as well. Our lass is a lot happier anyway.
AC: You say the kids have noticed a lot more?
Dominic: Yeah, yeah, yeah, and everytime. It's like one time, [they] wouldn't have their photograph taken with me, but it's all over now. I mean kids, fishing and all sorts, you know ... All drawn in face and looked poorly all time and you know what I mean? I were conscious about how I looked. Things like that.

For others such as Barry, there was a more conscious recognition of the existence of these negative feelings and the implications they had for his offending. An awareness of the need to control them emerged over time. Again, talking about how he is different from when he finished his probation order, he said he 'sits back and observes things more'. His assessment of this change was as follows:

It's much better, you know. I feel that I'm not so aggressive and more chilled. So yeah, no, it's better for me really ... I'm still an angry person. I don't think I've ever said that. I've always been an angry person, but I've only realized now later on that I am quite an angry person, you know. I get frustrated quite quickly, which is slowing down, but I still do, but I'm finding myself stopping myself, instead of going 'Aaargh!', do you understand what I mean?

He also identified the maintenance and control of these negative feelings of anger as being the result of his own efforts and conscious changes within himself over time, so he doesn't 'bottle things up' so much any more:

I think [probation] helped me to open up, and yeah, part of maturing as well. It also helped me to start talking about ... Before I used to bottle things up, you know. When I was a kid especially. But as I've got older and older, I find it more and more easier to talk about what's going on in my life, you know. Now so many things have happened, you know, there's nothing else can happen that'll be as bad as what has happened, you know.

The penultimate phase

Almost all of the cases that were placed in this phase had had quite entrenched offending careers, but had managed to stay (largely) crime free for three or more years. During this phase of the desistance process, more of our respondents started to talk about the shame and guilt they felt about their former lives (see also van Stokkom, 2002: 340). For some, despite the temptation to offend remaining with them, the emotions of guilt and personal shame provided a brake on them making a return to their previous offending behaviour. In this respect, guilt appeared to motivate respondents into taking responsibility for their past and future actions (see Retzinger and Scheff, 1996, cited in van Stokkom, 2002: 343). For Jamie, thinking about the wider implications of stealing a car again – the potential impact on its owners and the disruption he would cause – created an awareness of the feelings of guilt that would arise from pursuing such temptations:

> It's one big playground, innit? It's just the way it is, innit? There are plenty of opportunities out there for someone to get into trouble. It's just whether you can walk on by, innit? I mean, I walk on by ... passed a shop one time when I was with my missus and I said 'look out there', outside the dentist there was BMW convertible with the engine running sat in a car park. Back when I was seventeen I would probably have jumped straight in there and gone. I would have loved that but when I walk past now I would say things as 'look at that, fucking hell!', now I would see it as a sort of, err, I could be not like a crime avoider but a sort of a person that avoids the people and [tell others] what to do without getting your fucking car stolen. Because I wouldn't steal a car now because I know [that] the mortgage don't get paid and things like that, but when I was seventeen you don't realize about things like that. I thought it weren't harming no one. It was only a fifty pound Metro, it wasn't worth anything. But now I realize that fifty pound Metro is probably someone's wages for a week to get to work in and then you know, the kids don't get fed and shit like that and so ... And that's probably what's changed in me, I've grown up and realized that you can't do things like that no more, because no matter how less things are worth, it's always worth more to someone else than what it is to you, innit?

This guilt was not confined only to feelings about 'direct' victims. For Anthony, although he admitted feeling nostalgic for his 'rogue' days of heavy drinking and fighting, he could not see himself returning to it because of the shame it would bring to those closest to him, adding that 'you can't be a pissed up bum to your kids'. During this phase, some desisters identified shameful feelings about the suffering their behaviour had caused their family as the motivating force behind their starting the transformation away from offending.[5] Tony described the biggest change in his life as coming off drugs. He had this to say about what he feels is responsible:

> And me family as well, me mum, me mum hasn't been well. She's always in and out of hospital. They said a lot of that were caused through stress and that. Most of all her blood pressure or summut stupid, having heart attacks and that, said they're all caused through stress and that so me dad put that down to me, you know? Her worrying about me, so basically putting me mum in a grave as well as meself in a grave. I didn't think it [continuing to use drugs] were fair really.

Justin had the following thoughts:

> [Talking to my probation officer] made me think about it you know. I didn't want to be a bad person, you know, I never wanted to be a bad person but, err, that kind of thing isn't nice for anyone. So by her telling me that I'm upsetting my family by doing it, it made me realize that I should really cut down.

For those who suffered setbacks and relapses into offending and substance misuse, intense feelings of shame were often experienced. Al saw it as 'relabelling' him as a criminal:

> AC: How do you feel about that fine [for possession of unlicensed vehicle]?
> Al: Oh it done my head in. It's nothing to do with the fine it's to do with all the amount … the length of time I've been out of trouble to getting something else on my record. It's like I've not stayed away from it, you know what I mean, anymore. So now any judge or any policeman or anything like that they'll look at me and say, 'He's not changed, he's just not been caught.' And it's not right, you know what I mean.

But for others, like Peter, the unwelcome reintroduction of guilt provided a further incentive to desist from heroin use:

> You know, when I were on drugs, I didn't have a care, everything were great. You know, then when I wasn't on drugs, then just, it were complete opposite. So it were more to do wi' me moods but I just learnt to deal with it, I just thought, 'Well, you know, I don't wanna get back on drugs.' Because it, it perpetuates, you know, I would go and use drugs and then the following day, one, I would feel guilty for using drugs, which that in itself would put me on a downer and make me feel worse, which I'd, you know, there's more a propensity to go out and use again. And two, there's the physical side of it, the cold turkey side of it, and, you know, so I'd have to go use, so I didn't want to get back into that trap.

However, one of the most interesting emotions which emerged amongst respondents we placed in this phase was that of trust. Feelings of trust had not been mentioned by respondents in either of the earlier two phases, but was mentioned by six of the 11 respondents in the penultimate phase (see Figure 5.1).

The emotions of trust

Respondents in the penultimate phase described how, having desisted for a period of time, they found themselves increasingly trusted by family members. This emotion was an important incentive for their continued desistance. Whilst they had been offending, this trust was lost, but now that they had ceased for a reasonable period of time (often over three years) they could start to rebuild this trust. Peter described this as 'building bridges':

> I get on reasonably well with my brother. We have, overall, a decent relationship. Although, since then, I've built a lot of bridges, get on a lot better with me family these days.

Peter described the struggle he had had to endure in order to rebuild his relationship with his family:

> I think a lot of it at the time were the drugs, there were a lot o' mistrust. I mean, I've never actually done anything to me family. I mean like, I know people that have been in my situation and they've robbed their family blind, you know, but I, I've never done anything like that. You know, it's not like I'd give 'em reason, I think it, a lot of it were, it's just stigma, you know, stigmatized. And there were a lot 'o mistrust and because of that I, I isolated meself more than them isolating me, you know, because I didn't like going down to visit me brother, or visit me mum and then they'd be following me round the house everywhere I went, you know, and that made me feel bad. So that's why I actually stopped going [to visit them], you know, to save putting meself in that situation because then that put me on a downer, which were pointing more towards drugs and I were trying best I could to avoid triggers like that. 'Cos a lot of the reasoning why I got involved wi' drugs in the first place were through, through emotional issues, through family and things like that. So I were just trying to box clever and avoid them situations.

This process of losing and regaining trust was also described by Tony, who said his relationship with his family was now:

> More trusting, more helpful. They've always been supportive haven't they, me mum and dad? Tend to spoil me a lot more as well. Well they always spoilt me before didn't they? I've always been spoilt by them but when I were using before it would tend to stop, you know,

sort of. Didn't stop talking to me, but you could see an atmosphere there, do you know what I mean? And 'cos, I think it were 'cos they thought, 'Well if I buy him a pair of trainers he's only gonna sell them for drugs,' do you know what I mean? So when I come off of drugs and that they were more helpful and stuff. I mean if I didn't have no money and we were skint or whatever, phone them up and they'd bring us some shopping over or they'd take me shopping or whatever, do you know what I mean and stuff, like pay me bills and then I'd give it them back at the end of the month when I got paid. Before when I were using they wouldn't have done that, do you know what I mean? They thought, 'Well if you hadn't spent your money on drugs, you'd have had your shopping. At least now he sees it as well, he hasn't spent his money on drugs, I mean he's paid all his bills that's why he hasn't got enough money for the shopping or he's only paid half and half ...,' or whatever, do you know what I mean? So they'll help me out in lending me money and stuff so he's always there for me. Always.

For Tony, this new trusting relationship allowed him to build up social capital (see also Farrall, 2004). He now has access to greater resources, such as financial support, when times are hard. This help enables the continuance of desistance. The fact that being trusted is an enjoyable emotion in comparison to the unpleasant feeling of being mistrusted provides an additional incentive. Furthermore, the act of successfully rebuilding trust means that they have something to lose, itself an incentive to avoid reoffending (see also Sampson and Laub, 1993). These sentiments are echoed by Bill:

The main thing is, just look at your family first, and see how they'd feel. 'Cos once you've buggered up again then it all comes right back down to trust. And I've got a lovely relationship now with all my family, apart from my dad.[6] And I don't want anything to change that again.

This emotion of trust was not merely confined to relationships with family. Those offenders nearer the point of complete desistance, such as Niall, also described how they were now trusted by the authorities:

Niall: My allotment's down there and they take their police cars down there to wash 'em through the car wash. Whenever I'm down there they'll say, 'Oh, come on, Niall, let's have a look in your greenhouse then, what have you got growing?' 'cos, you know, they all know that I like a smoke [of cannabis]. And they all say, 'Are you still at it then?' I'll say, 'Well I smoke, but I don't grow it any more.' 'All right then, can we have a look in your greenhouse?' Just having a laugh with me, you know, it's...

AC: Do they have a look in your greenhouse?

Niall: No. No, they don't, no. I always offer them some rhubarb.
No, they wouldn't do. They just do it as a laugh 'cos I know
them. Well I've known 'em for years, you know.

The emotions of pride

Feelings of personal pride and a sense of achievement also featured
strongly towards the end of the desistance process. For the most entrenched criminals like Al, a pessimist whose offending escalated during the
first sweep and who admitted to having shoplifted every day of his life
from the age of 11 to 25, just having even managed to abstain for two
years was a sense of personal achievement:

> That's another thing I'm proud of myself. 'Cos from the age of eleven
> to twenty-five every single day I was a shoplifter. It was the only thing
> I knew how to do, after moving to [...]. I just changed my life. I
> couldn't even think about pinching a [sweet] or anything, man. If I
> see the kids anywhere near anything picking things I'm like 'move
> away from there, don't touch anything'.

Others were proud about having achieved their goals through conventional means of legitimate employment and described the difference
between 'now' and when they had started their original probation order:

> [I'm] a lot more healthier. I've got a lot more friends, my social life's a
> lot better. There's no dodgy people coming to t'house anymore. I go
> to work every day, like I earn an honest wage and stuff. I just stay out
> of bother, that's all I do.
>
> (Nick)

> I've got him [points to baby], I've got [partner], I make sure me bills
> are paid, me shopping's on, me food's on table. I've got me
> employment keeping, otherwise I'm not gonna be paid for that am I?
> Do you know what I mean? I mean, I haven't got much but, but what
> I have got, I can say I worked for. It's not as if I've stolen anything or
> owt, anything, I've bought and paid for I've worked hard for.
>
> (Tony)

There was also a pride in their achievements of 'respectable domesticity':

> I'm all right now. I'm happy with meself. I've got a nice house, I keep
> it that way. Reasonable garden.
>
> (Bill)

Ann said owning her own home was the biggest change in her life and
explained why this was important to her:

> Even though I've had all the problems that I've had and illness and ...
> and stuff ... this place is my own now, I can make it my own. I can

change it the way I want it to be. I can have whoever I want in here. Or if I please, not have them here. It makes me feel quite proud.

The respondents we placed in both the penultimate and the final phases also experienced an interesting variation in their hopes. Previously, most notably in the early phase, the hopes experienced had been for an 'escape' from an addiction or away from a particular lifestyle associated with offending. In the last two phases we see hopes becoming more concrete: people desire specific goals, such as their own businesses, a family (or children if they are in a partnership), a home which they own and so on. The hopes experienced towards the end of the emotional trajectory of desistance take on a different tone: the future is more certain now and particular needs and wants can be strived for.

The final phase: 'normalcy'

Those cases who had, to all intents and purposes, completed the process of desistance and that we had identified as being non-offending members of society were placed in the final phase of our schema. For these desisters, 'normalcy' is underlined by two themes that emerged from their responses. Firstly, they see their offending as being a 'long way away'. They regarded themselves in the present as very far removed from themselves at the time of their offending. Furthermore, when they talk about how the emotions of trust, guilt and shame encouraged their desistance – a trend which emerged amongst cases placed in the previous stage of the schema – these emotions were typically referred to in the *past tense*. Not just their offending but the journey of desistance was seen as something that *has* happened, rather than *is still* to happen. Six of the eight people we placed in this phase reported regrets about the past, suggesting that they are indeed rebuilding their 'selves' and strengthening other non-criminal aspects of their identities (Van Stokkom, 2002: 350). Secondly, where once they were involved in crime and in some cases, such as Ian and Terry, deeply entrenched in it, starting families, rebuilding bonds with parents and establishing successful careers has meant they are now more firmly entrenched in 'normality'. This new existence brings with it feelings of being rewarded as well as improved self-esteem and confidence.

While feelings of reward are reported by a few cases (e.g. Jimmy, Matthew, Clive, Dominic and Sally-Anne) in earlier stages of the schema, these exclusively involved persons with histories of either alcohol and/or heroin misuse. Given that addictions to these substances were previously perceived as powerful, malign forces responsible for driving their criminal behaviour, it is hardly surprising that those who have managed to desist or, in the case of Clive, control their consumption feel rewarded and have their self-esteem raised. Moreover, these feelings were specifically related to occasions when they have had the opportunity to offer their experiences for the benefit of others with drug and alcohol problems and to 'give something back' (Maruna, 2001). For example, both Dominic and Nick had been invited by local drug agencies to give a talk about their experiences of and since coming off heroin. Although they both declined, they said they were 'chuffed actually' (Nick) and 'came home proper buzzing' (Dominic) after being asked.

Others, such as Sally-Anne, did adopt this role of 'wounded healer' by becoming a volunteer key worker at the drug rehab she had graduated from. For her, the experience was a reward and a reminder: '[It was] really good for me, to see it from another side ... to see the heartbreak, and all the pain that families that have got people that are on drugs, what it does.'[7] Clive, however, took on the role of self-styled local do-gooder, 'passing on information to [the] younger generation', and said, 'It's really nice when someone thanks you for something ... when they say "Oh cheers for that" that makes all the difference.' Therefore, what all these cases (from the penultimate phase) have in common is not just that they were once heavy addicts and offenders, but that the feelings of reward they experienced were new, surprising, occurred in specific contexts and served as reminders of the incentives of continuing their desistance.

However, by the final phase of the schema, these feelings of reward and improved self-esteem were not uniquely confined to those with previous alcohol and drug problems. They were, in fact, much more widespread and included five of the eight cases we placed in this category. Furthermore, these feelings of reward were not merely the result of 'wounded healer' roles, of getting something back for giving something back, but owed their origins to the more continuous and subtle advantages of 'normal' life. This means, perhaps, that they have vested interests in maintaining the non-offending status quo of their current lifestyles, or at least not acting in such a way as to damage it in the long term. For Richard, falling in love and getting married and recently becoming a father had provided him with a completely different outlook and purpose in life:

Richard: I'm 42 nearly, that's a lot different. I'm married, I've got a child ... got a little dog over there ... It's, it's a world, a world of change. Everything is different.

AC: How do you feel about this change?

Richard: It's brilliant, it's ... that's why I'm alive now ... I'm alive. [Laughs] And I'm living a life. Whereas before I was just running through life, how it happened, you know, I didn't care how it ended up. Mattered not. 'Dead or alive? Who cares?' But now I wanna live, you know, I've got a purpose for stay alive for.

Others, like Mark, also considered that there was an appeal in the 'home comforts' of normality. This made even the thought of the behaviour in which he was involved previously, such as going out with his friends clubbing, drinking, taking drugs and fighting, now seem unappealing in comparison and hence for that reason much more unlikely to happen again. This is illustrated in response to the question, 'Is there anything that might make it hard for you to stay stopped?':

> Mark: No, I don't think so now. I've just sort of grown out of it now. It's like never lurking around at two o'clock in the morning and you know things like that. I'd rather be tucked up in bed. [Laughter] I don't even, you know, I don't even go nightclubs anymore, you know. It's just like, it feels as though you're getting a bit old and . . .
>
> AC: Yeah.
>
> Mark: I just can't be doing with it. [Laughter] It's terrible really . . . you know, you come out of a nightclub at two o'clock in the morning and you see people fighting and drunken people just falling all over the place, you know. No, I'd rather be at home with the kids, knowing that they're safe and tucked up in bed and, you know, it's things like that.

The notion that the distance covered had been too great to make a return to crime likely is seen in the attitudinal shift of Rajeev. He was 19 years old at the time of the first interview and on probation having been convicted of fraud and deception. Although officially his first offence, he informed us that it was preceded by a list of convictions prior to 17 for theft and drugs. At his fourth interview, he had not reoffended, had completed a university degree, had a 'good job' and was planning to buy a house. He described himself as 'totally different' and with a completely new set of goals (see above).

By the fourth interview, Terry, the only former drug addict and alcoholic in the 'normalcy' phase, had avoided alcohol and drugs for seven years and, as a Christian, was still an active member of his 'fellowship'. He was now working as a drugs worker for a clinic in the voluntary sector. In many ways his story is similar to the previously cited 'wounded healers' located earlier along the trajectory. However, Terry differs, as the following example illustrates, in that his 'reward' is continually reinforced 'every day', rather than intermittently. Interestingly, he also compares the 'high' he gets from his current job to the 'lows' he has suffered in the past, again a reminder of how far he has come:

> [Getting a job as drugs worker] made me feel ace, you know. Doing something that, you know, all me life, all me life I've done jobs . . . Me dad basically tried to mould me into, he tried to mould me into the building trade, 'cos me dad's a bricklayer. And he tried to mould me into himself. And I always come against that, I didn't want to be in the building trade. I didn't want to do that. And I used to do a lot of jobs that I hated. I used to go labouring on a building site and doing

different jobs but I didn't like it, you know what I mean. I used to get up on a morning, think 'I don't want to ...' I hated going to work ... a lot of work what I did I just didn't like. I worked in an office, I worked in factory. And doing really, I did some really crappy jobs. But now, the job that I do now, it's been tailor-made for me. It's just unbelievable. It's everything what I've gone through in my life. I'm actually helping people who are going through the same [that I did]. So I love coming to work, every day I love coming to work. To me it's just like me life, you know. And I'm getting paid for it, which is fantastic, you know.

For others, such as Meera, a 'one-off' white-collar offender convicted of embezzlement, the journey towards desistance had been one of *regaining* normality rather than trying to *gain* normality. She described herself at the time of conviction as feeling 'nervous, scared ... like a piece of dirt' and 'to be truthful, [I] was good for nothing'. Once detected she was dismissed from her job and felt intense shame for what she had done, saying that when she went out she had a 'fear that someone would recognize me'. She identified the turning point as her decision to file for bankruptcy, which gave her the confidence to look for work again and to start by applying for a place on a part time computer course. She described how doing this course made her feel:

Meera: Better, stronger.
AC: In what way?
Meera: Emotionally I felt more stable, as if I was, I suppose as if I was on a high, it was like, you know, 'I know I can do this,' so what was stopping me from going out and actually doing it for real, so to speak. Err, there was me previously, like independent, career-minded person, who'd turned into this very weak, insecure person and had no confidence in herself whatsoever. And, like I said, the course was, I suppose confidence building as well as getting the experience of trying to venture out to do something new.

Meera's experiences suggest that Seidler (1998: 209) is correct when he argues that it is only when a relationship has been lost that individuals realize what they have lost. She later went on to describe her feelings about her current financial situation as follows:

Good, positive. I don't think I've done too badly for myself over the last six years. I've got, like I say, I've got three lovely kids that I'm very proud of. I've got a job now which I thoroughly enjoy and I've been able to study and move forward with my life. And I've learnt that if I can survive on £200 a month, you know, in comparison to what, £900? I've got myself sorted. So if I can adapt from that difference of figure I know I don't need to spend recklessly. Because if I can manage that amount then I can manage my monthly salary, without it getting out of hand or anything like that.

Meera has undergone a long, slow journey, from being caught and charged with embezzlement to rebuilding her career. The experience, for all its faults, has been one of learning and she has managed to obtain something worthwhile. For others, previously painful emotions of shame and guilt were identified as having been responsible for prompting what had been for them a difficult change of direction and the desires 'to make a go of it' and 'to try going straight'. Ian, in talking about such feelings, reported that these were 'painful' and said that he felt that he was 'digging up old bones'. However, he has been able to rebuild trust with his daughter and this too has meant he has been rewarded in his 'new life':

Ian: My oldest daughter is now nine and in '99, when I served my last [prison] sentence, it was very traumatic for her. And I saw the pain she was going through and that is what gave me the strength to think, 'Well, I can't put myself in a situation where I ain't there for her because it's affecting her life and upbringing.' Whereas I want to give her a stable family, whereas I didn't have that stable thing and I felt that if I carried on now, then I'm just really showing her the path that I went down, and making history repeat itself maybe with her. Maybe she could, you know, anything could happen, she could be doing drugs or ... You know, there's always, you know, she and I thought to myself 'there's no more'. Whereas before it would be like, you know, 'daddy's away' or 'daddy's away working' or, you know, 'daddy's not here' for whatever reason. Whereas they're not stupid no more and I want to see my kids and if they come in to visit prison to see me, I am there, there, they can know, they know what's going on. They see it, they see it. I mean in '99, *Eastenders*[8] was on, you know, like with that boy in...

AC: Yeah.

Ian: You know, there was someone in without a bib on[9] whereas she's coming to see me with that on. So it was all real for her, do you know what I mean? And so basically I don't want to put her through that anymore and that's what gave me that, the attitude to think, 'Well, she can't see that no more.' Then, that's gone and, err, even my youngest, like, she was eight months when I went in and it's like both of my daughters I've been away for both them at a young age. And I think, you know, to say it's missing their and it took me, I tell you what it took me, I bet it took, it took me eighteen months to two years to actually build some kind of life. Err, no, she loved me but when she's tired she wouldn't want me and that has hurt me that like she wants her mother before me and I've always been the intruder whereas now it's not the case.

What Ian draws to our attention here is not only his own feelings and how they structured the process of desistance for him, but that the emotional aspects of desistance are not simply 'contained' within the desister. Like those involved with restorative justice conferences, distress is shared (van Stokkom, 2002: 343). The emotional trajectories of desistance are as much a part of the experiences that *others* around the desister feel (see the experiences related above by ex-substance users who refer to how their families had felt and how they now feel). Thus the emotional aspects of desistance are part of the feelings experienced by a wider social network of people other than the desister. It appears that, in many cases, the feelings experienced by the wider network were as important to desisters as their own feelings. Put simply, 'it takes two to trust'. Perhaps, therefore, these individuals were better able to desist than others because of the emotional ties which they had established (or re-established). If this is the case, then more work needs to be done (where appropriate) to help and support families with desisting sons, daughters, fathers and (occasionally) mothers. How this work ought to proceed and who ought to deliver it are questions for another day, but certainly there is an emotional component to desistance, and this, it would appear, helps to connect and reconnect potential desisters to wider social groupings.

Notes

[1] The terms 'positive' and 'negative' emotions, whilst setting up a somewhat false dichotomy (is pride positive or negative, for example?), are commonly used (see Tugade *et al.*, 2004; Frederickson and Joiner, 2002). We use 'positive' to refer to those emotions which are pleasurable to experience (happiness, for example) and 'negative' to refer to those emotions which are commonly held to be unpleasant (such as guilt).

[2] Following van Stokkom (2002), we group shame and guilt together in our discussion and schema (see Figure 5.1).

[3] Slang for the police.

[4] Although not victimization, it would appear (see Chapter 7).

[5] In this respect, there would appear, therefore, to be an even earlier phase which 'kick starts' the desires to get away from a particular lifestyle. Chapter 4 provides some clues on this phase.

[6] Bill and his father had fallen out over one of Bill's former girlfriends. Although Bill and she had split up, he and his father had yet to patch things up.

[7] See also Chapter 4 and Sandra's experiences with the alcohol group she had previously attended.

[8] A BBC TV soap opera.

[9] Prisoners often wear bibs around their tops to distinguish them from visitors during visiting times.

Further reading

de Haan, W. and Loader, I. (2002) (eds) Special Edition of *Theoretical Criminology*, 6(3).

Maruna, S. (2001) *Making Good: How Ex-Convicts Reform and Rebuild Their Lives*, American Psychological Association Books, Washington DC.

Maruna, S. and Burnett, R. (2004) So 'Prison Works', Does it? The Criminal Careers of 130 Men Released From Prison Under Home Secretary, Michael Howard, *Howard Journal of Criminal Justice*, 43(4): 390–404.

Simpson, C. (2004) When hope makes us vulnerable: a discussion of Patient-Healthcare Provider interactions in the context of Hope, *Bioethics*, 18(5): 428–7.

Citizenship values and desistance

> Here's the deal here. Hugh Benny has reformed his wayward life and
> has become a born-again Good Citizen.
>
> (Vincent Hannah, *Heat*, 1996, Michael Mann)

In Michael Mann's film *Heat*, the mean-talking police detective Vincent
Hannah, as part of an ongoing case and in order to extract information
relating to that investigation, assaults a known 'face', Hugh Benny.
Having extracted the information he needs, Hannah then calls one of his
colleagues to relay what he has learnt from Benny. Benny lies at Hannah's
feet, bloody and bruised, looking semi-conscious whilst Hannah utters the
lines above. Benny's 'reform' looks enforced and he himself hardly looks
the model of a 'good citizen'. In the film, we neither see nor hear of Benny
again. His 'reform', such that it was, remains problematic for all sorts of
reasons.

Recently, the relationship between being a 'good citizen' and one's
involvement (or otherwise) in crime has drawn much interest from
criminologists (e.g. Young, 1999; McNeill, 2000; Karstedt and Farrall,
forthcoming). Despite the inherent 'logic' of exploring the relationship
between citizenship and engagement in offending, very few of these
authors explicitly outline why they believe it important (or relevant) to
link the concept of citizenship with patterns of offending. In many respects
too, we feel, these investigations are carried out *in absentia* from the
messiness and complexities of data and, to some degree therefore,

operationalize citizenship in a rather unspecific fashion. Thus in the course of this chapter we wish to develop and explore two issues. We wish to state explicitly *our* case for exploring the relationship between citizenship and crime (or rather persistence or desistance from crime). Following this, we will discuss how both others and ourselves have measured citizenship and outline our findings on this topic as they relate to desistance from crime.

Why study citizenship and crime?

We believe that the emerging interest in citizenship and involvement in crime (in our case, most commonly expressed as offending or ceasing to offend) can be warranted as both legitimate and insightful for the following two reasons. Recent explorations into the relationship between offenders' attitudes towards the state have suggested that respondents who score highly on statements which are supportive of liberal citizenship values are less likely to have offended than are those who score highly on statements which reject such values (Karstedt and Farrall, forthcoming). In this study of the 'economic morality' of consumers, Karstedt and Farrall found that those people who supported liberal citizenship values were less likely to have kept the money when given too much change in shops, less likely to have cheated others in second-hand sales and so on. Respondents in their study whose answers suggested that they were disengaged from and/or distrustful of the state were more likely to have committed such crimes. Such liberal citizenship values also suggest an implicit support for those social and political institutions that attempt to uphold the law, redress imbalances in social justice and/or reduce harms in some way (expressed as trust in the police, local governments and the 'state' in general). As such, practices associated with citizenship are seen as fostering a 'social contract' which reduces social exclusion (McNeill, 2000).

Allied to these observations, and bringing us closer to our central focus (desistance), the following issues also help to provide a justification for a serious and sustained exploration of desistance and citizenship. Firstly, if offending and conviction are associated with the erosion of liberal citizenship values and social exclusion, then citizenship, in an active sense, may *also* be eroded as both individuals are repeatedly convicted and as larger numbers of significant groups in any population are convicted.

Also, as convictions are a static feature of an individual's life (Andrews, 1989), and are most often collected in the relatively early years of one's life, so the above processes may operate to create a group of people whose attachment to the state and civil society is weakened or broken relatively early on in their lives. Whilst we know that many such people will stop offending eventually, it is *not* known whether their feelings about the state and civil society also change as their offending patterns shift. If they do not change 'in line' with their engagement in offending, whilst *desistance* is possible, the possibility for full *reintegration* may be damaged for ever. On the other hand, as it is the state which prosecutes most offenders in the UK, so positive changes in citizenship values following a prolonged period of offending suggest a recognition on the part of the offender that their behaviour was wrong. This, in turn, suggests a level of 'forgiveness' or reconciliation towards the state on their part and that they are less likely to act in this way again. (See also Chapter 5 on feelings of trust and engagement in civil society.)

A criminologically informed notion of citizenship

In our discussion of the concept of citizenship, we draw heavily from a few key writers in this field (e.g. Plummer, 2003; McKinnon, 2000), bringing in other authors and commentators as we seek to 'flesh out' our definition. With such a voluminous topic as 'citizenship', leaving aside our wish to focus on only the most salient aspects of it, it goes without saying that we can only give the most cursory of glances to many important debates. In what follows, we deliberately side-step the debates about the inter-changeable use of words like 'citizenship' and 'nationality' (see Meehan, 1999: 239; Karatani, 2003: 16–18) as our goal is to develop a definition of citizenship suitable for use when exploring criminal careers rather than to discuss the concept and its usage more widely.

Plummer (2003: 51) reminds us that a number of models of citizenship exist. The first, a liberal tradition, emphasizes the rights and obligations of individual citizens. The emphasis in this model is placed upon those things that the citizen receives from their association with the state (e.g. care, respect, freedom of expression and so on) and those obligations (duties) that the citizen must agree to undertake (e.g. voting, paying taxes and so on). Commonly, as in the work of Janoski (1998), these obligations refer to specific arenas of the society in question. Legal obligations (upholding the rule of law), political obligations (voting), social obligations (tolerating social diversity) and participative obligations (such as respecting others involved in political processes) form part of Janoski's model. There would also appear to be some evidence to support this approach from studies of citizens themselves. When Wilkins (1999) asked postgraduate students what a 'good citizen' was, amongst the replies was the following:

> It sounds like, the individual ought to be *doing something* for society, things like, you know, going out to work and paying your taxes...
> (1999: 225, emphasis added)

A further model emphasizes the extent to which individual citizens are engaged in political processes. Sometimes referred to as the 'town hall' model, the emphasis here is on engagement in civil society (church, community groups and the like). This resonates with more recent work by the likes of Putnam (2000) on the 'death' of civil society in the USA and is, we feel, essentially concerned with measuring the extent to which an individual or a group of individuals is engaged at a behavioural level with the state and processes which support its work.

Of course, and it is important to acknowledge this point, there is much heterogeneity of thought when it comes to defining citizenship, a point emphasized by McKinnon (2000: 144). McKinnon herself relies heavily on the work of John Rawls, and in so doing widens the set of concepts. 'Good faith' (McKinnon 2000: 146) refers to the principle that a citizen ought not to take advantage of the law in order to promote their own interests at the expense of those of others. In this respect, the citizen is aware of the moral intention of society's laws and is able to refrain from the temptation to act in accordance with the letter of the law, if not the spirit of it. In some respects, the notion of 'good faith' resonates with Von Pufendorf's idea that the duty of the citizen is to 'live in friendship and peace' with other citizens (cited in Clarke, 1994: 91–2). Again, qualitative data from Wilkins' study supports this line of thinking:

> I don't think it's anything that a society should expect, through the sort of work you do ... it's up to the individual, living their lives ... I don't think it should be in terms of contribution to society, *it's more about tolerance and respect.*
>
> (1999: 225, emphasis added)

Another aspect of McKinnon's model is the ideal that the citizen ought to obey the law even if they personally disagree with it. This is because, if taken to the limits, law-breaking would create a high degree of instability; citizens ought to obey even those laws they dislike and instead seek to change them via democratic or legal procedures. Again this resonates with Von Pufendorf's claim that citizens ought to 'refrain from dishonesty' (cited in Clarke, 1994: 92) and Roosevelt's observation that, 'No man can be a good citizen ... who is not honest in his dealings with other men and women' (cited in Clarke, 1994: 153). However, another aspect of McKinnon's model (2000: 147–8) – civil disobedience – remains part of the apparatus of the 'good citizen', as he or she needs to act as a check against unfair or socially disadvantageous acts on the part of the state.

Voting, already a commonly cited dimension of citizenship, takes on a slightly different meaning in McKinnon's model, as Rawls argues that when voting the citizen ought to consider what is best for the *political community* (rather than just voting for what is best for themselves or what they believe in). A further aspect of Rawls' model of citizenship emphasized by McKinnon (2000: 148–50) is the moral duty to engage in reason when debating political issues with fellow citizens. This somewhat idealistic principle emphasizes the need for citizens to agree how to show respect for opinions which diverge from their own. Still others (e.g. Almond and Verba, cited in Clarke, 1994: 177) argue that citizens ought to be active participants in the political processes that underpin the state. However, they also claim that citizens ought to be 'loyal and respectful of authority' (cited in Clarke, 1994: 178), be obedient to the law and acknowledge their responsibility towards the wider community (see also Wilkins, 1999). Finally, Karatani (2003: 19) notes that since the rise of the New Right in the 1980s, citizens are also expected to be economically self-reliant.

From these writings we have developed what we have called a criminologically informed notion of citizenship. This takes into account many of the observations outlined above, but excludes those which are too clumsy to measure or which somehow appear to sit uncomfortably with our main focus. What, for example, are we to make of those people who vote for far right political parties such as the British National Party? Are we to hold such cases up as paragons of good citizenship on the basis that they are voting at a time when rates of participation are declining, or do we declare them the antithesis of this on the basis that they appear to hold little respect for the rights of others to express their views as they wish? Leaving aside such problems (which would divert us from our immediate concern), we feel that a criminologically informed notion of citizenship contains the following elements:

- Citizens are honest in their dealings with one another.
- Citizens are honest in their dealings with the state.
- Citizens uphold the law.
- Citizens are tolerant of others' right to be different.
- Citizens have a concern with the wider interests of 'the community'.
- Citizens are engaged in an 'ongoing dialogue' with the state (in which it is presumed one takes account of the other's opinions).

Our approach to citizenship includes, therefore, the following model of the 'good citizen': an individual who is honest and fair in their dealings with the state and with their fellow citizens and who tries to uphold the law, is respectful of others' wishes and desires to express their own identity (be it religious, ethnic, cultural or sexual) in whatever manner they chose, and who takes into account the needs and interests of the wider community (which may, of course in reality, be several communities) and, even at the most basic level, is engaged in public debate.

Our consideration of desistance and citizenship forces us to consider another aspect of citizenship: the socialization and resocialization towards key values. Our data, discussed below, strongly suggest that desisters are more likely to have liberal values when compared to persisters. This appears to hold independently of the usual range of explanatory factors (such as previous convictions, imprisonment, motivation and so on). Thus it would appear that our desisters are likely to have developed their citizenship values at around the same time that they were desisting.

Socialization and resocialization towards citizenship values

Some of the best research on political socialization was undertaken in the 1960s and 1970s, when research on this topic was at its most intense. However, much of what was reported from those studies holds a resonance with our own concerns and interests. In this section, we concern ourselves with the processes of socialization and (especially) resocialization as they are known to exist for the majority of adults. Dowse and Hughes (1986: 190) remind us that whilst socialization normally takes place during adolescence, it is a lifelong process. They refer to studies (1986: 201) that suggest that whilst American political representatives can recall early political experiences, they were not affected by these in their roles as elected officials (Prewitt *et al.*, 1966).

Amongst those engaged in radical political groups, Sigel and Hoskins (1977: 266) note that those aged 25–30 often experienced an increase in involvement in 'conventional' political groupings, a change which occurs in tandem with the assumption of family responsibilities. By this age, most men and women are married (they were writing in the 1960s one must bear in mind) and have developed concerns over taxes, mortgage rates and schools. In a statement that echoes many of those from ex-offenders, they cite an ex-radical union president as saying, 'It changes your outlook quite a bit when you have those mortgage payments, car payments and kids to feed.' They also cite evidence that in families where one person is interested in politics and votes regularly, their spouse will also vote (Glaser, 1959), suggesting that social institutions mediate engagement in political processes. Another of the key social institutions in contemporary life is the workplace, and there is evidence that this too influences political values and the 'colour' they take (see Sigel and Hoskins, 1977: 272–82 for a review). Studies of the unemployed suggested that, even amongst those who had previously been active in politics, they were likely to withdraw from political and community affairs after losing their jobs (Jahoda and Lazarfield, 1933, cited in Sigel and Hoskins 1977: 274). Similar processes were observed amongst those whose retirement was enforced (Sigel and Hoskins, 1977: 268).

Studies of social and geographical mobility also suggest that changes in political values and beliefs can be triggered by migration. Dowse and Hughes (1986: 204) report that the socially upwardly mobile take on the values of the stratum into which they move. Similarly, they find that migrants take on the values of the milieu they move into (1986: 205). Glaser and Gilens (1997) provide evidence that migrants from the southern US states to the northern US states change their beliefs about different ethnic groups in line with the communities they move to.

Taken together, these studies suggest that as people 'migrate', be it socially, geographically or in terms of their social status (employed/ unemployed, non-parent/parent and so on), so their outlook and political values are also likely to change. These processes of socialization and resocialization are important for our own consideration of desistance and citizenship values as they suggest that common changes (i.e. from offender to non-offender) are associated with shifts in values. Quite why this ought to be the case, and, perhaps more importantly, the causal ordering of this relationship, remains something of an enigma. However, this body of work suggests that there are good reasons to expect that shifts in offending and shifts in political values co-occur.

Desistance and citizenship

There have been relatively few explorations of desistance and citizenship. Mercier and Alarie reported that one ex-substance abuser related their reduction in drug usage to a new sense of civic identity:

> I am not a shame for society anymore. I am not living on society, giving back nothing. There was a time when my name did not appear on any computer, not even on social security databases, or electoral lists, or income taxes ... Anonymous, completely anonymous ... I did not want to be part of society, of the system ... And now, my name is on many files, I even voted, I quitted anonymity ... Now I have a bank book, my name is in the telephone book.
>
> (2002: 234)

In many respects, this quote echoes observations from Maruna (2001: 12), who reminds us that 'desisting ex-offenders emphasise the desire to make some important contribution to their communities', suggesting that the process of desisting encompasses feelings which can be characterized as 'active citizenship'. However, one of the most developed investigations of desistance and citizenship comes from Uggen *et al.* (2004). They start their contribution by outlining how criminal convictions in the USA strip the convict of their right to vote, hold elective office and sit on juries. Ultimately, they suggest that the self-concept of a reforming citizen is the principal mechanism for interpreting role transitions and desistance from crime. In this regard, Uggen *et al.* do not tap into their respondents' attitudes and social values as these relate to concepts of citizenship (as do Karstedt and Farrall, for example). Rather, Uggen *et al.* recast those relationships known to be associated with desistance as representing citizenship. In this way, employment is interpreted as representing 'productive citizenship', parenthood as representing 'responsible citizenship' and engagement in various civic organizations as 'active citizenship'.

Whilst we see (and applaud) the merit in adopting this line of thinking, we feel that there are some shortcomings with this approach and some of the wider aspects of this study. First of all, whilst we accept that citizenship *at some level* is about being a productive, responsible and active individual, we think that the values associated with citizenship go beyond this. That is to say, there are attitudes and beliefs that characterize any one individual's relationship with the various institutions which collectively are known as 'the state'. In this respect, Uggen *et al.*'s work is concerned very much with experiences of those processes which we think of as being about citizenship, rather than about attitudes towards notions of citizenship.

Above and beyond this, however, and despite our admiration for this contribution, we are not sufficiently convinced that the men and women interviewed by Uggen *et al.* actually represent desisters. In all, 33 men and women (23 of them serving prisoners) were interviewed (2004: 267). The remaining 10 interviewees were either on parole or on probation, and there was no effort (2004: 288) to ascertain whether or not these people were still offending. In this respect, the work by Uggen *et al.* raises some tantalizing findings and possibilities, which, as they acknowledge themselves, they are unable to resolve fully. In this chapter, we aim to take up some of these challenges.

Operationalizing and measuring citizenship

To what extent were the people we originally spoke to five or so years ago now 'model citizens'? Some 53 per cent were now engaged in full-time employment, with a further 8 per cent holding part-time jobs. Two-thirds had a partner and just under half also had a child. Some 45 per cent were listed in either the 2002 or 2003 electoral roll at the time that we were attempting to retrace them. Leaving aside this technocratic definition of citizenship, we explore in this chapter not so much their payment of taxes, etc., but rather their attitudes and values – attitudes and values from which we infer the nature of their citizenship.

During our interviews we asked respondents to agree or disagree[1] with a number of statements about citizens and their relationship with the state and 'the community'. Our aim was to measure those aspects of our model of citizenship as outlined above. This meant trying to place rather weighty concepts (such as tolerance or dialogue with the state) into language which would be readily understood. The statements we asked our respondents to consider were introduced with the line, 'How strongly do you agree or disagree with the following statements about being a citizen?' The six statements were:

1. 'People should not rely on the government, they should take responsibility for themselves'.
2. 'It does not really matter if you lie when dealing with state officials'.
3. 'Being a citizen is about becoming involved in your community'.
4. 'The government does not listen to people like me'.

5. 'People should obey the law'.
6. 'People should accept that others have a right to be different'.

Often without prompting, these items led to our interviewees discussing why they felt this way, giving examples of particular activities they felt were associated with citizenship, and other related topics. Statements similar to these had been used to measure citizenship values by Karstedt and Farrall (forthcoming). They found that two different sets of feelings emerged from these statements. One set of values emphasized western notions of liberal citizenship, chiefly taking responsibility for oneself and one's family, taking an active part in society and being tolerant of others' needs and wishes to, in some way, 'be different'. In opposition to this, Karstedt and Farrall found that statements such as 'It does not really matter if you lie when dealing with state officials' and 'The government does not listen to people like me' (statements identical to statements 2 and 4 above) were at best conceptualized as representing disengaged citizenship (i.e. a feeling that the state had turned its back in some way on oneself and that it was acceptable therefore to withdraw support for the state). The issue we wish to attend to is this: do desisters hold a different set of values from persisters, and if so, why might this be?

Let us commence our investigation with the examination of desisters' and persisters' answers to some of the questions we asked them. Desisters appeared to possess more liberal attitudes. For example, Mark, when asked the first of our questions about people taking responsibility for themselves rather than relying on the state, said the following:

Mark: I think some people just don't want to work, they just can't be bothered. So I don't think they should ... err ... rely on the government to give them hand-outs, you know, things like that.
AC: Sure.
Mark: I know some people are just not interested in working and there's plenty of jobs around but they just don't want to do it, do they? They've got enough money and ... but if they're not skilled in anything why should they be paid loads of money?
AC: Yeah.
Mark: You know, I know the minimum wage may be a bit low but ... Yeah, no, I agree, yeah.

Others, in this case George, when asked the extent to which he agreed with the statement 'It does not really matter if you lie when dealing with government officials', implied that one did not lie because it was against some internal set of personal ethics:

You shouldn't lie, you shouldn't lie. It's more for yourself, I think if you lie then you're being, you're lying to yourself, you know. And the end of the day if you want an end to the problems then you've got to be honest and the first place to start is be honest with yourself and certainly be honest with the people you're talking to. So I agree strongly that you should be honest.

Meera, when asked about 'becoming involved in the community', said the following:

Meera: Yeah, I agree with that because I do voluntary work, so, 'yeah'.

AC: Why is it important to be involved in the community?

Meera: Because there's always somebody who's worse off than you. Now I help out at the playgroup, I don't benefit from anything nor do the play leaders there but the children do.

Similarly, Justin believed that if one raised one's voice sufficiently, one would be heard by the government:

I disagree with that because if you want the government to hear you then there's ways of getting through to the government which is just most people don't know that. And they don't realize that persistently if you want to do anything, then it can be done. And you've just got to like carry on, carry on, even if it's like you're writing a letter and you never going to get a response, you just carry on, carry on, and make phone calls. If you really want to get through to someone, you can I believe.

Ben was asked the extent to which he agreed with the statement 'People should obey the law':

Ben: Yeah. There's no other way there, you got to.

AC: Okay, what makes you say that?

Ben: Well, you're just going to get into more and more trouble if you don't like.

Jamie, a desister with a girlfriend from a different ethnic background from his own, when asked about tolerance, said:

AC: 'People should accept that others have a right to be different.'

Jamie: Yeah that's fine with me.

AC: You agree with that?

Jamie: Yeah.

AC: Can you tell me a bit more?

Jamie: You have a right to be different. I play base guitar while my mate plays the drums. We're in a band, we're different than most people, and we go out on a weekend and go jamming. A lot of other people, cultures, Asians, whatever, they do their own thing, as long as it don't interfere with my thing, I haven't got a problem with no one.

Whilst this 'tour' of the responses we gained from our desisters is inevitably brief, the overwhelming impression is of a group of people who, by and large, hold liberal views which emphasize self-reliance, honesty in one's dealings with others, engagement in civil society and tolerance. Pesisters appeared to posses markedly less liberal attitudes, however. Danny provides an example of this:

AC: 'People should not rely on the government, they should take responsibility for themselves.'

Danny: The government really don't care, I mean they couldn't, they really couldn't give a flying fuck about you. At the end of the day, I've been trying to get a house for the last four years, they tell me I'm not sick, I'm not a asylum-seeker, I'm not [a] queer[2] and I haven't got a kid. Basically what they're telling me is, you can be born, pay taxes all your fucking whatless life or whatever whatless [inaudible] you've had, and you ain't got no rights, you can't get a house. So basically the government, the government really don't care. I don't see why I should listen to them or respect them or even vote for that man or whatever man who gets into office.

Here is an extract from the interview with John in which his feelings about dealings with state officials are probed:

AC: 'It does not really matter if you lie when dealing with government officials.'

John: Yeah, I'd agree wi' that ... to a certain extent. They fucking lie all the time themselves.

Although some desisters also reported feeling disconnected to their local communities, and while some persisters reported feeling heavily involved in theirs, generally speaking persisters appeared quite dismissive of the idea of there even being a local community for them to become involved with. Will gave a very direct response:

AC: 'Being a citizen is about becoming involved in your community.'

Will: Haven't got a community.

Danny was similarly dismissive of this aspect of his life:

AC: Okay, 'Being a citizen is about becoming involved in your community.'

Danny: No, I disagree. People really don't care, they don't know you and they don't care.

Fred, when asked his opinions about whether or not the government took an interest in his beliefs, expressed his conviction that government officials did not take much interest in people like himself who had an alcohol dependency:

> AC: Some people say the government does not listen to people like me?
>
> Fred: The government don't listen to people like me.
>
> AC: Yeah?
>
> Fred: Well really, if you're on the drink they don't. They've got things out there to help you but they don't really listen.
>
> AC: And what makes you say that?
>
> Fred: When I was going for me housing, and I went up to [my local] MP,[3] [...] He is up here and he, all he was interested in 'it's just my wife's birthday, come on hurry up, here's the form, go on, see you later'. And that was it, whereas, he didn't sit down and say 'right, you gotta fill it out like this ...' or whatever. He was more interested in going off for a drink with his wife. [laughs]. 'Cos that's his job really, innit, his job's there to advise and help you in whichever way he can.
>
> AC: Sure.
>
> Fred: Not hurry up and get out.

Even when persisters did express the belief that laws needed to be upheld, this was hardly done with much conviction:

> AC: 'People should obey the law.'
>
> Andrew: Err, the laws are like rules yeah? Obviously in general laws are there for a good purpose. They should be obeyed. Sometimes laws have to be bent or broken.

Tolerance, as discussed above, is an important aspect of contemporary citizenship, a fact not lost on the Home Office, whose declared mission is to build a 'safe, just and tolerant society'. When persisters did agree with the idea that people in society ought to be tolerant, they often responded in ways that suggested that they expected *others* to be tolerant of *them*. The wider notion of tolerance of others' sexuality, religion or culture did not appear often in their answers. Here is Will again discussing the matter:

> AC: 'People should accept that others have a right to be different.'
>
> Will: I've got the right to be different. It's human rights.
>
> AC: Can you tell me what you mean by that?
>
> Will: Yeah, I was chatting the other day and some geezer started having a go at me so I read this bit of advice at him. 'Section 4, paragraph 57, everyone has the right to freedom of speech.' And he flipped. Just flipped.
>
> AC: Was this guy another member of the public?
>
> Will: He was a Paki[4] [He whispered] ... an Asian. And he just flipped.
>
> AC: He flipped on you because you...?

Will: He stepped in front of me in the line, so I said, well you'd best get back there mate, and he went 'oh blah, blah, blah ...' and I said 'freedom of speech mate, Section 4, paragraph 57 it's human rights'. He didn't like it.

From Will, we get an immediate sense that it is *his own* rights which are at issue (*'I've* got the right to be different'), as well as a sense that the major impression of the man he had the altercation with was that he was 'a Paki'. This hardly suggests that Will is able to see much beyond his own perception of an individual's ethnic group. Let us look now at the quantitative data that the sorts of extracts above yielded.

After exploratory analyses (see the technical notes at the end of this chapter), we decided to sum the scores for five of our questions on citizenship to create one scale of citizenship. High scores indicate greater overall levels of liberal citizenship, whilst lower scores indicate higher degrees of civil disengagement. A T-test undertaken on the summed citizenship score to explore means scores between desisters and persisters yielded the results shown in Table 6.1.

Table 6.1: Desisters' and persisters' mean scores on the citizenship scale

Group	Mean score
Desisters:	18.14
Persisters:	15.38

$t = 2.572$, df = 46, $p = .013$.

It would appear, therefore, that desisters reported higher levels of liberal citizenship values than the persisters. Of course, the matter does not end there. These values could be the result of other variables, and hence we tested for age, previous prison experience and their motivation at the outset of their period of supervision.[5] These assessments are reported on in Table 6.2.

These variables relating to the previous criminal histories and demographic profile of our sample are all non-significant: that is to say, these variables do not appear to account for the observed differences in citizenship scores. Of course, it cannot 'prove' that we are correct in our assertions that liberal citizenship scores are associated with changes in patterns of offending. However, neither does this dispel our claim that desisters and persisters have different levels of liberal citizenship and that these differences stem from their different patterns of offending.

Table 6.2: Mean scores on the citizenship scale: explorations by age, motivation and previous prison experience

Variable	Group	Mean score	SIG
Motivation			
	Confident	17.40	NS
	Optimists	17.35	NS
	Pessimists	17.41	NS
Age			
	17–23	17.75	NS
	24–29	17.00	NS
	30–35	17.40	NS
Previous prison experience			
	Yes	17.28	NS
	No	17.29	NS

Assessment of motivation and age based on One-Way ANOVAs and that for previous imprisonment on a T-test. N = 47–48.

Accounting for the relationship between citizenship values and desistance

Having found a relationship between citizenship values and desistance, in this section we seek to account for the nature of this relationship. In short, we found that desisters were rather more likely to score more highly than persisters on our scale of liberal citizenship. Our hypotheses remain untested – data sets far more complex than ours will need to be utilized before any definite statements about the relationship between desistance and citizenship values can be made – but herein we outline some of the possible explanations for the findings we have reported above. Our hypotheses are presented diagrammatically in Figure 6.1.

Hypothesis A: desisters exhibit fewer self-centred values

Generally speaking, and in line with other research into the processes associated with desistance, we observed that desisters appeared to be less self-centred and to express a commitment to the welfare of others. This was sometimes embodied in specific people (offspring, parents or specific others) or as a concern for 'society' more generally. Our conceptualization of liberal citizenship (see above), and which emphasized honesty, tolerance and being involved with one's community, resonates with these concerns. In some respects, this mirrors the process of concern for others that Maruna (2001) identified and referred to as generative scripts. It is hard to imagine a causal ordering to the relationship between desistance

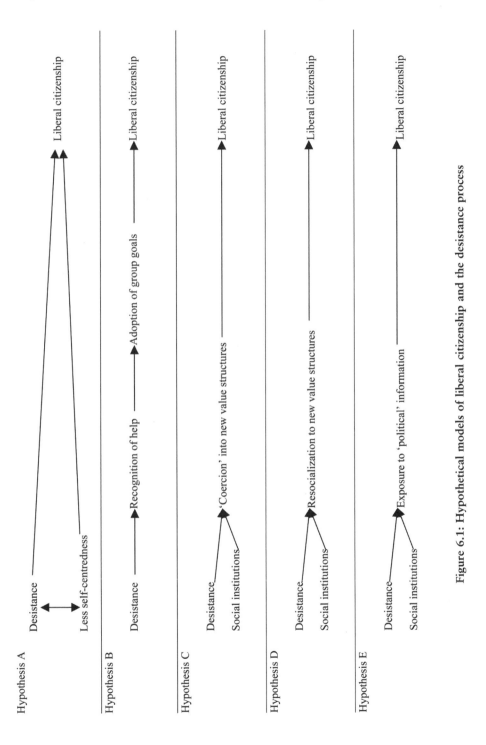

Figure 6.1: Hypothetical models of liberal citizenship and the desistance process

and citizenship such that one precedes the other, but rather, we suspect, it is likely to be the case that these values are developed as desistance occurs. One would expect to see an interaction between desistance and expressed concern for others, such that as expressed concerns for others increase, so the strength of the relationship between desistance and citizenship values ought also to increase.

Hypothesis B: desisters have experienced help from others and reflect this in their values

Rarely does desistance take place without reference to another individual or group. Partners, parents, employers and occasionally probation officers all assist to varying degrees in the processes by which an individual ceases to offend. This is not to dismiss the observation that 'you rehabilitate yourself', but rather simply to acknowledge the important roles which various others play in helping and motivating an individual to stop offending. In very few of the accounts of desistance does one find credible statements to the effect that 'I did it all by myself', although, of course, many desisters may try to claim their reform for themselves. In this respect, desistance is akin to a group accomplishment, reflecting group goals. Perhaps, then, this process of change helps desisters to appreciate, over time, how much they 'owe' to others, both immediate friends and family and (perhaps) the society in which they live.

Thus the relationship between desistance and liberal citizenship could be the result of the desister recognizing that others have assisted in their own reform. This could help to explain why it was that we found so many desisters who disagreed with the statement that people ought to take responsibility for themselves and not rely upon the state. For ex-offenders, this statement could sit uncomfortably with their experiences of the processes associated with desistance. If this hypothesis is correct, one would expect to see desistance emerge prior to the development of liberal citizenship values and for this to be strongest amongst those men and women who have received the greatest help from other people and groups.

Hypothesis C: liberal citizenship values are part of wider prosocial values

It could, of course, be that families and employment work in a different manner to that outlined in Hypothesis B. The 'hopeful' and 'optimistic' tenor of Hypothesis B is replaced with the rather more controlling outlook of C, which posits the following causal mechanism: liberal citizenship values are part of prosocial attitudes and, furthermore, engagement in families and employment coerce individuals into conforming behaviours (which includes prosocial attitudes). Just as the social migrants referred to by Dowse and Hughes (1986) above adopt the values of the milieu they move to, so desisters adopt and, to varying degrees, internalize prosocial attitudes. If this hypothesis is correct, one would expect to see desistance emerge *after* family formation and employment have commenced, but *prior* to the development of liberal citizenship values. Whilst this would be strongest amongst those men and women who spend the greatest time with other people and groups, if they are removed from the influence of these groups one may expect to see a return to previously antisocial attitudes (including offending). Evidence of similar processes comes from MacKenzie and Brame, who find that 'the imposition of direct controls may coerce offenders to participate in prosocial attitudes; the activities, in turn, may initiate changes in offenders that increase their ties ... to conventional behaviour patterns ...' (2001: 432).

Hypothesis D: social institutions encourage liberal citizenship values

Desistance, as is commonly recognized now, is associated with the formation of families and the adoption of adult public roles (most typically employment). Alternatively, therefore, desistance could *precede* the development of liberal citizenship values because desistance is associated with those social institutions (families and employment) that act to resocialize the individual towards mainstream values, which include liberal citizenship values. Evidence for this comes from a study of moral development amongst adolescents. Using longitudinal data, Pratt *et al.* (2003) found that those who reported being more heavily involved in community activities were subsequently more likely to increase the relative emphasis that they placed on prosocial moral values (which included a commitment to 'good citizenship') for themselves. If we think of child-rearing and employment as being akin to these community activities (in that they involve, to varying degrees, the use of one's own time to help others, the need to think of others' interests and the requirement to 'get along' with others), then engagement in families and the workplace could act to instil or to develop liberal citizenship values. If this hypothesis is correct, one would expect to see desistance emerge *after* engagement in families and employment (and analogous social institutions), but *prior* to the development of liberal citizenship values and for this to be strongest amongst those men and women who are most heavily engaged in their respective families and places of work.

Hypothesis E: engagement in civil society sees an increase in exposure to political information

Finally, it could be that engagement in the institutions of civil society (here families and employment) lead to an increase in exposure to political information (via concerns about school-related matters, pay negotiations, the funding of the health and welfare system and so on). This in turn leads to an increased interest in political decision-making and the development of liberal citizenship values. If this hypothesis is correct, one would expect to see desistance emerge *after* engagement in families and employment (and analogous social institutions), but *prior* to the development of liberal citizenship values and for this to be strongest amongst those men and women who are most knowledgeable about current political issues.

Summary

In this chapter, we have tentatively begun an exploration into the relationship between desistance and citizenship values. Our enquiries have been far from exhaustive. We have no idea, for example, of our sample's citizenship values prior to the fourth sweep of interviewing. Clearly, further work needs to be undertaken in this area. Our research has supported the findings presented at the start of this chapter, namely that some authors have found relationships between citizenship values and engagement in offending. Given the results reported herein, which hint at the operation of a relationship between citizenship values and desistance, we feel that further research in this area is warranted. Our outlining of five hypotheses is not meant to be exhaustive either, but they stand as candidate explanations for the observations we have made above.

Notes

1 The responses were coded as 'strongly agree', 'agree', 'neither agree nor disagree', 'disagree' and 'strongly disagree'.
2 Slang for homosexuals.
3 Member of Parliament.
4 An offensive slang word for someone of Pakistani descent.
5 See Chapter 1 and Farrall (2002: 99–114) for an outline of the creation of this scale.

Technical note: the creation of the citizenship scale

This note reports on the creation of the citizenship scale used above. The Cronbach's Alpha coefficient for the scale and the items in it are shown in Table 6.3. The Cronbach's Alphas indicate the extent to which a set of items can be thought of representing one scale. Alphas ought to be as high as possible, ideally above 0.7. The Alpha for the current items is therefore rather low (at .541), probably due to the relatively low number of cases available for analysis. However, by deleting the third item (on involvement in the community), we raise our Alpha to .561.

Table 6.3: Cronbach's Alpha coefficients for citizenship items

Item no. and short label	Alpha if item deleted
1 Take responsibility	.517
2 Lie with state officials	.501
3 Involved in community	.561
4 Government does not listen	.501
5 Obey the law	.369
6 Right to be different	.507

An initial principal components analysis (PCA) suggested that (after rotation) two components had been extracted from the five variables which we had entered. However, even before rotation, the five variables had loaded together on to one component and, therefore, we decided to sum the scores for the five items (1–2 and 4–6 above) to create one scale. It was this scale that we used in our analyses.

Further reading

Karstedt, S. and Farrall, S. (forthcoming) *Respectable Citizens – Shady Practices: Crime, Social Change and the Moral Economy.*

McNeill, F. (2000) *Soft Options & Hard Cases: Public Attitudes, Social Exclusion and Probation*, in Howard League for Penal Reform (eds) *Citizenship & Crime*, 9–12, London.

Uggen, C., Manza, J. and Behrens, A. (2004) '"Less Than the Average Citizen": Stigma, Role Transition and the Civic Reintegration of Convicted Felons', in Maruna, S. and Immarigeon, R. (eds) *After Crime and Punishment: Ex-Offender Reintegration and Desistance From Crime*, 261–93, Willan Publishing, Cullompton, Devon.

chapter seven

Criminal victimization and desistance from crime: in what ways are they related?

Overview
Desistance and victimization
Making sense of victimization, offending and desistance
What does this mean for victimology?

> There's no big sign up on my car saying 'oh yeah, I'm an ex-con don't come near me'. I get it just the same.
>
> (Ian, a desister, fourth interview)

In this chapter, we focus on the relationship between criminal victimization and desistance from crime. In an earlier publication stemming from this research (Farrall and Maltby, 2003), the relationship between victimization and offending was explored. Here we seek to extend these analyses to include desistance. In so doing, we are able to explore whether one 'desists' from victimization at or around the same time that one desists from offending.

Overview

In recent years, a number of studies have started to undermine the belief that 'offenders' and 'victims' form distinct groups in society (see, for example, Singer, 1981; Fagan *et al.*, 1987; Lauritsen *et al.*, 1991). Such studies, usually based on survey research, have suggested that engagement in offending behaviour is one of the strongest correlates of victimization, and vice versa (Van Dijk and Steinmetz, 1983; Gottfredson, 1984; Hartless *et al.*, 1995; Ballintyne, 1999).[1] Such research has produced a number of salient findings – for example, that violent offenders are the most likely to experience violent victimization (Singer, 1981; Fagan *et al.*, 1987; O'Donnell and Edgar, 1996a, 1996b; Wittebrood and Nieuwbeerta, 1999) and that an individual's lifestyle is a significant factor in mediating the nature of the relationship between their offending and victimization (Gottfredson, 1984).

One of the earliest studies which established a link between offending and victimization was that by Singer (1981). Using data drawn from a follow-up study of the Philadelphia cohort (Wolfgang *et al.*, 1987), Singer highlighted the significance of victimization in explaining the seriousness of offending careers. Singer's results suggested that victim experience was a major predictor of offending behaviour, particularly in the case of serious assault, where offending behaviour – he argued – was learnt through either repeat victimization or exposure to offending. In a similar vein, Van Dijk and Steinmetz's (1983) analysis of Dutch juveniles echoed Singer's findings and suggested that offending following victimization was contingent upon the victim having the *opportunity* to offend. As with Singer's findings, Van Dijk and Steinmetz highlighted the significance of lifestyles, which increased both the *opportunity* for offending and the *exposure to risk* of victimization.

Chief among the British studies that noted the importance of lifestyle was Gottfredson's (1984) analysis of the 1982 British Crime Survey. Gottfredson suggested that the social processes that contributed to high rates of offending corresponded with those that contributed to high rates of victimization. As such, where people lived, where they spent time and with whom they associated were highly predictive of both offending and victimization (1984: 17). From this, Gottfredson concluded that the lifestyles which were conducive to offending were also conducive to victimization. Peelo *et al.* (1992) threw further light on these relationships by suggesting that the situations that offenders placed themselves in were precisely those which exposed them to greater risk of victimization.

Building upon the earlier work in this field, Fagan *et al.* (1987) suggested that the social processes which contributed to offending were actually quite different from those which contributed to victimization. They suggested that although there was a relationship between being an offender and being a victim, this relationship varied between offence and victimization types. For example, violent offenders were more likely to experience violent victimization (1987: 600) – often as a result of their own offending. On the other hand, petty offenders were more likely to experience victimization randomly and for this to be less directly the result of their own offending (1987: 607–8). The relationship between violent victimization and offending has been further supported by a study which reported that being a victim of violence was associated with reconviction (May, 1999: 20) and by the work of O'Donnell and Edgar on victimization in prisons (1996a, 1996b).

Like many other areas of research, the establishment of precise causal relationships has, thus far, proved hard to establish. Whilst Singer (1981) suggested that victimization led to offending, he did so only with specific reference to serious assault and maintained the need for other factors to be explored. Similarly, Van Dijk and Steinmetz (1983) suggested a direct causal link between victimization and offending, but only when the situations that allow for adequate offending opportunity existed. A few studies have, however, been able to shed some light on this issue. Both Lauritsen *et al.* (1991) and Zhang *et al.* (2001) found evidence to support the proposition that offending behaviour had a direct influence on increasing the risks of victimization and that experiences of victimization increased involvement in delinquency (Lauritsen *et al.*, 1991: 286). Peelo *et al.* (1992) – one of only two UK studies to specifically address the victimization of probationers, the other (Farrall and Maltby, 2003) being based on the current sample – supported many of these findings with qualitative data. Several studies have noted that, with regard to petty theft (in particular), victimization may actually *lead* to offending as the 'victim' attempted to replace lost items (see also Tyler and Johnson, 2004).

Some methodological concerns

The vast majority of the investigations undertaken to explore the victim–offender overlap have employed survey methodologies. Several of these studies have relied upon either household surveys (Van Dijk and Steinmetz, 1983; Gottfredson, 1984; Mayhew and Elliott, 1990; Lauritsen *et al.*, 1991) or samples drawn from schools (Hartless *et al.*, 1995; Fagan *et al.*, 1987). The effect of this style of sampling procedure is to produce a sample which is likely to be drawn from those in stable accommodation and/or who regularly attend educational institutions. However, research has suggested that those living in hostels, temporary accommodation or with no fixed abode are particularly likely to be victimized (Peelo *et al.*, 1992: 6–7) and that those that do *not* regularly attend school are amongst the most likely to offend (Farrington, 1992: 129, Table 6.1). Additionally, most of the studies undertaken so far have focused their attention on the young (for example, Hartless *et al.*, 1995, studied 11–15 year olds, Fagan *et al.*, 1987, studied those of school age, as did Lauritsen *et al.*, 1991, whilst Van Dijk and Steinmetz, 1983, relied in part on data from a survey of 12–18 year olds). Whilst adolescents are undeniably amongst the most delinquent groups in society, as Moffitt (1993, 1997) and others have demonstrated, engagement in offending for the majority of young people is limited to no more than a few years. Because very few people manage to pass through life *without* either offending or becoming a victim, criminologists should waste little time with the short term and petty. A certain amount of offending *and* victimization is inevitable, and as such our attention should instead be drawn to those people who have high rates of engagement in offending and victimization.

Our aims

In revisiting the victim–offender overlap, we wish to address a number of issues which Farrall and Maltby (2003) were unable to explore. One of the major preoccupations of this current chapter is the fact that few studies have explicitly drawn links between victimization and desistance from crime. As Farrall and Maltby put it:

> This further raises the possibility of a section of the population who experience offending *and* victimisation across the life course [...]. This in turn raises a further series of questions: are there some people who are adolescent-limited victims as well as adolescent-limited offenders?; do offending and victimisation reduce *in tandem*?
>
> (2003: 49–50)

Because Farrall and Maltby relied upon data about victimization asked at the second sweep of interviewing, they could not know at that point whom from the sample had (or would) desist and who would continue to offend. Thus they were unable to explore the relationship between desistance from offending and reductions in victimization. We explore this topic now using data on victimization from sweeps two and four and our coding of respondents' offending trajectories based on up to four sweeps of interviews. We hope also to throw light on the following two questions, again both posed by Farrall and Maltby:

> If threats precede offending and offending precedes threats can causal orderings (ever) be discerned? Do causal orderings differ according to offence and victimisation types?
>
> (2003: 48)

> Are some lifestyles and patterns of offending associated with more serious levels of victimisation?
>
> (2003: 49)

Exploring these questions will allow us to 'unpick' the nature of temporal (if not causal) orderings and to assess the relationship between lifestyle and experiences of victimization and offending.

Findings from sweep two interviews

Instead of constructing entirely new questions to measure self-reported victimization, we have relied upon existing measures. In both the second sweep of interviewing and the fourth sweep, we employed questions concerning victimization developed by Graham and Bowling (1995) for the first Young People and Crime survey. This not only saved time (in that questions did not need to be piloted and so forth), but also meant that comparisons with the Graham and Bowling study could be made. The victimization questions used in both sweeps of our fieldwork were as follows:

In the last year...

> ...has anyone done any damage on purpose to your house or flat or to anything outside it that belonged to someone in your household? If so, how many times? **Damage**

> ...has anyone stolen or tried to steal anything from you, your home or car, or out of your pockets, bag or cases? If so, how many times? **Steal**

> ...has anyone, including people you know well, deliberately hit or kicked you or used force against you? If so, how many times? **Assault**

> ...has anyone threatened to hurt you or damage your things in a way that frightened you? If so, how many times? **Threats**

In all, 133 probationers provided useable answers to these four questions concerning their victimization in the past 12 months during the second sweep. These data are supplemented by an earlier study of the victimization rates of young people in a 'general'[2] population conducted by the UK Home Office (the main findings of which are reported in Graham and Bowling, 1995[3]). The current research, like virtually all previous research, is further limited in that 'street crimes' were the main focus of our enquiries.

We make two initial observations. Firstly, that rates of victimization amongst the probation sample are far greater than amongst the 'general' (i.e. household) sample of comparable age. This establishes that the probation sample is the more highly victimized[4] of the two samples and thus that the probation sample represents an appropriate sample with which to explore the relationship between offending and victimization. Secondly, it establishes, for those so interested, the rates of victimization experienced by those sentenced to probation *vis-à-vis* a 'general' (i.e. normal) population.

Because the 'general' population sample collected data from those aged 14–25 and the probation sample from those aged 17–35, the comparative rates presented herein are restricted *only* to those aged 17–25 in *both* of the samples (respectively 1,209 and 66),[5] thus enabling analyses which control for the effects of age differences between the two samples. The comparative victimization rates are shown in Table 7.1. As can be seen, in all instances probationers were significantly more victimized than the general population and all differences were significant at the .000 level.

Table 7.1 provides victimization data for the 'general' sample, those probationers aged 17–24 and all probationers. It indicates that more of the probation sample was victimized than the 'general' sample and that this ratio varied by victimization type. For example, when damage to property was considered, the difference in victimization rates between probationers and non-probationers was relatively small (33 per cent compared with 26 per cent). However, when theft from the person was considered, half as many probationers again were victimized (46 per cent compared with 31 per cent). When physical assault was examined, three times as many of the probationers were victimized (36 per cent compared with 12 per cent), and when threats were considered, around four times as many probationers were victimized (45 per cent compared with 13 per cent). Thus it appears that the victimization experienced by the probation sample was skewed towards violent victimization.

Table 7.1: 'General' and probation samples: victimization rates at sweep two

Offence type	'General' Sample		Probationers (17–24)		Probationers (all)	
	%	N	%	N	%	N
Damage to property	26	290	33	22	34	45
Theft from person	31	363	46	31	45	60
Physical assault	12	165	36	24	41	54
Threatened	13	175	45	30	39	51
Sample size		1 209		66		199

Over and above this, as Farrall and Maltby (2003: 49) note, the quality and seriousness of the victimization experienced by some probationers was truly horrific. For example, the ruthlessness of heroin dealers was brought home during the fieldwork when one of the probationers (who was a heroin user) was abducted by a man (presumed to be her dealer) and gang raped by him and his accomplices. Following this episode, she received death threats, presumed to be from this same man.

Findings from sweep four interviews

At the fourth sweep, respondents were asked exactly the same four questions again. The number providing useable responses was between 46 and 49 (some cases did not answer all questions and hence the range rather than an exact number). In all, 42 provided some level of data at both sweep two and sweep four. See Table 7.2 for the rates of victimization reported at sweep four.

Table 7.2: Probation sample: victimization rates at sweep four

Offence type	Probationers (all)	
	%	N
Damage to property	33	16
Theft from person	37	17
Physical assault	28	13
Threatened	34	16
Sample size		46–49

A comparison between the figures given for the probation sample in Table 7.1 and those in Table 7.2 suggests that, on the whole, the group had experienced less victimization in the year preceding their fourth interviews than had been the case for the year preceding their second interviews. Whilst the rate of damage to property remained stable at about a third (34 per cent at sweep two, 33 per cent at sweep four), other rates declined. For example, theft had declined from 45 to 37 per cent and threats similarly from 39 to 34 per cent. However, the biggest (in percentage point terms) was the decline in physical assaults, down from 41 per cent at sweep two to 28 per cent at sweep four.

As can be seen in Table 7.3, only a very few of the cases interviewed had been victimized at both sweeps two and four (around 15 per cent of the sample). Around a third to a half reported no victimization at either sweep (35–45 per cent). Therefore, respondents reporting victimization at just one of the two sweeps were most commonly reporting victimization at sweep two.

Table 7.3: Probation sample: victimization rates at sweeps two and four

Offence type	Victim at neither sweep % N	Victim at sweep 2 only % N	Victim at sweep 4 only % N	Victim at both % N
Damage to property	40 16	23 9	23 9	16 6
Theft from person	35 13	30 11	19 7	16 6
Physical assault	45 17	26 10	14 5	16 6
Threatened	45 17	23 9	16 6	14 5
Sample size		39–42		

Zhang et al. (2001), in an attempt to explore the causal relationship between victimization and offending, looked at the lagged effects of offending at time one on victimization at time two (and vice versa). They found that whilst offending at time one is associated with victimization at time two (2001: 138), victimization at time one is not associated with offending at time two. We, however, find no relationship (Tables 7.4 and 7.5) between victimization and admissions of any offending. Whilst a large proportion of those who offended at sweep two were victims at sweep four (74 per cent, Table 7.4), a large proportion of sweep two non-offenders were also victimized at sweep four (65 per cent). So, while more offenders were victimized than non-offenders, the differences were not statistically significant.

Similarly, there was no sign of a lagged effect of victimization on offending (Table 7.5). Over eight out of 10 of the sweep two victims became offenders by sweep four, exactly the same proportion of non-victims. Thus, whilst there may be a priori grounds for assuming that offending and victimization are causally related to one another at an individual level, this would not appear to be supported by our

Table 7.4: Lagged effects of offending on victimization

| | | Offend at sweep two | | |
		No	Yes	
Victim at sweep four	No	9 (35)	6 (26)	15 (31)
	Yes	17 (65)	17 (74)	34 (69)
	Total	26 (100)	23 (100)	49 (100)

Figures are N (%). Chi. Sq. p = .384

Table 7.5: Lagged effects of victimization on offending

| | | Victim at sweep two | | |
		No	Yes	
Offend at sweep four	No	2 (18)	5 (18)	7 (18)
	Yes	9 (82)	23 (82)	32 (69)
	Total	11 (100)	28 (100)	39 (100)

Figures are N (%). Chi. Sq. p = .654

investigation. This observation, as well as providing an answer to one of the questions we set ourselves above, brings us to the end of our general overview. We now wish to turn our attention to the chief concern of this chapter: the relationship between victimization and desistance.

Desistance and victimization

In this section we move on to explore desistance and victimization. Our measure of desistance is the characterization of the offending career of each individual at sweep four (see Chapter 2 for an outline of this). We had initially expected that as individuals desisted, so they would experience fewer and fewer episodes of victimization. Our reasoning was that as crime ceased to be a way of life for our respondents and more legitimate concerns came to dominate their lives, so they would cease to become exposed to situations or relationships in which they would be victimized. Our hunch appears to have been partially supported by the qualitative data. Here, for example, is an extract from the fourth sweep interview with Anthony in which the victimization that has happened to him is discussed:

SF: Again, in the last year, has anyone including people you knew well deliberately hit or kicked you or used force against you?

Anthony: Err, no, no. Like I said at the beginning I live a boring life now. We just keep ourselves to ourselves so don't really get into them situations.

He went on:

> Anthony: If I'm around it in a pub and someone wants to give me a smack then there's not a lot I can do about that.
> SF: No.
> Anthony: [But] I'm not very often in a pub, see.

However, whilst the qualitative data suggest that on the whole desisters had experienced fewer incidents of victimization than persisters, these differences did not reach statistical significance. Table 7.6 reports the mean number of victimizations reported to us by desisters and persisters at sweep four for each of the four victimization types we asked about. One sees, for example, that the mean number of times damage had been done to desisters' household was .50, whilst for persisters it was slightly higher at .54. Similarly, although again not to an extent that was statistically significant, persisters had experienced more physical assaults (with means of .26 and .75 respectively). Strangely, desisters appeared to have been the victims of theft more often than persisters had. Both groups had experienced similar amounts of total victimization. Although persisters had experienced a greater number of threats (an average of one each) than desisters, this was also not statistically significant.

Table 7.6: Mean victimization rates at sweep four: desisters and persisters

Offence type	Group	N	Mean	Std Dev	Sig
Damage to property	Desisters:	36	.50	.878	NS
	Persisters:	13	.54	.776	
Theft from person	Desisters:	35	.51	.781	NS
	Persisters:	11	.36	.674	
Physical assault	Desisters:	35	.26	.505	NS
	Persisters:	12	.75	1.422	
Threatened	Desisters:	35	.34	.591	NS
	Persisters:	12	1.00	1.706	
Total victimization	Desisters:	35	1.63	1.477	NS
	Persisters:	11	2.73	3.717	

NS = not significant.

It is clear from foregoing statistics that the desisters in our sample did not experience a statistically significant lower rate of victimization than the persisters. Thus the rule would appear to be a rather depressing one: 'once an offender, always a victim'. Desisting would not appear for very many people to have resulted in a reduction in their rates of victimization. Why might it be the case that desisters did not experience a reduction in the rates by which they were victimized? Two closely related processes form the backdrop to our explanation: lifestyles and area of residence.

Area of residence

Although desisters had made significant changes to their own lives, they often found themselves living in marginalized and impoverished areas. These areas, frequently ex-council housing estates, were home to some of the worst social and economic conditions in the UK and, naturally enough, often the location of much crime. Anthony (who was again classified as a desister), for example, recounted the tale of an attempted burglary at his own home (which was indeed on one such housing estate):

Anthony: Two weeks ago someone kicked in my back door and tried to break in the house at 4 o'clock in the morning. I was in bed, I heard a bang, I sat up and she [Cleo, his partner] heard it as well and said to me 'what was that noise?' And I thought something had fallen off the wall or something and then there was another bang and then I realized that someone's fucking booting the door in. So I ran downstairs but they legged it and ran round the front trying to get the front door open and it sticks and I couldn't get out, so by the time I got it open they'd long gone. So I had to get the old bill out and they come out and finger printed and all that shit.

SF: Right.

Anthony: But apparently someone had been on a little thieving spree round here. It's the first time it's happened round here mind since I've lived here...

SF: Right.

Anthony: ... to us.

SF: Right.

Anthony: I've had my car damaged before that's about it.

SF: Sure. That's a bit unfortunate.

Anthony: Yeah, that's just how it is round here, petty criminal damage, kids innit?

SF: Right. But you phoned up the old bill and what did they say?

Anthony: Yeah. The same old shit, some scag-head[6] looking for some money for a fix. You already knew it anyway, it's just procedure really to get the council number to come and fix the fucking door otherwise you wouldn't even bother with the old bill. Do you know what I mean?

SF: Yeah, yeah.

Anthony: It's not worth it, they ain't going to do shit are they?

Another desister, Ian, expressed a similar sense of resignation, albeit for different reasons, when recounting damage which had happened on his housing estate:

Ian: You might have a kid kick a ball and smash your window in your car or something but I wouldn't call that vandalizing.
AC: Right.
Ian: I just call that just life, just life. Living in a crammed, a crammed up estate where you know the kids have got nowhere to do nothing and they've not got a big back garden or mummy take them down the sports club or whatever, they're quite deprived and they got to do everything in one space.

In general, desisters, whilst they experienced victimization as regularly as the persisters, appeared to experience it randomly, rather than as victims who had been targeted:

AC: With regards to your push bike, what happened exactly?
Peter: It just went missing from out back, it were chained to ... erm, to fall pipe at back, cast iron drainpipe, got up next morning it had gone.
AC: Did you report it to the police?
Peter: No.

And again, Tony said:

I put all new window locks on and everything to stop people getting in, clothes go missing off of line, amount of his footballs what kids pinch out of garden are unbelievable...

Persisters, on the other hand, appeared more often to have been targeted in some way:

Danny: Yeah I've been, I've had a gun stuck in my face.
AC: When was that?
Danny: That was when I was selling drugs. I mean two junkies tried to rob me.
AC: So what happened? How did that happen?
Danny: That was, that was the situation where I was working in a drugs-house. And basically, basically I let them in thinking they was a plain old punter and they pulled out a gun, tried to rob me, the gun jammed and I was fighting one of them and in the end I ended up getting robbed basically. I was robbed for two hundred of crack with a gun stuck in my face.

And again:

AC: In the last year has anyone threatened to hurt you or damage your things?

Gordon: Every day.

AC: What happens?

Gordon: Yeah, it's people I've robbed in the past and you know. Not every day but ... Yeah, I've done some things bad and you run into these obstacles in life. [...]. They are just threats. Yeah, just threats, nothing's going to happen.

Another case, John, who was well known in the area in which he lived and reported several fights with others in the local area, reported the following when asked if, in the last year, anyone had threatened to hurt or damage his possessions?

John: Yeah, they have ... a good few times. Nothing ever come of it but they threatened. That just pisses me off that. Don't scare me or intimidate me at the end it just pisses me off.

AC: What's a typical example?

John: Someone drove past giving me shit and ... when they pulled back up and they seen that I was up for it they drove off [saying] 'You're getting ...' this that and the other. 'You're getting chopped up' Dah dah dah. Through [my] door, and it just pisses me off, it's just ... it's empty threats, it's full o' shit, that's all I feel that is, if you're gonna threaten someone don't need to threaten [them] – just do it.

In these cases it would be appear that prior offending was related to subsequent victimization, although, as noted above, this was not supported by the quantitative data analyses. Peter, although now classified as a desister, reported a previous victimization in which he was very much targeted for being a persistent drug user:

I've been the victim of vigilantes, but that, it wasn't, it wasn't in last 12 months though, it were about, just before I left [...] about three year ago. I was stood outside a shop waiting for a dealer. A car pulled up, three guys I'd never seen before got out and leathered me, two of them held me, other one beat shit outta me. Broke me nose, knocked all me teeth out ... broken ribs, cracked jaw, cracked cheekbone. I made, I tried to make a claim through Criminal Injuries Compensation and basically they sent me a letter and it, it wasn't actually that blatant, but it were words to the effect that I was a disreputable character. Apparently they run a totting up scheme and because of the, me convictions and things, I wasn't eligible to claim for criminal injuries. So [laughs] yeah, I've been a victim of crime.

This is not to imply, of course, that desisters were never targeted (as the quotes below demonstrate) or that crime did not befall persisters randomly either, but merely to report that persisters appeared to be more likely than desisters to be *targeted*. Desisters who were targeted included the following two cases:

> AC: In the last year has anyone threatened to hurt you or damage your things?
>
> Bill: [...] It was my neighbours from upstairs. Well the gist of it is that they liked to play their music on a weekend slightly loud after eleven o'clock, when it's supposed to be quiet. And I wrote to the council and complained. And by rights they shouldn't tell you who complained, but they said, you know, 'We get any more letters, you complaining, the next time I knock on your door it won't be the door that I'll be knocking on.' So the threat was implied.

> AC: In the last year, has anyone done any damage to your house, flat or to anything outside?
>
> Dominic: Yeah. Property on the other side, fences got kicked down, this is what I were telling you about, this crowd. They kicked me fence me down and I say they were still selling drugs, selling drugs to kids. And then, erm, they then started on kids, he's in to smack dealing and all, you know what I mean, kids and all have told him to 'fuck off'. Because they haven't been getting nowhere, I were outside shop one day. And he come out of the shop, like nine of them, all surrounded shop and that, chased me, I got as far as I could, got in to the stable, a shop where I knew there were loads of cameras, you know what I mean. So I just got into middle of all cameras, and I thought, 'Right I'm going to do it.' See it on camera, they broke my nose, they broke my ribs, gave me a right kicking.

In each of these cases it appears that the desisters were targeted not because they were known offenders who were being sought for retribution or who were 'in the wrong place at the wrong time', but rather because they were in some way opposing the criminal or antisocial activities of others.

The influence of lifestyle

Disentangling lifestyle from where one lives is an almost impossible task. However, we focus here on those aspects of lifestyle which go beyond postcodes. In this way we are exploring episodes of victimization in which family members, friends, old associates or the places one chooses to frequent play a central role. Again, desisters and persisters reported similar experiences. First, examples from two persisters:

> AC: In the last year has anyone tried to steal anything from you or your home?

Fred: Have done, yeah.

AC: What happened?

Fred: Nothing. I didn't report it, it was family. [...] They stole for addiction. They come round here and they stole two watches and a gold ring ... But I didn't report it.

AC: In the last year has anyone, including people you know well, deliberately hit, kicked you or used force against you?

Will: Yep.

AC: In the last year has anyone threatened to hurt you or damage your things?

Will: Yep.

AC: OK, can you tell me about the last two? Who deliberately hit, kicked...

Will: Er, I broke his legs.

AC: Can you briefly describe the event leading up to it.

Will: He owed me some money, er, another fella. He owed me some money, I lent him some money, £2,000, and he didn't [pay it back] so I put his knee on the kerb and jumped on his knee.

AC: OK, but did he assault you?

Will: Oh yeah. Came on strong a bit.

AC: So how did that happen?

Will: He punched me.

AC: Who threatened to hurt you or damage your things?

Will: He did, he threatened to hurt me dad.

AC: Was the guy known to you?

Will: Yeah.

AC: So he was a friend?

Will: One of me best mates.

AC: Did you report either incident to the police?

Will: No, I'm not a grass.

Desisters' victimization again seemed to be more random and less targeted than the victimization experienced by persisters. Jamie, for example, was robbed whilst on a night out, whilst Niall had things stolen whilst away on holiday:

I was pissed up one night, come in [to the pub in which he was being interviewed] from work on a Friday, me and my mate both got pissed up, come in here in the afternoon about 1 o'clock, stayed there all night. I had a pair of work trousers on, overalls sorry, had my clothes on underneath, took my overalls off, chucked them in the windowsill in the back. [At the end of] the night, I put my overalls back on, looked in my pocket and my wage packet was gone, three hundred and twenty quid gone.

(Jamie)

I'd gone away, I took [partner] away for two weeks, I took her to [...] last year for a couple of weeks. And I had a lodger at the time, and he had a party, and him or his friends sold some very silly things, some seashells that I'd got out of the sea from [...] when I was in there last time. And an old plastic crocodile that I've had since I was a little kid, and I've still got it. But they used to sit on the shelves in the bathroom. And that annoyed me more than if they'd stolen my gold watch. I can replace that. I couldn't replace these. So I didn't get angry so much, I just rang him up. I kicked him out actually first. And then I found the stuff had gone.

(Niall)

Peter reported how, despite stopping offending and no longer using heroin, he was still approached by other users who turned to him for help. Requests which, when refused, brought threatening responses:

AC: In the last year has anyone threatened to hurt you or damage your things?

Peter: That, when I were saying that lad came the other week wanting to come in here, well it were last week, about a week, ten days ago, he tried everything to get me to let him in house. Apparently he had no electric in his flat and he were wanting to sort himself out. He's saying, 'Oh well, you know what it's like, you've been there, don't be like that, let me in', and I'm saying, 'Well no, I've been clean for a long time, I don't need it plus this is me grandma's flat.' So then he started threatening me then. He's going, 'Alright then matey, I'll be seeing you around', and all this lot and I'm like, 'Well, yeah, perhaps you will.' And I just shut door on him, so yeah, he did threaten me, yeah. Not that it had any ... any influence over me like. I just humoured him and shut door.

These 'lagged effects' of Peter's past perhaps also go part of the way in accounting for the victimization of desisters. As another of our respondents, Ian, said:

There's no big sign up on my car saying, 'Oh yeah I'm an ex-con don't come near me.' I get it just the same.

Victimization in some of the estates in which our respondents lived was all too common, and in this respect desisters did not stand out from persisters. Desisters' victimization, however, did appear more often than not to be random rather than targeted at them directly, whilst the opposite was broadly true of persisters.

Making sense of victimization, offending and desistance

How ought we to make sense of the victim–offender overlap and desistance, especially in the light of the fact that desisters seem no less likely to be victimized than persisting offenders? In seeking to understand the processes by which desisters (and persisters) remain criminally victimized, we turn to the work of Sandra Walklate and of Tim Hope. In a series of publications, Sandra Walklate (Walklate, 1996, 1992; Mawby and Walklate, 1994) has proposed a 'critical' approach to exploring victimization. Her proposed agenda calls for empirically based research, an integration of quantitative and qualitative methodologies, and comparative and longitudinal studies which are able to explore those social processes which 'go on behind peoples' backs' (1996). Such an endeavour ultimately seeks to understand (amongst other things) and explore the processes associated with victimization in such a way that their socio-economic and cultural contexts were acknowledged (Walklate, 1992, 1996). This then is the framework in which we locate our work.

Tim Hope (and in particular Hope, 2001) reminds us of the embeddedness of both crime and crime risk.[7] Certain behaviours, in this case crime, are to be found with an alarming regularity and frequency in certain communities. The occurrence of certain forms of crime in some of the poorer housing estates in the UK is disproportionate to the frequency with which these crimes are found elsewhere. In short, in some housing estates where the poorer members of society are to be found living there is an excessive amount of criminal activity or behaviours that support such behaviour (see Hagan, 1997, for an overview of these processes). Our sample members, it ought to be remembered, by and large lived in such housing estates. But how did they come to be living there?

Several criminologists have started to chart the ways in which the early onset of offending behaviour 'knives off' (Moffitt, 1993; Sampson and Laub, 1993, 1997) future opportunities for 'early starters'. This 'knifing off' refers to the process of the accumulation of disadvantage and prevents such individuals from ever fully escaping the stigma of their pasts. Given that all of our sample had been convicted of at least one offence, and some of them of very many offences, many of them had probably experienced such 'knifing off' of the opportunities which would have enabled them physically to have moved home to better-off housing estates. The process by which the future chances become limited is referred to by Anthony:

SF: What are your ambitions for the next year?
Anthony: I don't have ambitions. I never have ambitions. What's the point? I take one day at a time. There's no point. I never had ambition. The only ambition I had is ... it's probably too late to do it, you know what I mean, so there's no point in doing it. I'd like, I'm not dumb, if I

> can ... I know I've got a brain I choose not to use it, I
> choose to fucking smother it with cannabis or whatever,
> you know what I mean, or I'm too lazy to use it. I would
> like to go back and get a decent bit more of an education,
> you know what I mean, learn a bit more. Do you know
> what I mean? Do something interesting like, I dunno,
> history or something like that...

Thus Anthony finds himself in a situation whereby not only does he now
feel regret at not working harder at school, but also in a situation in which
he feels it impossible, in his case, to take further classes. In this respect,
desisters, and indeed persisters, become in housing terms 'socially caged'
in 'clear, fixed, confined social and territorial boundaries' (Mann, 1986:
38). That many of these people grew up on such housing estates makes the
inevitability of their ultimate destinies seem all the less remarkable to
them.

As Hope (2001: 200–1) outlines, different housing estates have differing
income levels and, accordingly, face different opportunity/risk matrices.
Affluent housing estates have more valuable goods to be stolen and, by
virtue of the fact that far more of the residents of such areas are working,
are more likely to have homes which are unoccupied during the day. Such
houses may also be easier to enter unobserved due to their being detached
or in 'leafy' suburbs where cover is plentiful. On the other hand, affluent
areas can minimize their risk by using some of their financial resources to
purchase household security (extra locks, alarms and so on). They may
also take more precautions against crime which individually and collectively reduce this threat.

Poorer neighbourhoods, like the ones on which many of our sample
became 'socially caged', may have fewer valuable household goods (or less
expensive goods) and are more likely to have people at home during the
day. Such houses are (arguably) harder to enter without being seen. Of
course, and set against this, fewer of these homes will have their own
alarm systems and the residents (by virtue of the fact that they are renters)
may be less inclined or prohibited from adding security devices. Such areas
are also more likely to have active property and personal offenders living
within them, hence also increasing the risk of victimization. Of course, the
affluent living in poor areas may face an increased risk because they are
more exposed to offenders (by virtue of where they live) and because they
are more likely to have more of the desirable goods which such offenders
seek.

We argue that, in some respects, desisters can be thought of as being
akin to the affluent who live in poorer areas. The desisters in our sample
are, of course, not *absolutely* affluent, but rather are and can be thought of
as being *relatively* affluent when compared to some of their neighbours.
Why is this? We know from studies of desisters that they are more likely
than persisters to be in stable partnerships (which would mean that it is

more likely that they will have access to two household incomes) and more likely than persisters to be working (which will mean a stable, regular income – Pezzin, 1995). True, they will also have children (but then so do many people who offend). Desisters will probably be no more or less 'affluent' than many of their neighbours (many of whom will not have been as heavily engaged with the criminal justice system). However, they probably *will* be more affluent than those who are not working (e.g. the long term ill) and/or are reliant on benefits (e.g. the elderly) or the 'shadow economy' for their incomes, all of whom will be key groups in such estates, albeit with different trajectories of arrival.[8] In this respect – along with a lot of other people living in poorer housing estates where crime is embedded – desisters will be amongst the more affluent groups. However, unlike the truly affluent groups, our desisters will probably have different spending patterns with regards to home security. Unlike the truly affluent, who may divert some of their income towards home security, our desisters are less likely to do this. This is because of the heightened status that such goods as televisions, video and DVD players may have in that cultural milieu. It is also because the same set of cultural values will instil in them a sense of fatalism and a desire to 'live for the day' – values which we see hinted at in Anthony's quote above.

Thus desisters become 'socially caged' in poorer housing estates where crime is prevalent and embedded. They are probably better off than some of their neighbours (and in this respect they represent attractive targets), but are unlikely to have either sufficient spare resources or the cultural value systems which suggest to them that home security is worth purchasing. In any case, living in rented accommodation – in which many of them would be – would make this an unattractive option. In this respect, persisters and desisters experience the same levels of victimization as one another because, despite their differing levels of engagement in offending, they both live in areas in which crime is common. Persisters seem to be slightly more likely to be targeted for who they are, whilst desisters appear to be caught up in the crime which occurs on such estates and are (arguably) more attractive targets by virtue of their household goods.

We wish to outline some of these processes by way of two very short case studies. Both of our case studies are desisters (Anthony and Meera). We chose to include Anthony here because he was included in an earlier report of these processes (Farrall and Maltby, 2003) and as such there is much to be gained from longitudinal qualitative research with the same people. We include Meera as she successfully moved home and as such highlights the importance of local area in an understanding of victimization and desistance. Let us start, however, with Anthony.

Anthony

Anthony was classified as a desister as part of the earlier study (Farrall, 2002) and he continued to show signs of a downward trajectory in his offending. He had pretty much stopped drinking in pubs and night-clubs and reported not being able to remember the previous time he had had a fight. He continued to smoke cannabis and to drive without a driving licence (but the car was taxed and MOT'd). To all intents and purposes, then, he was very close to having stopped offending. However, in terms of his victimization, Anthony had not been so lucky. He had suffered an attempted burglary on his home in the previous year (see above) and had had his car damaged by local kids. Interestingly, when asked about the burglary he said that 'you can't really do much about' home security, reinforcing a point we made above. Other than these episodes he could recall no others.

Anthony lived in a poor housing estate (where he had also grown up) and which, according to a report by the local council (Thamesdown Borough Council, 1994), had the following telltale signs of deprivation: 41 per cent of the local residents were owner-occupiers; 55 per cent were renting from their local authority; 47 per cent of families had no car; and 15 per cent were unemployed. Almost 14 per cent reported suffering from a long term illness. The most recent crime statistics available (for 2002) suggested that the area which Anthony lived in experienced slightly higher than average rates (for England and Wales) of theft from a vehicle, burglary and sexual offences. Thus Anthony lived in rented accommodation in one of the area's least desirable housing estates. His desistance was therefore of little use as a protective factor in avoiding further victimization.

Meera

Meera, on the other hand, was living in an equally poor part of London when she commenced her period of probation supervison. The Ealing, Hammersmith and Hounslow Health Authority (which covered the area in which she was living) reported in 1995 that about 11 per cent of its resident population had a limiting long term illness (below the national average of 13 per cent), about 12 per cent were unemployed (the national average was 9 per cent at that time) and about 23 per cent of the children in this area were living in households defined as 'low earning' (the national average was 19 per cent). Some 30 per cent of children in the health authority were living in 'unsuitable' accommodation, with 20 per cent in overcrowded households. The area was a rather run-down one in which there appeared to be a number of injecting drug users. Another respondent [035] who lived in the area, and who was himself an injecting drug user told, Farrall (at the second interview) that he had been at a comedy show in a local pub in which a local (Asian) comedian had told the following joke: 'My father, when he first came here, had absolutely nothing. Absolutely nothing. It was, however, three kilos of *very good absolutely nothing*' – the inference being that he had arrived from the Asian subcontinent with three kilos of heroin. We repeat this 'joke' simply to underline the extent to which drug use was perceived amongst the local community to be extremely common, even to the extent that it was openly joked about. This, then, was one aspect of the area in which Meera lived.

At the second sweep of interviewing, Meera reported that she and her family had had problems with the neighbours over a disputed house extension. The neighbours had damaged her garden and thrown dirty nappies into it. Following this, Meera and her family moved to a different area. When asked about this she said:

> ... one of the main reasons that we did move was because our road was getting very rough. Every other day there was police down because of whatever reasons etc.

When probed in further detail, the following emerged:

AC: What was up with your street, your area, what sort of problems?

Meera: Err, they built a load of council flats just around the corner and I'm not being discriminating when I say this but the council flats were full of Somalians. So we always had a couple of families down our road, Indian families where their sons were very rough and so were their friends that they hung around with and because there was conflict between the two there were still fights.

AC: Yeah.

Meera: Err, you would find needles, etc. down the side of our house which was on ... We were an end-terraced on the side of this little alleyway and things like that. I didn't let me daughter play outside in the garden because of the fear of this.

AC: Sure.

Meera: She might pick something up or someone might throw something in the garden and I'm not going to know about it. Err, and like I say, [the] police [were] coming down every other day, just didn't want it, didn't want to know about it.

Meera was able to move to a housing estate that she preferred. The area that she moved to (according to 2002 data) had lower rates of theft from vehicles, theft of vehicles and robbery. The areas were comparable in terms of their respective rates of burglary and of sexual offences. When seen at the fourth sweep, she reported no victimization in the previous year. There are, of course, differences between Meera and Anthony. They are of different ethnic backgrounds, live in different towns and had committed different offences (Meera had embezzled her employer of several thousand pounds). Nevertheless, here one sees evidence that movement away from one particular area into another can lead, for desisters at least, to reductions in victimization.

What does this mean for victimology?

An earlier essay on this topic by Farrall and Maltby ended on a somewhat combative note:

> Because an accurate victimology is desirable [...], we, as scholars, need to tackle one of the most common findings of victimology, namely that victims and offenders are often drawn from the same population 'pool'. Because this ultimately means grappling with offending behaviour as much as it does victim behaviour, it begs the following question: Can victimology ever really distinguish itself from criminology? The authors' feelings are that it cannot. It could be argued that it was precisely *because* victimology attempted to establish itself as a separate discipline from criminology, and that in so doing it aligned itself with certain political and policy positions, that the victim-offender overlap was quietly dropped from its research agenda. This omission can no longer be sustained.
>
> (Farrall and Maltby, 2003: 50)

We feel, in the light of much of the above, that victimology stands guilty of the accusations we made previously. That is, that by continuing to ignore one of the most common findings from studies of offenders and victims (that they are often one and the same) victimology has taken a rather lop-sided view of the nature of crime and victimization. Our research agenda, namely desistance from crime, has highlighted both the inadequacies of much victimology and the problems facing people who stop offending. Victimology needs to get to grips with the fact that many victims are also offenders or ex-offenders (and vice versa) and we repeat again our calls to victimologists to turn their attention to this field of enquiry.

Notes

1   See also Mayhew and Elliott (1990: 92), who find only partial support for this 'overlap' in their data.

2   The term 'general' is used throughout to refer to the Graham and Bowling data. However, it should be noted that this sample is not truly general in that it was a sample of 14–25 year olds.

3   There are certain limitations to the data employed. The 'general' population was reported by Bowling *et al.* (1994: 47) to 'somewhat' over-represent younger respondents, students, the unemployed, those on youth training schemes and those not living in poorer localities, but in other respects it is representative of 14–25 year olds living in England and Wales at that time.

4   Given that all of the probation sample had, by the very fact of being on probation, been found guilty of an offence in the last 12 months and that Graham

and Bowling reported that 28 per cent of males and 12 per cent of females in the 'general' sample had admitted to offending in the previous 12 months (1995: 11–12), it is assumed that the probation sample was also more frequently engaged in offending than the 'general' population.

5 The 66 cases selected for comparison with the Graham and Bowling study did not differ greatly in terms of gender or the offence for which they started probation. In the main probation sample, 87 per cent of respondents were male, but for the sub-sample of 66 this figure was 88 per cent. The offences for which they started probation were also very similar, although there were some notable differences. The sub-sample of 66 were more likely to have started probation for either robbery (4 per cent) or drug offences (12 per cent) and less likely to have started probation for a summary offence (10 per cent). For the main probation sample these figures were respectively: 2 per cent, 9 per cent and 17 per cent (see Table 7.1).

6 Slang for heroin addict.

7 Hope's chapter deals with property offenders, but we feel that the general principles he outlines can be applied to personal crimes too.

8 The elderly, for example, may have first moved to the estates when they were 'respectable, working class areas' and have been overtaken by social and economic change.

Further reading

Hagan, J. (1997) 'Crime and Capitalization: Toward a Developmental Theory of Street Crime in America', in T. Thornberry (ed) *Developmental Theories of Crime And Delinquency*, Transaction Press, New Brunswick.

Hope, T. (2001) 'Crime Victimisation and Inequality in Risk Society', in R. Matthews and J. Pitts (eds) *Crime, Disorder and Community Safety*, Routledge, London.

Lauritsen, J., Sampson, R. and Laub, J. (1991) The Link Between Offending and Victimisation Among Adolescents, *Criminology*, 29(2): 265–92.

chapter eight

Understanding desistance from crime: agency, structures and structuration in processes of reform

Structuration theory
Applying structuration theory to desistance
Process one: imprisonment
Process two: community supervision
Process three: feelings of citizenship and inclusion
Process four: victimization and desistance
Process five: the structuration of place
Process six: the structuring capacities of emotions
What ought to be done?

> Given a simple choice, no one in his right mind would choose to be a homosexual.
>
> (Donald West, *Homosexuality*, 1955: 154)

Our aim in this chapter is to outline our thinking on the relationship between agency, structure and culture with regards to desistance from crime. The relationship between agency and structure is one that has seen much debate in social scientific research in the recent past. We are fortunate in that we have been able to draw upon the insights generated not only by sociologists and social theorists (e.g. Giddens; Bourdieu), but also by criminologists, especially those working on desistance (e.g. Giordano *et al.*, 2002; Laub and Sampson, 2003; Bottoms *et al.*, 2004).

Several key social theorists have in recent years attempted to move away from the simple agency/structure divide and have sought explanations that develop the interplay between agents and structures. Chief amongst the social theorists that have engineered these 'theories of the middle range', as some have called them, is Anthony Giddens. Whilst it was true a few years ago that it was mainly at the theoretical level that Giddens' efforts had received sustained interest within criminology, the picture has changed considerably. Smith (1986) was one of the first who drew upon elements of structuration theory in her discussion of crime in Birmingham. Bottoms (1993) and Bottoms and Wiles (1992) provided an excellent manifesto that both outlined structuration theory and suggests the ways in which criminologists could make use of it. Insights from this theory have informed our understanding of: victimology (Walklate, 1996); prison research (Sparks *et al.*, 1996); racial violence (Bruce *et al.*, 1998); sentencing decisions (Henham, 1998); and various other topics germane to the study of crime (see Messerschmidt, 1997, for a discussion of similar approaches to resolving 'agents' and 'structures' within criminology). In our review below, we outline some of the main organizing principles of structuration theory as put forward by Giddens and highlight some of the most innovative and useful additions to this body of work which others have suggested.

Structuration theory[1]

The starting point for Giddens is that it is a fundamental mistake to see agents and structures as being separate: neither the agent nor the structure truly 'exists' independently of one another. The creation (and continual recreation) of both 'agents' and 'structures' occurs at the same moment via the same mechanisms. Both are bound up in the very reproduction of each other. From this basic point, Giddens develops an elaborate theory of the interplay between the individual and society. In this review, we outline only those aspects of the theory which we rely upon most heavily.

Central to the theory is the concept of the 'duality of structure' (1984: 297). Giddens conceptualizes structures as both the medium and the outcome of the conduct of individuals. Giddens writes that '... the structural properties of social systems do not exist outside of action but are chronically implicated in its production and reproduction'. Brewer (1988: 146) summarized Giddens' position nicely when he wrote that, 'This duality occurs because knowledgeable agents are seen as reproducing in action the structural properties of society, allowing social life to be reproduced over time-space.' As such, Giddens sees humans as knowledgeable agents who understand a great deal about the conditions and consequences of what they do in their everyday lives and who are able to describe what they do and their reasons for doing these things (1984: 281). The agent's ability to describe the motives for particular courses of action Giddens calls 'discursive consciousness' (1984: 290–1). This knowledgability is bounded on one side by the unconscious and on the other by unacknowledged circumstances and unintended consequences (1984: 282). As such, all humans make decisions under conditions in which they are unaware of all of the constraints they act under and all of the potential outcomes of their actions. Closely related to this concept is the concept of 'practical consciousness'. This refers to the individual's ability to know how to accomplish daily tasks, but not necessarily to be able to describe or discuss this knowledge.

'Rules' (which Giddens, 1984: 18, maintains cannot be conceptualized apart from resources) are the everyday guidelines which allow individuals to continue their day-to-day existences. As Giddens (1979: 67) puts it, borrowing from Wittgenstein, 'to know a rule is to "know how to go on"'. 'Resources' we shall use in the sense of being something that social actors can rely upon and use in achieving certain ends. Thus the structuring aspects of society are not merely *constraining* – they are, at the same time, *enabling*. An example may clarify the distinction. Imagine that a disruptive student is bored of their school class. He or she wishes to 'escape' from the tedium of the class and sees any avenue of escape as being worthwhile. Knowing that the rules of the school call for good, attentive behaviour in class, which allows all to learn, the disruptive student can deliberately set about causing so much mayhem that the teacher is forced to expel the student from the class. Thus knowing the rules allows one to use these rules as a resource for achieving one's own goals. By undertaking such behaviour, the student ultimately reproduces these rules by demonstrating the need for such rules.

A key part of social action is power – the power to act and to achieve specific goals. 'Power ...,' wrote Giddens (1984: 283), '... is the means for getting things done and, as such, directly implied in human action.' Power, of course, relates to an individual's (or group's) ability to be able to 'structure' the behaviour of themselves and others, and to be able to resist the 'structuring' capabilities of others. Bauman (1989: 46) accuses Giddens of 'leaving in the shadow' the fact that some agents are in different positions to one another in terms of their ability to resist the structuring forces that they are subject to. In other words, the abilities to 'structure' and to 'be structured' are not evenly distributed throughout society. As Farrall and Bowling (1999) demonstrate, whilst Bauman may be correct in his criticism, his observations only go half the way. Not only are there differences between individuals' *abilities to structure* and avoid *being structured* at the same moment, but there are also differences in the abilities of any *one* given individual during the course of their own lifetime. Position-practices are the behaviours *normally* expected from a particular individual as a result of their social identity. In his formulation of structuration theory, Giddens notes that:

> Social identities, and the position-practice relations associated with them, are ... associated with normative rights, obligations and sanctions which, within specific collectivities, form roles.
>
> (1984: 282–3)

Thus social identities are indicative of, and are associated with, particular forms of behaviour ('position-practices'). An individual's position-practice is the result of what they and others *normally* expect of someone occupying that particular position. Giddens' work resonates with John Coleman when he writes that '... there will be expectations and prescriptions of behaviour appropriate to roles such as son, daughter, citizen, teenager, parent and so on' (1992: 5). For example, 'parents' are *normally* expected to love, nurture, care and provide for their children. In other words, each social identity describes an appropriate series of roles for members of that identity: in Giddens' terminology these are 'position-practices'. Over time, some position – practices become routinized. Giddens (1984: 282) defines 'routine practices' as the basis of what most people do most of the time. Through routines one gains a sense of security and well-being. Giddens defined critical situations as being '... a set of circumstances which – for whatever reason – radically disrupts accustomed routines of daily life' (1979: 124). For Giddens, these events are characterized by the radical disruption of routines (which incorporate a corrosive effect upon the normal behaviours of the actor concerned), leading to anxiety or fear. Conversely, critical situations could create new, positive opportunities for changes in behaviour. The notion of critical situations (developed by Giddens in 1979: 123–8, but thereafter largely ignored) is central to our use of structuration theory in relation to the life-course approach.

Despite the innovative territory mapped out by Giddens, there are 'holes' in his theoretical work as it applies to structuration (as Giddens acknowledges himself, 1990: 300). In some respects, however, this is one of the attractions of structuration theory for us. New insights and suggestions for improvements are always possible, and indeed, as we shall demonstrate, the literature on social theory is littered with them. Theoretical development is the order of the day. In this respect, applications and evaluations of structuration theory must embrace the literature and theoretical work undertaken on the theory '*après*-Giddens' (so to speak) and also those which have emerged from Giddens himself in response to the various critiques of his work.

Here we focus on the work of three writers: Rob Stones (1991, 1996) develops the issues surrounding methodological bracketing and contexts; Ira Cohen (1989) has much to say on methodological bracketing and other topics germane to structuration theory; and Doyle Paul Johnson (1990) is one amongst a number of authors who sympathetically attempt to introduce a theory of motivation into structuration theory (see also Willmott, 1986, on motivation; New, 1994, on social transformations).

In the paragraph above, we introduced the term 'methodological bracketing'. Here we outline it in greater detail, explain why it is important, how it fits into structuration theory and why the contributions of Rob Stones and Ira Cohen are so important to structuration theory. Giddens suggests that two levels of analysis are possible within structuration theory (1984: 288). The first of these, which emphasizes the action of the agent, he referred to as the 'analysis of strategic conduct', whilst the second, 'institutional analyzis', emphasizes the way in which structures are reproduced. The analysis of strategic conduct focuses upon how agents reflexively monitor what they do and how they draw upon rules and resources in the course of social interactions (this is largely the approach adopted by Farrall and Bowling, 1999). Institutional analyses, on the other hand, are less concerned with individual agent's motivations, skills and actions, instead focusing on how social institutions are reproduced over time. Some critics (Mouzelis, 1997) have argued that by introducing such concepts Giddens merely reverts to the micro/macro divide which he intended to transcend. We must admit that we are in two minds about this. Giddens states that there is 'no clear-cut line' between the two forms of analyses, but it is tempting to view these elements as representing a return to the micro/macro of old. However, despite these shortcoming on Giddens' part, we feel that the work of Stones and Cohen provides useful additions to forms of methodological bracketing which *do* indeed transcend the micro/macro divide.

When he proposed 'systems analysis', Cohen was originally attempting to 'fill the gap' in structuration theory left by the failure of Giddens to consider the 'time-space patterning of social systems' (1989: 89–93). In other words, 'systems analyses' should be concerned with how agents help to reproduce certain social systems. For example, how agents help to reproduce the systems, whereby a guilty person is processed from finding or admission of guilt at court, through to pre-sentence report, recommendation of sentence, consideration of extraneous factors (e.g. previous 'good character') and eventual sentencing. Clearly, although agents such as clerks of the court, probation officers, judges and so on *are* involved in these processes, they are not *continually* involved in them, in that one passes responsibility for the next stage of the process to another until the task (in this case appropriate sentencing) has been completed.[2] This form of methodological bracketing, we feel, is an important consideration because it helps to form a bridge between the rather 'macrological' institutional analysis and the rather 'micrological' analysis of strategic conduct. In addition, it demonstrates that, whilst agents *are* active, what is at the heart of structuration theory is the issue of being productive and/or reproductive, rather than just being active.

Stones' work emphasizes the agent's understanding of the situation(s) in which they are operating, which he refers to as agent's context analysis.[3] Just as Cohen developed system analysis as a partner to institutional analysis, so Stone developed agent's context analysis as a partner to Giddens' strategic conduct analysis. Strategic conduct analysis, observes Stones (borrowing heavily from Thrift, 1985), 'leads us back to the agent', as opposed to locating the agent and his or her actions in wider spheres, or to quote Stones, '... outwards into the social nexus of interdependencies, rights and obligations, and asymmetries of power' (1991: 676). Stones suggests that it should be employed when '... a knowledge of the terrain ... that faces or faced an agent and that constituted the range of possibilities and limits to the possible ...' is needed (1991: 676, 1996: 98).

This, we feel, helps social analysts 'get inside the heads' of actors to understand more fully how they viewed the landscape of opportunities which faced them and what they were trying to achieve. This leads us to a greater understanding of why people acted in the ways which they did and, as such, gets to the heart of how agents help to reproduce structures or make innovations. This is, in many respects, the sort of analysis employed by Farrall and Bowling 1999 in their article on structuration processes and desistance (see especially the section which relates to Russell and his desistance, 1999: 261–2).

Our discussion of Rob Stones' contribution brings us neatly to the question of motivation and its place in structuration theory. We are not going to make any bones about this: Giddens *was* poor at addressing motivational issues and his efforts to do so (which appear to revolve around the desire for security) we find, at best, partial.[4] In this respect, we think that criticisms of Giddens' original outline of structuration have some validity on this issue. Of course, we are not alone in the recognition that Giddens has skimped on this topic. Cohen (1989: 227–8) was one of the first to recognize this, and went as far as stating that it was the 'most serious' problem with Giddens' work in structural constraint (but suggested that this did not compromise the overall project of structuration).

Thus the work of Doyle Paul Johnson (1990) has been a particularly welcome addition to the development of structuration theory. We would like to devote more space than we are able to in discussing Johnson's work. It is enormously important for the theory of structuration and we are more than a little surprised that the article has not been more widely referenced. In a nutshell, Johnson proposes that Giddens' work on motivation (culled from Giddens, 1976, 1979a, 1982, 1984) revolves around two key issues: the need for security and the need for autonomy (Johnson, 1990: 112). He argues that there are two issues which require attention. Firstly, that the need for security and the need for autonomy may contradict one another; secondly, that Giddens' concentration on the need for security has meant that he is more concerned with those social practices which *reproduce* aspects of social life, rather than those which transform or modify it (1990: 118). Johnson points out that this bias means, for those wishing to develop structuration theory, that it is just as important to focus upon 'deliberate departures from routines. .. as it is to focus on their repeated enactment', (1990: 118). Johnson adds the following summary of his intellectual efforts:

The basic idea [contained within the article] reflects a fuller and more dynamic view of the complexities of human motivation and development than Giddens' emphasis on security needs, and it provides an opening for exploring the numerous ways in which autonomy can be expressed. In addition, this expanded view [of motivation] allows us to give equal theoretical weight at the level of human motivation to

practices that *change* social systems and those that *reproduce* them,
thereby correcting Giddens' tendency to conflate these two processes.'
(1990: 119, emphasis in original)

It is our belief that the addition of work on institutional analyses and
agent's context analyses helps us to avoid the criticisms that structuration
theory has reimposed the macro/micro divide which Giddens sought to
transcend. In addition, Johnson's work on motivation adds an important
missing element in structuration-inspired analyses.

Whilst we *do* believe that agency can be influenced by structure, and
vice versa, Giddens was trying to do more than just this when he wrote
about structuration theory. He was trying to explain how these processes
occurred *simultaneously* (through structuration) and *over time*. We
therefore present Figure 8.1 as a diagrammatic summary of a model of
structuration theory.

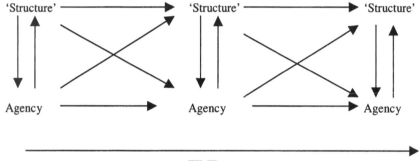

Figure 8.1: Diagrammatic representation of structuration theory

There is a somewhat complicated structure to Figure 8.1 – hinted at by the
mass of arrows. This enables the following sorts of social processes to
occur: structures and agents to simultaneously influence one another;
agents to influence the reproduction of structures over time; structures to
influence the reproduction of agents' actions over time; and, most cru-
cially of all, agents' actions influencing the reproduction of structures,
which in turn influences the reproduction of agents' actions. We could
also have added a further set of arrows – running from, for example, the
top left-most 'structure' to the bottom right-most 'agent' – to indicate long
term influences. This, we feel, is what structuration theory is about.

Applying structuration theory to desistance

Applying structuration theory to desistance poses something of a conundrum. Structuration theory, at least as originally conceived, is an

attempt to explain why certain societal practices are chronically *repro-duced* over time (as acknowledged by Johnson, 1990: 118). What we are interested in, however, is how some people (desisters) manage to create *change* in their lives. 'Reproduction' and 'change' appear to be mutually oppositional and, therefore, explaining the two simultaneously becomes a tricky conceptual problem. It is indeed Johnson himself, along with several criminologists, who we turn to in resolving this conundrum.

As Maruna and Farrall (2004) note, human beings want to achieve or attain various things and at various stages of their lives these desires change or are modified in some way. They cite Moffitt (1993: 686–7), who describes the five-to ten-year 'role vacuum' that many teenagers and young adults encounter during which 'they want desperately to establish intimate bonds with the opposite sex, to accrue material belongings, to make their own decisions, and to be regarded as consequential by adults'. However, adolescents frequently find that they are 'asked to delay most of the positive aspects of adult life' until they 'grow up', 'are older' and so on. Under such frustrating circumstances, delinquency and other analogous behaviours that express these frustrations, provoke responses from adults or 'make something happen' (Matza, 1964), take on an unusually compelling appeal (Agnew, 1985; Katz, 1988). Hence we see a common pattern amongst many European and North American teenagers: expressions of frustration, boredom, hostility towards authority and, not least of all, engagement in petty crime and other misdemeanours (such as alcohol or drug consumption) are common during teenage and early adult years.

As humans age, however, two not unrelated processes take hold. On one level, many find that they are more able to achieve the goals they craved (and indeed that they are encouraged to do so, hence alleviating some of the frustrations previously experienced). At another level, however, a different set of wants and desires also emerges. Security, comfort, meaningful relationships and a concern with future generations and diffused 'others' start to emerge for many people as desirable aspects that could improve their lives and the lives of others whom they care about. Hence we also see, for males at around the time of their early to mid-20s and earlier for females, a channelling of energies towards family formation and career building, aspects of life that often go hand in hand with desires to lead a 'quieter life' or to 'settle down'. Also at around about this time, rebelliousness dissipates as people start to make choices that will minimize disruption to their lifestyles or to their sense of well-being. People seem to make choices to lead more normal and less 'hectic' lifestyles.[5] From our perspective, then, these sorts of changes are part of the process which is often called 'maturation' and which represents not so much a radical break or discontinuity, but rather an ongoing process which is age-graded and which, naturally, means that desires and goals change over time.

Where do these desires come from? Certainly, in one sense, they come from 'within' the individuals concerned. The desire to belong to or to 'have' a family are so widespread that we must assume that this represents some basic instinct to which human beings are 'hardwired'. Similarly, the desire to 'do something', and especially 'something constructive', is common to many people living in many different societies and cultures. Taken together, some have argued (Bottoms *et al.*, 2004), such desires can be thought of as the 'English Dream'. This 'dream', which is inspired by the notion of the 'American Dream' and which we see as eminently transferable, with care, to many other national cultures, consists of acquiring a job, a home and a family (Bottoms *et al.*, 2004: 384). Thus this 'dream' provides very many people with a set of specific goals to be achieved, namely partnership, child-rearing and employment (or a legitimate alternative role such as homemaker). The existence of such a 'dream' is, we feel, the unspoken and often unacknowledged motivation behind many people's chosen paths through life.

Meeting life partners and starting work have unintended consequences for those who experience them. These features of peoples' lives often result in pressures to conform to societal norms. Antisocial behaviour, the poorly structured use of time and intermittent physical presence are not tolerated by most partners and employers. The motivating factors which 'lock' many people into relationships and jobs may be as crude as the desire for an income, and, in the case of relationships, the security which it represents.[6] In this respect, we concur with Giddens' claim that most behaviour is not *consciously* motivated (1984: 6). These desires (for income and security) mean that many men, both those who had previously offended and those who have not, help to reproduce the constraints on their behaviour via their own actions, or in 'Giddenese':

> Constraint . . . operate[s] through the active involvement of the agents concerned, not as some force of which they are passive recipients.
>
> (1984: 289)

That these actions may result in the reproduction of particular social institutions (e.g. the family and hegemonic masculine identities) is a byproduct of the coming together of individuals' desires and their attempts to fulfil these desires (see Gadd and Farrall, 2004). Gadd and Farrall outline the processes (both 'internal' and 'external') that two violent men go through in their progression from 'troubled youths' to 'protecting, but fallible family men' (2004: 142). Each man's desire to avoid becoming more like their fathers than they already had done is clearly apparent (2004: 140). In many respects, Gadd and Farrall combine with a psycho-social perspective elements of systems and agents' context analyses.

Ethnographic work, in part, perhaps also explains why some people embark on lengthy offending careers. The work of Willis (1977) in the UK and MacLeod (1995) in the USA suggests that, knowing that they are 'destined' to 'dead end jobs' some school children, and especially males, spend their schooling 'dossing off'. This thereby ensures that they achieve the 'dead end jobs' which they had anticipated, and, of course, reproduces the belief structure that such jobs are all that people in their position can hope for, thereby helping to legitimate a future generation's 'dossing off' at the same time. Expressing this in the language of structuration theory, Giddens writes:

> The unintended ironical consequences of their 'partial penetration' of the limited life chances open to them is actively to perpetrate the conditions which help to limit those very life chances.
>
> (1984: 293)

Of course, it is not simply the case that once one has achieved employment, partnership and parenthood, one will automatically stop offending. Whilst the evidence (e.g. Laub *et al.*, 1998, on marriage; Farrington *et al.*, 1986, on employment; Hughes, 1997, on parenthood) suggests that these processes act in such a way as to severely curtail offending behaviour – and if not 'producing' (as such) desistance then certainly starting the processes which ultimately lead towards desistance – it takes more than this. Numerous obstacles impede the travel from offending to non-offending lifestyles. Chief amongst these remain the status of the individual desister in the eyes of both his or her former associates and the 'long arm' of the law (should they have become involved in the criminal justice system). If friends fail to recognize or deliberately ignore the desister's pleas that they have changed their ways or no longer wish to be associated either with them or with certain behaviours, then the would-be desister may resign themselves to continued offending (Rumgay, 2004: 416). As Ebaugh (1988: 22) notes, following Erikson 1959: 89, confidence in one's ability to maintain the same identity is partly dependent upon others' perceptions of oneself. If an individual's friends frequently pay visits to their home offering stolen goods for fencing and if no alternative sources of income emerge, how long will it be before this individual gives up resisting and takes them up on their offers? Similarly, if the police refuse to accept that an individual has given up offending, that individual may feel they have little to lose from continuing to offend. Many, but not all, of these processes are described in Chapters 3–7. Here we recap and summarize the most important of these processes.

Process one: imprisonment

The major impact of prison on the desistance process is, arguably, to disrupt the journey of 'going straight'. This is created via the removal of people from structures that favour 'maturation' (such as employment, family and the home). As such, imprisonment suspends the possibility of the benign reproductive processes, whereby people's involvement in those structures listed above encourages actions that reduce offending and favour desistance. These processes, in turn, can embed people further into structures that, over time, assist desistance. When people are imprisoned, those processes which encourage desistance are replaced by a more malign set of processes of reproduction, where structures and agents interact to reduce the chance of successful desistance. For example, incarceration completely transforms the potency of an individual's agency, leaving them with few resources at their disposal. Furthermore, ex-prisoners find new structural impediments to desistance imposed when they re-enter mainstream society following their release. Steady employment, a place to live and a steady relationship are frequently damaged by custody (if they existed prior to imprisonment). Moreover, for those who have lost and those who have still to establish such roles as father/mother, husband/wife, breadwinner, the experience of prison often means that they find it more difficult to establish these roles because of the stigmatizing label that being an 'ex' prisoner attaches. Barry described his experience:

> Well, yeah, basically, when you get out everyone knows you've just got out of prison, no employment wants to touch you, as such. Well they do, you get [work] on building sites [but] it does, it closes a lot of doors once you've been in prison. You know, people look at you different.

Prison also arrests 'maturation' and outlooks that help to encourage desistance. For example, whilst in prison inmates are subject to strict regulations, where activities such as meals, exercise and visits are conducted around strict rules of time and place. Therefore, prison rules place people under an institutionalized routine that virtually suspends their power: 'when you're in prison, you don't make any decisions for yourself'. This disempowerment creates a mentality that is not well suited to overcoming the structural impediments that many face upon release from prison. According to Richards and Jones (2004: 203), this means ex-prisoners 'may have little memory traces of societal rules and resources (memory of social structure) with which to reciprocate in the practice (social integration) of day-to-day life (routinisation)' and consequently may lack confidence and trust in the world they re-enter. Furthermore, this deficit of the resources and power to cope with legitimate society is contrasted with the newly acquired resources in terms of criminal knowledge and networks of contacts that have been gained from prison and can be brought 'back to the streets' (Richards and Jones, 2004). John, who at the most recent interview was expecting to receive a prison sentence for another driving offence, is conscious of this process of structuration exacerbating his deviant behaviour:

> And I know as well if I go to jail I'll come out twenty times worse off, I'll think 'bollocks to it, I've been there, I'll come out and I'll just be worse'. Know what I mean, it's just, I know that's gonna happen,

that's why I don't wanna go really. 'Cos it's gonna be one o'them, I'll go in there and I go in for, for driving, but it's classed as driving while disqualified 'cos bringing the charge back up and I'll go in and I'll come out and I'll be back in court coupla months later and it'll either be for driving or summat worse. It'll probably be robbery or something, 'cos I've got friends what I've cut meself off from, the ones that I've done, like was in trouble with back then. I've cut myself off from them years ago and they're all in prison and things like that. And I'll meet back up with them and I'll go straight back to it and I'll end up worse.

The irony here is that by being conscious of the fact that he will face severe structural constraints when released from prison, and that prison will renew relationships with previously lost criminal contacts, John accepts that he'll 'think bollocks to it' and commit further crimes. His awareness of the consequences of prison and being involved in crime means the 'realistic' outlook he adopts actually increases the chances that his pessimistic prophecy will be fulfilled. In this respect, John's predicament resonates with that of 'Super', one of MacLeod's (1995: 225) respondents, who was 'pushed from behind and pulled from the front by structural forces'. John is 'being pushed to jump'. In short, using Barry's analogy (see Chapter 3), prison 'closes a lot of doors' and increases the likelihood of further involvement in crime, which, in turn, forecloses future opportunities and makes persistence more likely (see also Moffitt, 1997: 23).

Process two: community supervision

Farrall (2002) concluded that whilst probation was of little direct help to many probationers, its indirect impact – by allowing naturally occurring changes in employment, accommodation and personal relationships to develop – played a significant role in assisting desistance. In contrast to prison, probation leaves 'good roads open' and allows for the completion of processes of maturation. However, this study has demonstrated that probation is sometimes responsible for other long term impacts on desistance (see Chapter 3) by planting seeds of help that can be drawn on when needed.

Probation can help desistance by what it does *not* do, namely not constricting the ability of individuals to meet and strengthen their relationships with partners, as much as by what it *does* do. As outlined by many studies of desistance, marriage and partnership are strongly related to desistance. This process operates by structuring individuals' lives away from offending. On the one hand, they have less time to spend with criminal peers and friends (Warr, 1998) with whom they might become involved in heavy drinking and drug taking. By removing would-be desisters from such activities, their partners also remove them from the 'night-time economy' that provides the context for much of their offending. On the other hand, the structures of marriage and new relationships with partners also form new social bonds that represent new forms of informal social control (Laub and Sampson, 2001; Horney *et al.*, 1995). Individuals who wish to preserve these bonds consequently take actions to strengthen them (e.g. staying in, looking after children, avoiding going out with certain friends and so on). Through taking these actions they strengthen their relationships and, by so doing, (re)produce the very structures that tie them into desistance (Laub *et al.*, 1998). This process is illustrated by the case of Bryan.[7] Going to the cinema as part of a couple and having nights in watching videos took him away from key criminogenic locales (see also Process five). Here he describes how becoming involved in a new relationship led to a shift in his social identity:

> I look at relationships a lot differently now. I'm actually looking at the girl I'm with now and thinking I could marry her. [...] I used to be adamant that I would never get married. [...] Another thing is that I'm starting a pension up. [...] I'm looking at things a lot more realistically, I'm thinking this job could not make it. So I've got to do something else. I've got to have some security. [...] Which I wouldn't have thought about before. I think about things a lot more.

In effect, Bryan has chosen to allow his social identity to be restructured so that he becomes tied in to other structures, like pensions and marriage, that will – in all probability – cut him off further from his past offending (see also Rumgay, 2004, on 'scripts'). Through his agency he constructs a positive, future oriented self-identity (Maruna, 2001; Laub and Sampson, 2001).

Probation also, again indirectly by not imposing restrictions in the same way imprisonment might, allows individuals the opportunity to enter or remain in the labour market. This again enables the process of desistance to develop. Tony, describing how probation helped him, said:

> Tony: Yeah. Keeps me employment as well, don't it? I mean 'cos they actually give me deferred sentence with this order where I had to comply with probation and stay in full time employment, so it gave me more of an incentive as well with deferred sentence on it.
>
> AC: Yeah.
>
> Tony: 'Cos I knew if I gave me job up I'd go to prison. If I didn't go to probation I would have gone to prison, I would have gone to prison for at least three or four years if I'd breached all that. I mean working's not really as bad as going to prison for three or four years is it?

Of course, on the surface working is recognized, at least for those convicted, as preferable to prison but, more importantly, behind this are processes that allow desistance to develop. Being engaged in work structures individuals' lives so that, like those with partners, there is less time and opportunity for offending. Employment means less time is available to be spent with criminal peers, and individuals find themselves in a routine that means they have less time to spend engaged in criminal activities (Farrington *et al.*, 1986).

Work also structures and constrains individuals' behaviour by subjecting them both to new rules and to position-practices, such as 'income provider', 'company representative' and 'responsible taxpayer' (see Process three), that come with being employed. Aware of these rules (or 'skeleton scripts': Rumgay, 2004), individuals can act in ways that provide a resource to be used to their advantage. Many jobs, and the job market in general, have informal and formal rules and regulations that do not favour the continuation in many forms of criminality. In this respect, many individuals, it would appear, commit themselves to avoiding offending because that would undermine their future employment. For example, Chas[8] gives his reasons for not wanting to offend any more as follows:

> I've got more to lose. I need a good reference from work if I want a decent job and I'm looking for a decent job because I'm looking for a graduate job, so I wouldn't really want to jeopardize that.

Chas recognizes the things that will get him a good job and, by so doing, he takes actions that will reproduce this. For those in jobs which they perceive as being 'good' jobs, like Rajeev, who worked in the IT sector, the good behaviour of his colleagues was seen as helping to develop a welcome shift in his identity:

> Everyone [at work] is really professional which is very good because they're turning me into a professional. If I start hanging round with people like that then I'll gain more and more experience and I'll start acting more like a professional, you see.

This suggests that work involves the development of new position-practices, such as that of 'the professional', which is in many cases the antithesis of 'the offender'. These position-practices are by their definition more 'responsible' and 'adult'. Thus probation enables the maturation process to be more fully completed. Mature adults have good reason not to behave in ways that would undermine their 'mature' status (often seen as the results of their own actions), as Jamie explains:

> When you get to the age of twenty-one you've got no excuse for going in prison. You're an adult, you shouldn't have to do stupid things, you're grown up, good enough to get a job, deal with it, not ... When you're younger, that's different, you're a little, you're just a kid, aren't you? Messing around like a little tiger, playing around with ...

Now when you get to an adult, you've got to be sensible and act like an adult...

It is precisely these benign processes that imprisonment prevents from happening by imposing structural and agentic impediments in the way. However, probation has another role in encouraging desistance. As the case studies of Mark and George in Chapter 3 demonstrate, probation officers *can* raise the consciousness and knowledge of those they supervise in such a way as to increase the resources they can draw upon. While factors such as employment and family formation structure their desistance, the advice that their probation officers had given them on making choices and mapping out their futures begins to resonate as these life changes take hold. This advice appears to act as a resource that helps motivate them in ways which reinforce their commitment to maintaining the conventional structures of work, partner and family.

Process three: feelings of citizenship and inclusion

As individuals move from unemployment to legitimate employment they find themselves subject to taxation via their salaries. Rachel[9] provides an example of the impact of this:

Once you start paying taxes or things like that, and then you think you're paying for all these services, so when that bus shelter over there gets smashed it's taxpayer's money. Or the bus fares go up to pay for the glass getting smashed and there's no real reason to smash the glass. Kids say 'I was bored, so I smashed the glass'. A lot could be done, if you're growing up round here, and you're a teenager, you've got nothing to look forwards to.

Paying her taxes fed into Rachel's appreciation of the importance of taxation and helped to instil in her a concern with acting in a responsible manner. Like other 'responsible' working adults, who also pay their taxes and with whom she now perceives herself as sharing an affinity, Rachel regularly provides a proportion of her income to pay for wider services. Paying for such services means she feels that she is 'responsible' in some way for them. To be a 'responsible' taxpayer, she feels morally obliged to act in specific ways that accompany her new identity, like not damaging the services she has helped pay for. These rules act as useable elements of a new social identity. By following them, Rachel is able through her actions (such as caring for public property) to reinforce to others (and perhaps herself) her new 'responsible' identity. By contrasting her new identity with that of the 'bored' kids responsible for criminal damage, Rachel emphasizes her own 'respectable' identity, but at the same time demonstrates an awareness of how their bored routines are responsible for encouraging their behaviour and how it impacts on her sense of place ('round here').

This can be seen as evidence to support Hypothesis A, as outlined in Chapter 6. Desisters exhibit fewer self-centred values because as their expressed concern for others increases, so the strength of the relationship between desistance and citizenship values increases also. Jamie, who said that he strongly agreed with the statement, 'Being a citizen is about becoming involved in your community,' explained his reasons as follows:

Jamie: Because your community is your community. If you don't look after your community then the community is not going to look after you and then you'll end up a nobody in society. So you've got to look after your own community, definitely.

AC: Have you done anything like that?

Jamie: Looked after my own community? I look after my own community by working and paying taxes. That's how I help my community.

Legitimate work is both the cause and effect of Jamie's attitude: it requires him to contribute to his community, but at the same time strengthens his non-criminal identity as a 'hard working citizen' who is responsible for helping where he lives and his wider community.

Process four: victimization and desistance

In Chapter 7, we saw how few of our desisters had been able to escape victimization. They appeared to be housed in 'sink estates' where crime was routinely embedded and where victimization was common. The entrapment of our desisters in these estates is partly a function of their social class origins (whereby members of the working class frequently remain living in lower quality housing, often close to where they grew up), of the 'kniving off' of future options (Moffitt, 1994) and of wider social policies (Murie, 1997). We see the second half of Chapter 7 as essentially structurationist in manner and method, and so merely summarize our thoughts here. That criminal victimization was common in these places suggests a further process of structuration, whereby 'desisters', once victimized, 'strike back' at their assailants, at once reproducing the victim–offender overlap for themselves and the party who originally offended against them. This observation perhaps in part explains why it takes many people a long time to desist fully from offending, in that the opportunities and motivations for offending are common in some areas of our towns and cities (see Hagan, 1997).

Process five: the structuration of place

In all of this discussion we have yet to mention what we feel to be an important aspect of the desistance process that holds another resonance with Giddens' work, namely the importance of place. Giddens (1984) puts great emphasis on the importance of places in the reproduction of social forms. Other commentators writing within the criminological arena have similarly noted how important specific places are in the production of criminal events generally (e.g. Sherman *et al.* and Reiss, quoted in Bottoms and Wiles, 1992) and, moreover, as a central concept in structuration theory (Bottoms and Wiles, 1992: 19). Hagan's (1997) work suggested that there are certain meso-level social or community structures which influence individuals' desires, motivations and abilities to engage in, or refrain from, offending.

A similar, but often neglected dimension can be found in the work of Meisenhelder (1977), who refers to the spatial dimension of desistance. Not all 'places' (e.g. bars, snooker halls, railway stations, churches) are equal in terms of their ability to either facilitate or confirm a would-be desister's status as an 'ex-offender'. For example, some places (bars, gambling halls, snooker halls or certain street corners) have a negative effect, suggesting that an individual has not recanted their old ways and is still engaged in illegal or 'shady' activities. Other places are suggestive that an individual has made the break with crime, and these include churches, reputable employers, domestic family homes and other 'conventional' civic associations. Still other places may convey neither positive nor negative messages (e.g. a large out of town supermarket or a railway station).[10]

The explanation given by the likes of Meisenhelder (1977) and Goffman (1963) is that the places where an individual lives out their life communicates some element of 'who' they are and 'what' they do. Time spent in snooker halls or certain bars suggest a routine engagement with others who may themselves continue to be engaged in illegitimate endeavours. On the other hand, routinely spending time in stable employment, engaged in childcare duties, with other 'benevolent' bodies such as churches or civic groups, or engaged in some other 'constructive' use of one's leisure time can help to create (at least) the image of a reformed or reforming character.

In this section, we shall discuss how developing notions of place and what it means to the people who inhabit and act out their lives in these 'places' is of use in developing an understanding of desistance. We shall present data which show the ways in which place can impact upon an individual's propensity to reoffend. In the following quote, Graeme,[11] whose offending was related to fighting, often after drinking, explains how the size of the town in which he lives affects his preparedness to get into further fights:

There's no point is there. I'm alright giving someone a hiding one night, but I can't stand facing them the next day. I don't like thinking, 'I'm going to bump into that bloke down the high street, oh shit, what am I going to say?'. And this place is so small, it's such a small town if someone's hit someone the whole town knows about it the next day. And it just causes too much trouble.

Staying out of trouble is thus related to the dilemma brought on by bumping into the victim later on, which is all the more likely given the size of the town. 'Places' can thus (as in this case) act as regulating forces, discouraging offending. In other instances, avoiding a specific place, commonly public houses, was also observed to be related to changes in patterns of offending. This extract is from the same interview with Graeme:

Interviewer: If you had to put your finger on the one thing which made you stop getting into fights, what would it be and why was it?
Graeme: Women.
Interviewer: But what is it about the women which is making you stop?
Graeme: Being in a relationship I suppose. That's all that matters to me when I'm in a relationship, is the woman. [...] And I tend to stay away from the pubs and all that when I'm with a woman.
Interviewer: So, it's as much avoiding situations where a fight could start as being in those situations and avoiding the fight?
Graeme: Yeah.

Whilst spending time with his partner took Graeme away from a situation in which he could potentially get into trouble, for one respondent (Trevor)[12] merely having his partner with him negated any effects of being in certain situations.

Everytime I go out on my own I'd end up fighting. Everytime *we* go out you're fine.

As the following quote shows (taken from an interview with Bryan),[13] no longer visiting one particular place can end abruptly:

There was a pub that was a centre of violence and I'd been going out with this girl from there, but we fell out, and I just never went up there again.

Changes in where and when an individual makes visits to a particular place do not need only to relate to 'deviant' or 'dangerous' spaces. Anthony, when interviewed as part of the current project, reported how changes in his use of the local town centre shifted over time – changes which appeared to be part of his process of desistance:

Anthony: If I go out and drinking or something or even in fucking town when I walk through town, you know, people say how you doing and that. 'What are you up to nowadays?' [they ask]. You just give them 'fine, yeah, see you later', that kind of thing.

SF: So when was the last time you actually went into town?

Anthony: What drinking in town?

SF: Well, no, not drinking, just went into town?

Anthony: Last week. I go into town all the time. The town centre is only down there from us, innit?

SF: Right, so you go in there shopping?

Anthony: All the time yeah, shopping or whatever, getting some clothes or whatever yeah.

SF: Right.

Anthony: My bank's in town you know ... so I go to the bank or whatever.

SF: So when you went, the last time you went to town last week I mean what time of day was that?

Anthony: It was about dinnertime because I went to the bank.

Anthony's relationship with the town centre had changed dramatically. Unlike during previous interviews with him (see Farrall, 2002, 2003; Farrall and Maltby, 2003), Anthony had been working at the same job for a number of years. As such, his relationship with the town centre ceased to be one of 'drunken entertainment' and started to become one characterized by the daily routines of life. During these forays into the town centre, Anthony encountered some of his old friends. This brings with it certain dilemmas: maintaining cordial relationships (if not actual friendships) with old acquaintances whilst not risking his 'respectable' identity:

Anthony: [I've only got] to across the road and I can see two kiddies sat on the bench who I know, so that's, you know, what I mean. The kind of thing I don't like nowadays.

SF: Right.

Anthony: I'd rather be ignorant and uncommunicating to people now. I still don't like people, people who are too sly, too devious.

SF: Oh, did you go over and talk to them or...?

Anthony: No, no. I said 'alright' but I can't remember. They were begging on the benches at lunchtime so I didn't stop and have a chat. Do you know what I mean? Don't do your street-cred much good. [Laughter] But they're mates. I've known them for years but, like I said, I told you about them earlier, scag-heads now. One of them in particular begs in town all the time.

SF: Right.

Anthony: He floats from spot to spot. One of his spots happens to be outside my bank.

These extracts tell us several things, not least of all that most of the 'dangerous' places are public houses and that the offences being referred to are exclusively related to violence against the person (Graeme, Trevor and Bryan's interview extracts all refer to these aspects). In addition to this, Anthony's interview extracts suggest that, over time, as an individual moves from being 'an offender' to 'a desister' to 'an ordinary person', so their relationship with physical spaces changes. Anthony used to view the town centre as somewhere in which fights could be watched and engaged in and women pursued (see Farrall, 2002). This relationship of 'deviant consumption' has transformed into one of 'respectable reproduction' as he visits the town centre to buy clothes, visit his bank and so on. These quotes, taken as a whole, also point to the fact that places are key in understanding how desistance occurs for some people. As Bottoms and Wiles (1992) note, places are crucial in understanding patterns of offending and, in particular, how places are important *generators* of actions and not merely *venues* in which actions are performed.

Violent places too attract a reputation. Thus people wanting 'a scrap' or wishing to experience the anticipatory excitement of being where a fight may erupt know where to go, as do the police. Similar processes can be seen to operate with regard to the sale of, say, illegal drugs or prostitution. Certain pubs, street corners, shop arcades and such like are known locally as places where, commonly, drugs or sex are available for purchase. Often this knowledge is shared by those who use these services, those who disapprove of them and those who are charged with policing them. In some instances, these seemingly hostile groups co-operate together in order to reserve these places exclusively for these sorts of activities.

Process six: the structuring capacities of emotions

Emotions provide a useful means through which individuals, such as those in our sample, are able to process a wide range of information about themselves and their wider world and, significantly, the relationship between the two. In doing so, they may help in delivering a moment of 'realization', where individuals reflect on their previous actions and evaluate these in the light of their feelings about such actions. In this respect, emotions help individuals to make sense of their pasts and their potential futures. If they feel unhappy, guilty or ashamed about their behaviours, these feelings inform them of their emerging values and goals (Douglas, 1984; Ebaugh, 1984). In turn, these may prompt an appraisal of their lives, the direction they are heading in and the implications of their behaviour (Maruna, 2001).

Via these processes, emotions may shift the boundaries of consciousness in favour of greater levels of self-awareness. While people are capable of appraising these feelings, the intensity of emotional states, coupled with the possibility that such feelings can often be confusing, means that individuals are often forced to 'make sense' of their feelings over time. The insights derived from this process allow offenders to establish how far they have 'travelled' towards a non-criminal lifestyle and how much further they have still to travel. Given that many desisters appeared to experience setbacks, such feelings help to reinforce in the would-be desister's mind that their behaviour is at odds with their values (see Chapter 5). Whether desisters are ultimately successful will depend on the support of others, such as friends and family, but agency is crucial in initiating the desistance process (Maruna and Farrall, 2004: 25), whilst emotions, it would appear, play an important role in formulating and maintaining the resolve to stop offending.

That emotions play a role in motivating offenders towards desistance is demonstrated in Peter's description of when he decided to make an effort (once more) to stop his heroin use and associated offending:

> [My drug use] just gradually went downhill, it got worse and all me, what I woulda considered to be me genuine friends gradually turned away, i.e. people who were not involved with drugs – so-called decent people. They gradually turned away. So I ended up, got more *isolated* as time went on. This [pause] took me up to about the year 2000 [pause] and it were actually Millennium eve when I decided enough were enough. At midnight on Millennium eve I found meself sat at home, about five to midnight I thought I'll go for a walk round and as midnight struck I could see fireworks, people partying and I could hear, you know, people enjoying themselves etcetera and I were cold turkey and *I felt absolutely terrible.* And it crossed me mind to go jump in't river, pretty much. And that were when I decided that it were time, time to change, you know, it were either up or all the way down. So I thought right, now's the time to change.

Other people's enjoyment made Peter acutely conscious of his own isolation and loneliness and this was made even more intense by the physical effects of withdrawing from heroin. These emotions were not only responsible for producing 'a moment of clarity' that made him aware that he needed to take action to change his situation, but because they were so uncomfortable, they provided the motivation to see this change through.

While not all desisters undergo an epiphany, and indeed for many the realization was an incremental process, at some stage they came to the belief that there was an alternative to offending. For those at the beginning of the process of desistance, as seen in Chapter 5, this belief was maintained through the emotion of hope. This provides them with the vision that an alternative 'normal' life is both desirable and, ultimately, providing they overcome the obstacles and uncertainties that remain, possible. For hope to be meaningful, the object or situation desired must appear attainable at some level. Therefore, for those in the early phase of desistance, their hope had its origins in and was promoted by their conduct in a range of social situations. For Frank and Tom, this was their success at finding and keeping employment. For others, like Ben, Ron and Paul, hopes were reinforced by their relationships with their respective partners. While for Jimmy and Matthew, who had both recently stopped misusing alcohol and drugs, it was their continued involvement with their respective rehabilitation programmes and the emotional support they received which grounded their hopes in reality.

These processes also work in the other direction, with hope reinforcing actions, which in turn reproduces and reinforces desistance-favouring structures (Burnett and Maruna, 2004: 397–9). As Simpson (2004: 441) reminds us, there is an 'action component' of hope that means that hope has behavioural implications for agents who possess it. 'A person with hope will act in a manner that supports (or minimally does not foreclose) ... hope,' writes Simpson (2004: 441), and this extends to include taking actions that 'sustain one's hope' and which are aimed 'towards realising the hope'. The three types of actions she describes are all relevant to those who hope they can desist from crime: firstly, *doing* something to maintain the hope (such as avoiding criminal peer group or not relapsing into drug use); secondly, re-evaluating one's hopes as circumstances change (such as accepting the termination of a relationship or dismissal from a job); and, finally, the recognition that a person's hopes may depend on the actions they do *not* take (such as continuing to avoid certain areas or individuals). Hope provides a feedback loop which reinforces behaviours likely to bring about whatever is desired, which in turn may serve to maintain the original hopes – and, over time, build upon them (Chapter 5).

Structuration theory can also highlight the role that other emotions play in further embedding the desistance process. Maruna and Farrall (2004) argue that the feelings of 'intrinsic reward' found in non-criminal activities such as parenthood, coaching or painting provide an alternative to the 'extrinsic' and fleeting rewards provided by crime. This, they argue, can help lulls in offending to become longer periods of 'secondary' desistance, particularly when the person's new non-criminal behaviour is recognized by others and reflected back in a 'de-labelling process' (Trice and Roman, 1970). This process is illustrated by the experiences of Jimmy, who here describes the reaction of an 'old couple' he has got to know through his voluntary work as a repair man:

Jimmy: ... I've built a relationship up and I said I'd put [their wall up] for them. But they find it very hard – me doing it for nothing. But I have to say to them, 'look I need to do it. I need to do some of this good', 'cos I, and I explained my past. Oh I don't, I don't, I don't hide anything.

AC: What's their reaction when you tell them?

Jimmy: It blows them away. Well, no, um, well, they say, um, 'you're not like that now. We accept you as [the] Jimmy of to-day [. . .] You obviously, you have done [wrong], but a lot of people have got pasts, unfortunately'.

AC: Yeah.

Jimmy: And they try and encourage me very much, you know what I mean? To stick with what I'm doing today. And they all say if I need to talk to anybody just go and talk to them. It don't matter what about just go for a chat.

For Jimmy, voluntary work and the rewards it brought helped him to establish a new social identity for himself which not only organized his previously chaotic life but also allowed him to 'pay back' his debt for his previous behaviour. However, through his voluntary work Jimmy was able to meet others – networks of support from the respectable, non-criminal community such as the old couple – whose faith, trust and confidence in him helped reinforce his developing identity further. This seems likely to increase the likelihood that he will continue to act in ways that will support his non-criminal view of himself. Moreover, as this process continues over time, desisters appear to develop strong emotional attachments to and identifications with the individuals, institutions and organizations to which they are 'bonded', such as marriage and employment (Hirschi, 1969; Laub and Sampson, 2001). As seen in Figure 5.1 (p. 109), for those ex-probationers in the last phase of the emotional trajectory towards desistance, it is their involvement in 'normal' life that provides their own 'intrinsic' sense of reward. Their extrinsic rewards are now provided by their achievements in 'normal' life, such as job, home, children, mortgage and holidays, and the fact they have all been gained on 'normal' terms reinforces this non-deviant identity.

What ought to be done?

What we wish to do now is to reflect upon what our exploration of desistance tells us about policy matters. We have, at various points above, addressed this issue when it has arisen. However, this section is intended as a more 'distanced' consideration of policies in the criminal justice and social arenas.

We think it fairly obvious that we agree with David Downes' assessment that 'informal social controls are far more effective than formal social control' (1997: 1). That is, that the role of families, communities, friends, work colleagues and so on is more important for the prolonged maintenance of 'good order' (at macro, meso and micro levels) than is the input from, for example, probation officers. Yet, conversely, some aspects of the criminal justice system, most notably the use of imprisonment, are extremely effective in helping to damage those social institutions (family and employment) that do most to foster 'good order'. We have elsewhere demonstrated that life changes are more important than the work of practitioners in fostering desistance (Farrall, 2002). Our thoughts on these matters have not altered greatly as a result of the most recent sweep of interviews. In this respect, criminal justice policy needs to attune itself more directly with efforts to reinforce key aspects of informal social control. In this case, employment and family formation are the key to this. As Downes writes, 'the absence of future employment prospects de-legitimises school and results in many pupils becoming cynical, bored and rebellious' (1997: 3). Similar processes (which we understand as a further process of structuration) have been observed by others working with those who have left school and are seeking employment (MacLeod, 1995; Hagan, 1997). Where employment is unavailable, engagement in anti-social behaviour becomes more likely. For this reason, we welcome the renewed interest in the New Careers Movement (see Maruna *et al.*, 2004: 228), the notion of 'co-operative employers' (Kakizawa, 2004, cited in Court, 2004) and further evidence that employment schemes can help people make the bridge between offending and non-offending lifestyles (Berk *et al.*, 1980; Liker, 1982; McSweeney *et al.*, 2004: 28; see Krienert and Fleisher, 2004, for an overview of this literature).

We are *not* suggesting that getting a job will suddenly make the world a better place, providing the motivation for offenders to desist and for ex-offenders to remain desisters. However, in the light of the available evidence, it would appear that employment *is* one of the aspects most commonly associated with desistance about which central and local governments can reasonably do something, and, given the importance of informal social controls noted above, about which one might have reasonable hopes for sustained changes at the individual level (Downes, 1997). We therefore applaud the publication of the Home Office's outline of the work of the National Offender Management Service, which suggests that just over £30 million is to be spent on education, training and employment schemes in the period 2004–05 (Home Office, 2004: 15). The order of the areas for intervention (accommodation, education, training and employment, mental and physical health, drugs and alcohol, finances and debt, families and lastly 'attitudes, thinking and behaviour') gives hope that the days of the exclusive focus on cognitive behaviouralism are starting to recede. There are no quick fixes to entrenched social problems, as those working in other fields (see Brown *et al.*, 2004, on education) have started to recognize. The overly structured and often restrictive cognitive-behavourial programmes may serve to raise hopes only for them to be dashed quickly once it is realized that social, economic and cultural processes are more important than the operation of the criminal justice system (Downes, 1997:1). Some of these processes we have outlined immediately above, and, in short, they appear to make some people's efforts to desist doomed to failure.

We do not, however, wish to suggest that desistance is the result only of macro and meso level social processes. Clearly, much of what we have described above relates to those actions (or 'inactions') pursued by individuals. It remains our contention, however, that (to paraphrase Giddens paraphrasing Marx) people make their own choices in circumstances which are not of their own choosing. How then ought probation officers to intervene? Actions aimed at solving practical problems delivered in one-to-one sessions (an unfashionable mode of action we admit) strikes us as providing not just solutions to the problems faced by probationers, but also (reflecting on what we have learnt from Chapter 3) an opportunity for probation officers to start the process of 'chipping away' referred to by Anthony. The 'talk' which went on between officers and probationers, we admit, got a rather poor press based on the evidence collected during the first three sweeps (see Farrall, 2002: 141). We can only report what is told to us, and five years on it appears that *some* of our ex-probationers now viewed the discussions which they had with their officers in a more positive light. In this respect, we adhere to Maruna *et al.*'s call to take words seriously (2004: 227, echoed by McNeill, 2004: 243). 'Words' eventually 'filter through'. In the light of our research, however, this appears to take several years (reinforcing our claims that quick fixes and those who peddle them are misguided) and may in part be dependent upon there being a growing resonance between what an officer has said to an individual and that individual's ability to apply these insights in their daily lives. In short, time is required for changes in both the outlook and the life circumstances of ex-probationers to take place before these changes and the advice of their officer becomes 'aligned' and, as such, meaningful for the recipients of such advice.

One way of reorganizing (both conceptually and substantively) state-sponsored interventions is the re-emerging 'strengths based' perspective (Maruna and LeBel, 2003). This perspective argues that the key to successful state-sponsored reintegration is to ask, 'What are the positive contributions that this individual can make?' (instead of the usual question which is something like, 'How do we manage the risks this individual poses?'). Maruna and LeBel (2003) outline a number of activities that ex-offenders and ex-prisoners have undertaken which express the goals of the strengths based perspective. These include building homes for low-income families, repairing computers and fighting forest fires. These tasks, in essence, produce goods and services which the wider community wants and needs and simultaneously do two things. Firstly, they reduce crime in general by improving the environment for the local community (e.g. making alleyways safer and providing accommodation for those at risk of homelessness); and, secondly, such schemes help to (re)introduce offenders to the labour market. Although not designed with the strengths based perspective in mind, we place the calls for desistance-focused interventions (Farrall, 2002; McNeill, 2003; see also Chapter 3) in this broad family of approaches.

These approaches, however, have another element contained within that has not always been explicitly acknowledged, but which, from our analyses above (Chapter 5), seem increasingly important in assisting desistance and reintegration – namely providing would-be desisters with a sense of hope. As recognized by some US scholars (Maruna and LeBel, 2003; Sherman, 1993; Ritchie, 2001 – the latter two cited in Maruna and LeBel, 2003), a sense of hope in the future as a place where one would wish to live plays a key part in the avoidance of further offending. Providing people with hope, especially in a consumerist society in which employment provides the key to unlocking the door to resources, may well mean providing people with employment which pays a decent wage and from which the individual derives some sense of satisfaction (Shover, 1983: 213). The key point here, however, is that this means *looking to the future* and helping probationers and ex-prisoners to *make plans for 'who' they want to be in the future* and not continually revisiting the past. We ought not expect these processes to be completed during the terms of a probation order: they may not even be *started* during this period (see Chapter 3). However, this does not mean that we advocate extending periods of supervision. It simply means that we have to be a bit more realistic about the time it takes people to change. This needs to be reflected in our evaluations of such policies too.

We started this chapter with a quote from Donald West – the opening line from the chapter entitled 'Treatment for the Individual' from his book on homosexuality. At the time that West was writing, homosexuality was still a criminal offence, and such individuals are at points in his book referred to as 'freaks' (1955: 57) who suffer from 'abnormal inhibitions' to the opposite sex (1955: 12) and who cause various 'social problems' (1955: 12–13). Whilst these words today cause offence and are not in keeping with more tolerant attitudes towards gays and lesbians, we wish to use this example to demonstrate the notion that 'who' and 'what' is considered deviant and therefore in need of 'correction' is time- and context-specific.

Just as we as a society have altered our position on the so-called 'treatment' of homosexuality, so we need to re-examine some of our notions about the reform of offenders. Put succinctly, state-sponsored efforts at reform may not be as successful at encouraging and enabling naturally occurring personal changes to occur. This book, and the previous book written about this cohort, suggests that investments in informal social controls or, at very best, non-custodial, non-programmatic interventions (i.e. the now unfashionable notion of 'social work') may be the most effective way of enabling desistance from crime for many men and women. This is not to argue for a *laissez-faire* style of radical non-intervention, but rather to accept that the most effective motivations for desistance come from 'within' the individual and are fostered by social interaction with others in the community. As such, interventions need to become more closely directed to social interventions (Burnett and Maruna, 2004: 400–1) and less concerned with cognitive-behavioural ones.

Notes

1. This section draws upon Farrall and Bowling (1999).
2. A more thoroughly described and supported example of this sort of analysis, although clearly one which preceded Cohen's intervention, is provided by Sarre *et al.* (1989) in their discussion of the housing position of the various ethnic groupings which migrated to Bedford. Although Sarre *et al.* did not use the term 'systems analysis', we feel that the analyses they report closely resemble our own understanding of what such a style of analyses would 'look like'. It is, in any case, a fascinating book. See also Murie (1997: 28) on social housing and crime, which also illustrates how agents' actions aimed at reproducing an existing structure can create change by exaggerating aspects of that structure (28–9 on social housing and 'tipping').
3. Readers need to be warned here: Rob Stones *initially* introduced his conceptual apparatus as 'strategic context analysis' (1991), but later (1996: 98) renamed this 'agent's context analysis'. There is no discernible difference between the two and we refer to the latter as it is the most recent.
4. One explanation for this neglect can perhaps be found in Giddens' assertion that 'much of our day-to-day conduct is not directly motivated' (1984: 6) and his wider attempt to 'de-centre' the acting subject (Cohen, 1989: 227–8).
5. We have encountered examples of this throughout the course of this book. See, for example, Sandra in Chapter 4 on the existential aspects of desistance or George in Chapter 3 on the long term impact of probation.
6. Security here can be thought of both as emotional security and purely financial security.
7. Bryan was interviewed by Stephen Farrall in the early 1990s as part of his initial interest in desistance.
8. Chas was interviewed as part of the Home Office's Young People and Crime Survey: see Graham and Bowling (1995).
9. Rachel is another of those interviewed as part of the Home Office's Young People and Crime Survey: see Graham and Bowling (1995).
10. See also Goffman (1963: 102) on spaces.
11. Graeme was interviewed as part of the Home Office's Young People and Crime Survey: see Graham and Bowling (1995).
12. Trevor was interviewed as part of the Home Office's Young People and Crime Survey: see Graham and Bowling (1995).
13. Bryan was interviewed by Stephen Farrall in the early 1990s as part of his initial interest in desistance.

Further reading

Bottoms, A. and Wiles, P. (1992) 'Explanations of Crime and Place', in D. J. Evans, N. R. Fyfe and D. T. Herbert (eds) *Crime, Policing And Place*, Routledge, London.

Downes, D. (1997) What the next government should do about crime, *The Howard Journal of Criminal Justice*, 36(1): 1–13.

Giddens, A. (1984) *The Constitution of Society*, Polity Press, Cambridge.

Hagan, J. (1997) 'Crime and Capitalization: Toward a Developmental Theory of Street Crime in America', in T. Thornberry (ed.) *Developmental Theories of Crime And Delinquency*, Transaction Press, New Brunswick.

Mair, G. (2004) 'The Origins of What Works in England & Wales', in G. Mair, (ed.) *What Matters in Probation*, Willan Publishing, Cullompton, Devon.

Maruna, S. and LeBel, T. P. (2003) Welcome Home?: Examining the Reentry Court Concept from a Strengths-based Perspective, *Western Criminology Review*, 4: 91–107.

Meisenhelder, T. (1977) An Exploratory Study of Exiting From Criminal Careers, *Criminology*, 15: 319–34.

Richards, S. and Jones, S. (2004) 'Beating the Perpetual Incarceration Machine', in S. Maruna and R. Immarigeon (eds) *After Crime and Punishment: Ex-Offender Reintegration and Desistance From Crime*, 57–82, Willan Publishing, Cullompton, Devon.

Rumgay, J. (2004) Scripts for Safer Survival: Pathways Out of Female Crime, *Howard Journal of Criminal Justice*, 43 (4): 405–19.

Relocating our sample

This appendix outlines the characteristics of those people interviewed as part of the original study and the follow-up study. Issues relating to the representativeness of the sample, the attrition rate and the honesty of the responses gathered are accordingly discussed. Some of the processes by which probationers were traced and interviews with them secured are also covered.

The original sample

In all, some 199 probationers and their supervising officers were recruited into the original sample. The methodology built upon that employed in an earlier study of recidivism among prison inmates who had recently returned to the community (Burnett, 1992, 2000). Probationers aged 17–35 and who were starting probation or combination orders of six to 24 months' duration between the start of October 1997 and the end of March 1998 were eligible for inclusion in the study (see Farrall, 2002, Chapter 3, for a full outline of the methodology of the original research). The age range of 17–35, it was anticipated, would produce a high number of probationers who were experiencing a number of salient life changes, such as marriage, entry to the labour market and moving away from the parental home, which were expected to be related to whether or not they desisted from further offending. Indeed, this was the case – see Farrall, 2002, Chapter 9. The achieved sample of probationers had the socio-demographic characteristics illustrated in Tables A1–A3.

Table A1: Sample characteristics: gender

	N	%
Males	173	87
Females	26	13
Total	199	100

Table A2: Sample characteristics: age

	N	%
17–23	88	44
24–29	62	31
30–35	49	25
Total	199	100

Table A3: Sample characteristics: main offence

	Achieved sample N	%	National data %
Violence	20	10	9
Sexual	2	1	2
Burglary	22	11	10
Robbery	4	2	1
Theft/handling	64	32	28
Fraud/forgery	11	6	5
Criminal damage	7	4	2
Drugs	17	9	–*
Other indictable	19	10	12
Summary offences	33	17	33
Total	199	100	100

* The Home Office includes drug offences in summary offences, hence the discrepancy.

The single largest offence type was crimes of dishonesty – with burglary, theft/handling and fraud/forgery accounting for some 49 per cent of cases. The average Offender Group Reconviction Scale (OGRS) for the sample was 58 per cent, just above the national average at that time of 55 per cent (Home Office, 1996: Annex 1). Probationers were grouped into four types of previous conviction experience – 'no previous', '1–3 previous', '4 or more' and 'unknown'. They were similarly grouped into four types of previous custodial experience (the right-hand side of Table A4).

Table A4: Sample characteristics: previous convictions and custody

Convictions	N	%	Custody	N	%
No previous	43	22	No previous	121	61
1–3 previous	51	26	1–3 previous	50	25
4 or more	98	49	4 or more	22	11
Unknown	7	3	Unknown	6	3
Total	199	100		199	100

Because of the desire during the earlier research project to interview both officers and probationers, consent was required from all probationers involved in the research. Like any other research that relies upon consent, this meant that certain unavoidable biases were built into the research. However, as a check against biases, the achieved sample was compared against national statistics in relation to age, gender, commencement offence, OGRS and previous convictions. These suggested a sample that was not too greatly different from the national statistics and, therefore, that the findings may have some general relevance. Attrition during the subsequent sweeps of the original project (sweeps two and three) was found to be sufficiently randomly distributed not to introduce non-random biases into the research (see Farrall, 2002, Chapter 3).

Individual sweeps during the original research never achieved less than a 60 per cent response rate. These rates can be regarded as very good, taken in light of the fact that many of the respondents were highly mobile, often with no fixed abode, urban living, with drug and alcohol problems, and with good reason to conceal themselves (i.e. their past criminal record). Osborn (1980: 60) reported that delinquents in the Cambridge Study in Delinquent Development were more likely to move than non-delinquents (a finding supported by Gottfredson and Taylor, 1988: 79). Attempts to follow up similar groups of people have often yielded low response rates. For example, Cordray and Polk (1983) reported that attrition rates in surveys of crime were anywhere between 5 per cent and 60 per cent, whilst Capaldi and Patterson (1987) reported that the average attrition rate in surveys with four to 10 year follow-up periods was 47 per cent. Wolfgang *et al.* (1987) were only able to trace 58 per cent of their sample after three years of searching, whilst Laub and Sampson (2003) retraced 11 per cent of the cases from the Gluecks' original cohort after 35 years. In addition, recent data suggest that there is a tendency for respondents in more deprived areas to be most likely to refuse to be interviewed (Thorogood *et al.*, 2002).

Of course, any research that asks people directly about sensitive topics such as criminal behaviour must take steps to ensure that the data collected are as reliable and truthful as possible. Despite our assurances during both the original study and the follow-up that anything said in the interview was confidential (a common practice intended to increase truthful responses), it could have been that probationers still concealed some things from us. It is assumed that any concealment, if it existed at all, was *most* likely when probationers were asked about their offending. Some respondents may have suspected, despite our assurances of confidentiality, that any admissions of undetected offending made during an interview would be relayed to their supervising officers or the police. However, an analysis of the responses given to us by interviewees during the earlier study with Offenders Index and Police National Computer data sets suggested that 'the relationship between self-reported offending and officially recorded convictions was ... very close' (Farrall, 2005: 121).

The sweep four follow-up interviews

Our funding budget restricted us to a maximum of 75 fieldwork trips in order to secure 50 interviews with members of the previous sample (on the assumption that there would be some fruitless trips). All of our interviews were recorded and transcribed in full. The use of Sony minidisk recording machines made the process of transcribing interviews infinitely easier. In tracing sample members, we relied on a number of sources of information:

- Our recontact details from the previous fieldwork, which listed respondent's home address and telephone numbers and those for a number of their relatives.
- Current probation case load records (which were searched at the start of the efforts to retrace sample members during autumn 2003).
- Current prison inmate records, which were searched twice – once in early autumn 2003 and again in early 2004.
- Local area telephone and electoral roll databases.

Convenience and necessity dictated that priority was given to tracing those people who appeared most likely to be available for interview. This included those who, according to the prison or probation records, had recently been sentenced to community or custodial sentences. Probation offices and prisons provided both a point of contact and (thanks to the helpful co-operation of staff) a useful medium through which to make direct contact with such cases. These sample members needed to be contacted as a matter of priority before their sentences were terminated or their whereabouts became unknown to the authorities. The following criteria were therefore used for prioritizing cases to be selected for follow-up:

- Cases currently serving community penalties.
- Cases currently serving prison sentences and who might shortly be released into the community and therefore possibly lost to the study.
- Cases who had previously given us a greater number of contact addresses and phone numbers and who were therefore likely to be easier to find.

So as to avoid producing an overly biased sample based on the above criteria, we also undertook intensive searches for all cases in one area and as many cases as was possible in all others. Once all telephone numbers had been called, last known addresses were searched on the electoral and telephone databases. Following this, all known (and presumed) telephone numbers were tried, including those for friends and relatives. Where no telephone number was available, sample members (and/or their respective contacts) were written to at their last know address(es) and, wherever practicable, visited several times in person.

In all we were able to secure interviews with 51 respondents interviewed as part of the original sample. Of these, five had not been interviewed since the very first sweep. This brings the number of cases reinterviewed at least once to 162 (81 per cent). Table A5 gives a breakdown of the outcomes of the fourth sweep for the full sample.

As can be seen from Table A5, some 37 per cent of the original sample were located (n = 73) and of these 51 interviewed. A large number of people were untracable (39 per cent in all). However, due to time

Table A5: Fieldwork outcomes*

Outcome	N	%
Located and interviewed:	51	26
Located but not interviewed:		
...refused to be interviewed	7	4
...in prison since previous interview	4	2
...left the UK	3	2
...no time to interview	3	2
...high risk of harm to interviewer	3	2
...repeatedly missed interviews	1	–
...had died	1	–
Sub-total located:	**73**	**37**
Untraceable: whereabouts unknown	72	36
Untraceable: contacts refused to help	6	3
Sub-total untraceable:	**78**	**39**
Not interviewed: no time to start search	30	15
Not interviewed: contacts tried, no time to interview	18	9
Sub-total untraceable:	**48**	**24**
Total	**199**	**100**

* Figures are not exact due to rounding.

constraints, we were unable even to start to look for around one-quarter of the sample. Respondents were paid £20 for participation in the interview, which was felt to have made the fieldwork much easier (very few individuals failed to attend interviews and when they did so this was often due to circumstances beyond their control). Interviews lasted between an hour and an hour and a half.

Details of achieved sample

Our achieved sample of probationers had the socio-demographic characteristics illustrated in Tables A6 and A7.

Table A6: Sample characteristics: gender

	N	%
Males	45	88
Females	6	12
Total	**51**	**100**

Table A7: Sample characteristics: age

	N	%
Originally 17–23	21	41
Originally 24–29	20	39
Originally 30–35	10	20
Total	**51**	**100**

We maintained a representative sample with regard to the gender of our respondents (compare Tables A1 and A6) and did reasonably well with their age (although our sample is biased towards those who were aged 24–29 when they were first interviewed: see Tables A2 and A7). Most of our sample were white (81 per cent at first interview and 90 per cent for this follow-up), but our ethnic minority groups contained very small numbers and so achieving a representative sample at the follow-up was hard. We also found that our sample was biased towards those cases who had been given longer sentences. Table A8 reports on the main offences for which our achieved sample had been convicted when they were originally recruited into the sample. This shows that we slightly oversampled people originally sentenced for violence, burglary and criminal damage and undersampled those found guilty of summary offences (compare Tables A3 and A8). However, this is not felt to be of major significance. In short, given the small N of cases (which made sampling exact proportions of cases hard to achieve), a reasonably representative sample was followed up.

Table A8: Sample characteristics: main offence

| | Achieved sample | |
	N	%
Violence	6	12
Sexual	0	0
Burglary	10	20
Robbery	0	0
Theft/handling	12	24
Fraud/forgery	2	4
Criminal damage	5	10
Drugs	5	10
Other indictable	5	10
Summary offences	6	12
Total	51	100

The nature of the interviews

The interviews started by reminding the interviewee of the earlier study and attempted to get each respondent to cast their minds back to the previous interview by summarizing what we know about their personal and social circumstances at that time. We asked respondents to clarify or amend these details and to provide us with an update of their lives since that time. We were seeking not just factual information, but also their *opinions* of their current life and the changes that they had experienced. We also asked each respondent to reflect on the biggest change in their life since we had previously interviewed them and on how they were different now to when they had started and finished probation.

We tackled head-on the issue of their offending immediately after this and asked respondents to reflect on why they had or had not been able to stop offending. We also asked them about times when they had got close or had been tempted to become involved in offending. At this point respondents were also asked about how they felt about having stopped (or not stopped) offending. Those who had continued offending were asked about any other court disposals they had experienced and the impact of these on their lives and offending.

We deliberately revisited their earlier probation order (i.e. the one which had made them eligible for inclusion in the original study) and probed respondents for its impact on their offending careers and lives more generally. We also asked them to reflect on their earlier probation order and to consider what, if anything, they felt they had gained from probation. The obstacles to desistance that they had nominated we also revisited.

Respondents' desires and abilities to desist and changes in these since their previous interview were similarly explored in depth, as was the topic of who or what might help them stop offending (or stay stopped). Their ambitions for the future were also explored. Wherever appropriate during the interview, we asked respondents to think back to their previous answers and to try to reconcile differences between their answers when previously interviewed and their current answers.

We then moved on to consider their values with regard to citizenship. This was achieved via their answers to six items (given as open-ended answers and coded by ourselves). These were introduced with the question, 'How strongly do you agree or disagree with the following statements about being a citizen?' The six items were:

1. People should not rely on the government, they should take responsibility for themselves.
2. It does not really matter if you lie when dealing with state officials.
3. Being a citizen is about becoming involved in your community.
4. The government does not listen to people like me.
5. People should obey the law.
6. People should accept that others have a right to be different.

Following this, respondents were asked four questions about their victimization during the past year (and one more open-ended question):

1. In the last year has anyone done any damage to your house/flat or to anything outside?
2. In the last year has anyone stolen/tried to steal anything from you, your home or your car?
3. In the last year has anyone, including people you know well, deliberately hit/kicked you or used force against you?
4. In the last year has anyone threatened to hurt you or damage your things?
5. Have you ever been a victim of crime?

These items, all of which were probed in detail, repeated those items used during the second sweep of interviewing for the original fieldwork and were deliberately chosen to be identical to those used in the Home Office's Young People and Crime Survey I (see Farrall and Maltby, 2003).

The mechanics of finding sample members

This section outlines, using two case studies, the nature of the processes by which ex-probationers were located, followed up and interviewed at each of the three sweeps of interviews and then retraced as part of the current research. Whilst of some interest to those wishing to undertake follow-up studies themselves, the cases also illustrate to some degree the complex lives of those who have at some point 'been on probation'. We ought also to mention that fieldwork of this nature requires time and patience and needs to be extremely well-resourced.

Anthony

Anthony was seen at all four sweeps. His 12 month order started on 4 December 1997 and he was interviewed at the probation office from which he was being supervised on 20 January 1998 (by Stephen Farrall, who conducted all interviews relating to this case). His second sweep interview took place at his home (he had moved from his previous address, but he gave his officer permission to release his new address), on 2 July 1998. At the start of the third sweep (in January 1999), his order was due to have been completed, but in fact he had failed to attend all of his sessions since the start of the autumn and was in breach (a warrant was out for his arrest). He was written to at all of his previous addresses on 20 January 1999, and on 22 January Farrall called at all of his previous addresses. These included the address at which the probationer had been interviewed the previous summer (empty, and where neighbours said he had left suddenly some months before), his sister's address (where no one answered the door, but at which neighbours said his sister still lived) and another previous address (where the new occupants had not heard of him). On 22 February Farrall called again at the probationer's sister's address. She was in and tried to call the probationer at his new address. Despite the fact that he was out when she called, the probationer's sister gave the interviewer his new address and telephone number. The interviewer called the number later and spoke to the probationer, who agreed to an interview and was seen the next day (23 February 1999). The address he was living at turned out to be one he shared with his partner.

During the fieldwork for the fourth sweep, Adam Calverley called at Anthony's previous address in the autumn of 2003. Anthony was not in, and Calverley was told by his partner that they had recently split up and that he and the rest of his family had gone to live in a city some miles away. She said that she did not have any forwarding addresses for him and that they were no longer in touch. Disappointed by this news, we tried to trace Anthony at the city in question by searching local telephone and electoral registration databases for his name. This brought us several leads, all of which went cold. Because our sample members were originally clustered together in various small areas (see Farrall, 2002), 'call-backs' were relatively easy as members of the sample frequently lived near one another. This was also the case with Anthony. Whilst looking for another case, Calverley called again at Anthony's home in December 2003. Again Anthony was out and again Calverley was told that he had moved away. Shortly after this, Anthony called Calverley on the latter's mobile telephone to say that he *was* still living at his original address and was prepared to be interviewed. Farrall called Anthony immediately and learnt that the story of him leaving was a smoke-screen regularly put up to ensure that he was not found by (unspecified) people whom he would rather did not find him. Farrall and Anthony arranged an interview for January 2004, which was duly completed as arranged.

Al

Al was seen twice by one interviewer in the Manchester area (sweeps one and two), once by Farrall after the probationer had moved to the south (sweep three) and once by Calverley (sweep four). His first interview was conducted on 16 February 1998 (his order had started on 12 December, 1997). He was interviewed in the office from where he was being supervised. Shortly after the first interview, the probationer moved to the south coast. He was, however, caught shoplifting and had his probation order breached and replaced with a 12 month custodial sentence. His whereabouts at the time of the second sweep were not known to the officer (who had not seen him since the spring of 1998) and for a while it appeared that he would be lost to the study. However, a telephone call to his father revealed that he was in prison, where he was interviewed in late October 1998. At the start of the third sweep (January 1999), the probationer was believed to be homeless, having lost his accommodation in the south, and so his father was called (late January 1999). He did not know where the probationer was, but agreed to call if he heard anything. A further telephone call to his father about a month later revealed that the probationer was back in prison, having been released just before Christmas 1998, returning to the south coast briefly before being rearrested and sentenced for a further offence. A letter was written (on 16 March 1999) to the probationer and sent via the Prisoner Location Service. However, a week later, on an off-chance, the interviewer again telephoned the probationer's father. The probationer was there, having been released from prison that day. He stated his intention to return to the south coast and agreed to an interview with Farrall (it being too far for the original interviewer to travel). He gave an address and was telephoned about a week later to arrange an interview for 8 April 1999. Farrall travelled to see the probationer, but at the last minute the probationer had to attend a DSS interview (he called to cancel the interview). The author telephoned his old address, where a new number was given and a further call to this number resulted (at last) in a successful interview carried out on 22 April 1999.

Efforts to contact Al for the fourth sweep of interviewing began on 23 April 2004, when Calverley phoned the last number Al had previously been contacted on. It was no longer in use. His father's telephone number still worked, but despite repeated attempts there was no answer. Probation service records had a different last known address to our records, so both sets of addresses were searched on '192.com' (an electoral role and telephone database). These searches produced no results for probation records' addresses or for its wider postal area, but did confirm that his father was still on the electoral roll at the same address as last time. Calverley called Al's father once more (on 10 May 2004) and managed to speak to him. He took details and promised to pass the message on to Al. On 18 May, Calverley received a voicemail message on his mobile telephone from Al who was himself using a mobile, but who left a land line number for him to be contacted on. This number was answered by a woman who said she had never heard of Al. She then passed the phone on to a man called Dave who said that it was a wrong number. The missed call on Calverley's mobile was called next, and immediately answered by Dave, who said he had misheard and that he *did* know Al and would pass on the information. Over a month later and still no direct contact had been made with Al. Hence a letter was written to his father. On 28 June 2004 Calverley made a further call to Al's father, who confirmed that he had received the letter but that he did not have a contact number or address for Al because 'he comes and goes, don't know when I'll hear from him'. On 23 July Al phoned Calverley's office number (it was the first time he had done so): a contact address and phone number were taken, meeting time agreed to and interview was completed on 29 July 2004 at Al's house. It was the last interview of the sweep four fieldwork to be completed.

Summary

The purpose of this appendix was to introduce to the reader the 'nuts and bolts' of the study. It has outlined: some of the characteristics of the probationers recruited into the original sample; the characteristics of the probationers relocated and interviewed; and some of the reasons for, the extent and impact of sample attrition, and the nature and ordering of the questions asked during interviews. By recounting the efforts we went to in order to trace original sample members, we have outlined some of the circumstances of the respondent's own personal lives and illustrated the efforts which one is required to go to in order to retrace such cases.

Bibliography

Adams, K. (1997) 'Developmental Aspects of Adult Crime', in Thornberry, T. (ed.) *Developmental Theories of Crime and Delinquency*, Transaction Press, London.

Adler, P. (1985) *Wheeling and Dealing*, Columbia University Press, New York.

Adler, P. (1993) *Wheeling and Dealing* (2nd edn), Columbia University Press, New York.

Agnew, R. (1985) A Revised Strain Theory of Delinquency, *Social Forces*, 64(1): 151–67.

Aitken, J. (2003) *Pride & Perjury*, Continuum, New York.

Andrews, D. (1989) Recidivism Is Predictable and Can Be Influenced, *Focus on Correctional Research*, 1(2): 11–18.

Arrigo, B. A. (1998) 'Shattered Lives and Shelter Lies?', in Ferrell, J. and Hamm, M. S. (eds) *Ethnography at the Edge: Crime, Deviance and Field Research*, Northeastern University Press, Boston.

Athens, L. (1995) Dramatic Self Change, *The Sociological Quarterly*, 36(3): 571–86.

Aust, R., Sharp, C. and Goulden, C. (2002) *Prevalence of Drug Use: Key Findings from the 2001/2002 British Crime Survey*, Home Office Research Findings, 182, Home Office, London.

Ballintyne, S. (1999) *Unsafe Streets*, IPPR, London.

Barbarlet, J. M. (2002) Moral Indignation, Class Inequality and Justice: An Exploration and Revision of Ranulf, *Theoretical Criminology* 6(3): 279–98.

Barclay, G. (1990) The Peak Age Of Known Offending By Males, *Research Bulletin*, 28: 20–3, Home Office, London.

Bauman, Z. (1989) 'Hermeneutics and Modern Social Theory', in Held, D. and Thompson, J. (eds) *Social Theory of Modern Societies: Anthony Giddens and His Critics*, Cambridge University Press, Cambridge.

Becker, H. S. (1963) *Outsiders*, Free Press, New York

Berk, R., Lenihan, K. J. and Rossi, P. H. (1980) Crime and Poverty: some experimental evidence from ex-offenders, *American Sociological Review*, 45: 766–86.

Blumstein, A. and Cohen, J. (1987) Characterizing Criminal Careers, *Science*, 237: 985–91.

Bottoms, A. (1993) 'Recent Criminological and Social Theory', in Farrington, D. P., Sampson, R. J. and Wikstrom, P-O. (eds) *Integrating Individual and Ecological Aspects of Crime*, National Council for Crime Prevention, Stockholm, Sweden.

Bottoms, A. and McWilliams, W. (1979) A Non-Treatment Paradigm for Probation Practice, *British Journal of Social Work*, 9(2):159–202.

Bottoms, A. and Wiles, P. (1992) 'Explanations of Crime and Place', in Evans, D. J., Fyfe, N. R. and Herbert, D. T. (eds) *Crime, Policing And Place*, London, Routledge.

Bottoms, A., Shapland, J., Costello, A., Holmes, D. and Muir, G. (2004) Towards Desistance: Theoretical underpinnings for an Empirical Study, *Howard Journal of Criminal Justice*, 43(4): 368–89.

Bowling, B., Graham, J. and Ross, A. (1994) 'Self-Reported Offending Among Young People in England and Wales', in Junger-tas, J., Terlouw, G.-J. and Klein, M. (eds) *Delinquent Behaviour Among Young People in the Western World*, Kugler, Amsterdam.

Braithwaite, J. (1989) *Crime, Shame and Reintegration*, Cambridge University Press, Cambridge.

Brewer, J. D. (1988) 'Micro-sociology and the "Duality of Structure"', in Fielding, N. (ed.) *Actions and Structure: Research Methods And Social Theory*, Sage, London.

Brogden, M. and Harkin, S. (2000) Community Rules Preventing Re-offending by Child Sex Abusers – A Life History Approach, *International Journal of the Sociology of Law*, 28: 45–68.

Brown, K. M., Anfara, V. A. and Roney, K. (2004) Student Achievement in High Performing, Suburban Middle Schools and Low Performing, Urban Middle Schools, *Education and Urban Society*, 36(4): 428–56.

Bruce, M., Roscigno, V. and McCall, P. (1998) Structure, Context and Agency in the Reproduction of Black-on-Black Violence, *Theoretical Criminology*, 2(10): 29–55.

Bull, J. (1972) *Coming Alive: The Dynamics of Personal Recovery*, Unpublished PhD dissertation, University of California, Santa Barbara.

Burnett, R. (1992) *The Dynamics of Recidivism*, Centre for Criminological Research, University of Oxford, England.

Burnett, R. (1994) 'The Odds of Going Straight: Offenders Own Predictions', in *Sentencing, Quality and Risk: Proceedings of the 10th Annual Conference on Research and Information in the Probation Service*, University of Loughborough, Midlands probation Training Consortium, Birmingham.

Burnett, R. (2000) Understanding Criminal Careers Through a Series of In-Depth Interviews, *Offender Programs Report*, 4(1).

Burnett, R. (2002) 'To Reoffend or to Not Reoffend? The Ambivalence of Offenders', in Maruna, S. and Immarigeon, R. (eds) *After Crime and Punishment*, Willan Publishing, Cullumpton, Devon.

Burnett, R. and Maruna, S. (2004) So 'Prison Works', Does it? The Criminal Careers of 130 Men Released from Prison under Home Secretary, Michael Howard, *Howard Journal of Criminal Justice*, 43(4): 390–404.

Burnett, R. and Maruna, S. (forthcoming) Trusting prisoners to 'do good': pre-release voluntary work and the development of pro-social identity, *Criminal Justice*, Special Edition on Life after Punishment.

Bushway, S., Piquero, A., Boidy, L., Cauffman, E. and Mazerolle, P. (2001) An Empirical Framework for Studying Desistance as a Process Desistance, *Criminology*, 39(2): 496–515.

Caddle, D. (1991) *Parenthood Training for Young Offenders: An Evaluation of*

Courses in Young Offender Institutions, Research and Planning Unit Paper 63, Home Office, HMSO, London.

Capaldi, D. and Patterson, G. (1987) An Approach to the Problem of Recruitment and Retention Rates in Longitudinal Research, *Behavioural Assessment*, 9: 169–177.

Carlen, P. (1992) 'Women's Criminal Careers', in Downes, D. (ed.) *Unravelling Criminal Justice*, Macmillan, Basingstoke.

Churchill, W. (1910) Debate in the House of Commons, 20th July, *Hansard*, Fifth Series, Vol XIX, Sixth Volume of Session 1910, p1353.

Chylicki, P. (1992) *To Cease With Crime: Pathways out of Criminal Careers*, Unpublished PhD thesis, Department of Sociology, Lund University, Sweden.

Clark, C. (2002) 'Taming the "Brute Being": Sociology Reckons with Emotionality', in Kotarba, J. and Johnson, J. (eds) *Postmodern Existential Sociology*, Altamira Press, Oxford.

Clarke, P. B. (1994) *Citizenship*, Pluto Press, London.

Clarke, R. V. and Cornish, D. B. (1985) 'Modeling Offender's Decisions: A Framework for Research and Policy', in Tonry, M. and Morris, N. (eds) *Crime and Justice: An Annual Review of Research*, University of Chicago Press, Chicago.

Cohen, I. (1989) *Structuration Theory*, Macmillan, Basingstoke.

Coleman, J. (1992) 'Current Views on the Adolescent Process', in Coleman, J. (ed.) *The School Years* (2nd edn), Routledge, London.

Copleston, F. (1972) *Contemporary Philosophy: Studies in Logical Positivism and Existentialism*, Continuum, London.

Cordray, S. and Polk, K. (1983) The Implications of Respondent Loss in Panel Studies of Deviant Behaviour, *Journal of Research in Crime and Delinquency*, 20: 214–42.

Court, D. (2004) Applying the findings of the *Liverpool Desistance Study* in probation practices: Views from the front-line 2, *Probation Journal*, 51(3): 237–40.

Cromwell, P. F., Olson, J. N. and Avary, D. W. (1991) *Breaking and Entering*, Sage, London.

Crow, I. (1996) 'Employment, Training and Offending', in Drakeford, M. and Vanstone, M. (eds) *Beyond Offending Behaviour*, Ashgate, Aldershot.

Cusson, M. and Pinsonneault, P. (1986) 'The Decision To Give Up Crime', in Cornish, D. B. and Clarke, R. V. (eds) *The Reasoning Criminal*, Springer-Verlag, New York.

Dale, M. W. (1976) Barriers to the Rehabilitation of Ex-Offenders, *Crime and Delinquency*, 22(3): 322–37.

Davies, M. (1969) *Social Work in the Environment*, HMSO, London.

de Haan, W. and Loader, I. (2002) (eds) Special Edition of *Theoretical Criminology*, 6(3).

Denzin, N. (1987) *The Recovering Alcoholic*, Sage, London.

Denzin, N. (1989) *Interpretive Biography*, Sage, London.

Ditton, J. (1977) *Part-time Crime: An Ethnography Of Fiddling And Pilferage*, Macmillan, London.

Donaldson, W. (2003) *Brewer's Rogues, Villians and Eccentrics*, Cassell, London.

Douglas, J. (1977) 'Existential Sociology', in Douglas, J. and Johnson, J. (eds) *Existential Sociology*, Cambridge University Press, Cambridge.

Douglas, J. (1984) 'The Emergence, Security, and Growth of the Sense of Self', in

Kotarba, J. and Fontana, A. (eds) *The Existential Self in Society*, Chicago University Press, Chicago.

Douglas, J. and Johnson, J. (1977) 'Introduction', in Douglas, J. and Johnson, J. (eds) *Existential Sociology*, Cambridge University Press, Cambridge.

Douglas, J. and Johnson, J. (1977) (eds) *Existential Sociology*, Cambridge University Press, Cambridge.

Downes, D. (1997) What the next government should do about crime, *Howard Journal of Criminal Justice*, 36(1): 1–13.

Dowse, R. E. and Hughes, J. A. (1986) *Political Sociology*, Wiley, London.

Eaton, M. (1993) *Women After Prison*, Open University Press, Buckingham.

Ebaugh, H. R. F. (1984) 'Leaving the Convent: The Experience of Role Exit and Self-Transformation', in Kotarba, J. and Fontana, A. (eds) *The Existential Self in Society*, Chicago University Press, Chicago.

Ebaugh, H. (1988) *Becoming an Ex*, Chicago University Press, London.

Elliott, D. (1994) Serious Violent Offenders: Onset, Developmental Course and Termination – American Society of Criminology 1993 Presidential Address, *Criminology*, 32: 1–22.

Erikson, E. H. (1959) Identity and the Life Cycle: Selected Papers, *Psychological Issues*, 1: 5–173.

Ezell, M. E. and Cohen, L. E. (2004) *Desisting From Crime*. Oxford University Press, Oxford.

Fagan, J. (1989) 'Cessation of Family Violence: Deterrence and Dissuasion', in Ohlin, L. and Tonry, M. (eds) *Crime and Justice: An Annual Review of Research*, Vol. 11, Chicago University Press, Chicago.

Fagan, J., Piper, E. and Cheng, Y-T. (1987) Contributions of Victimisation to Delinquency in Inner Cities, *Journal of Criminal Law and Criminology*, 78(3): 586–613.

Farrall, S. (1994) *Desistance From Offending*, Unpublished MSc dissertation, Department of Sociology, University Of Surrey.

Farrall, S. (2000) 'Introduction', in Farrall, S. (ed.) *The Termination of Criminal Careers*, Ashgate, Aldershot.

Farrall, S. (2002) *Rethinking What Works With Offenders*, Willan Publishing, Cullompton, Devon.

Farrall, S. (2003) J'accuse: Probation Evaluation-Research Epistemologies (Part Two: This Time It's Personal and Social Factors), *Criminal Justice*, 3(3): 249–68.

Farrall, S. (2004) 'Social Capital and Offender Reintegration: Making Probation Desistance Focussed', in Maruna, S. and Immarigeon, R. (eds) *After Crime and Punishment: Ex-Offender Reintegration and Desistance From Crime*, 57–82, Willan Publishing, Cullompton, Devon.

Farrall, S. (2005) Officially Recorded Convictions for Probationers: The Relationship With Self-Report and Supervisory Observations, *Legal & Criminological Psychology*, 10(1): 1–11.

Farrall, S. and Bowling, B. (1999) Structuration, Human Development and Desistance From Crime, *British Journal of Criminology*, 39(2): 253–68.

Farrall, S. and Maltby, S. (2003) The Victimisation of Probationers, *Howard Journal of Criminal Justice*, 42(1): 32–54.

Farrington, D. (1992) 'Juvenile Delinquency', in Coleman, J. (ed.) *The School Years*, Routledge, London.

Farrington, D. P. (1997) 'Human Development and Criminal Careers', in Maguire,

M., Morgan, R. and Reiner, R. (eds) *The Oxford Handbook of Criminology* (2nd edn), Clarendon Press, Oxford.

Farrington, D. P., Gallagher, B., Morley, L., St. Ledger, R. J. and West, D. J. (1986) Unemployment, School Leaving and Crime, *British Journal of Criminology*, 26(4): 335–56.

Feld, S. L. and Straus, M. A. (1989) Escalation and Desistance of Wife Assault, *Criminology*, 27: 141–61.

Feld, S. L. and Straus, M. A. (1990) 'Escalation and Desistance of Wife Assault', in Straus, M. A. and Gelles, R. J. (eds) *Physical Violence in American Families: Risk Factors and Adaptations to Violence in 8,145 Families*, Transaction Publishers, New Brunswick, NJ.

Ferrell, J. (1998) 'Criminological Verstehen', in Ferrell, J. and Hamm, M. S. (eds) *Ethnography at the Edge: Crime, Deviance and Field Research*, Northeastern University Press, Boston.

Flood-Page, C., Campbell, S., Harrington, V. and Miller, J. (2000) *Youth Crime: Findings From the 1998/99 Youth Lifestyles Survey*, Home Office Research Study, 209, HMSO, London.

Folkard, M. S., Smith, D. E. and Smith, D. D. (1976) *IMPACT Intensive Matched Probation and After-Care Treatment, Volume II*, Home Office Research Study, 36, HMSO, London.

Fontana, A. (1980) 'Toward a Complex Universe: Existential Sociology', in Douglas, J. *et al.* (eds) *Introduction to the Sociologies of Everyday Life*, Allyn & Bacon, Inc., Boston.

Fontana, A. (1984) 'Introduction: Existential Sociology and the Self', in Kotarba, J. and Fontana, A. (eds) *The Existential Self in Society*, Chicago University Press, Chicago.

Fontana, A. (2002) 'Short Stories from the Salt', in Kotarba, J. and Johnson, J. (eds) *Postmodern Existential Sociology*, Altamira Press, Oxford.

Ford, G. (1996) An Existential Model for Promoting Life Change, *Journal of Substance Abuse Treatment*, 13(2): 151–8.

Frederickson, B. L. and Joiner, T. (2002) Positive emotions trigger upward spirals toward emotional well-being, *Psychological Science*, 13(2): 172–5.

Friendship, C., Mann, R. and Beech, A. (2003) *The Prison-Based Sex Offender Programme – An Evaluation*, Home Office Findings 203, Home Office, London.

Gadd, D. and Farrall, S. (2004) Criminal Careers, Desistance and Subjectivity: Interpreting Men's Narratives of Change, *Theoretical Criminology*, 8(2): 123–55.

Giddens, A. (1976) *New Rules of Sociological Method*, Hutchinson, London.

Giddens, A. (1979a) *Central Problems in Social Theory*, University of California Press, Los Angeles.

Giddens, A. (1979b) 'Agency, Institution And Time-Space Analysis', in Knorr-Cetina, K. and Cicourel, A. (eds) *Advances in Social Theory And Methodology*, Routledge, London.

Giddens, A. (1981) *Contemporary Critique of Historical Materialism*, Macmillan, Basingstoke.

Giddens, A. (1982) *Profiles and Critiques in Social Theory*, University of California Press, Berkeley.

Giddens, A. (1983) Comments on the Theory of Structuration, *Journal of the Theory of Social Behaviour*, 13: 75–80.

Giddens, A. (1984) *The Constitution of Society*, Polity Press, Cambridge.

Giddens, A. (1990) 'Structuration Theory and Sociological Analysis', in Clarke, J., Modgil, C. and Modgil, S. (eds) *Anthony Giddens: Consensus and Controversy*, Falmer Press, London.

Giddens, A. (1991a) 'Structuration Theory: Past, Present and Future', in Bryant, C. G. A. and Jary, D. (eds) *Giddens' Theory of Structuration: A Critical Appreciation*, Routledge, London.

Giddens, A. (1991b) *Modernity and Self-Identity*, Polity Press, Cambridge.

Giordano, P. C., Cernkovich, S. A. and Rudolph, J. L. (2002) Gender, Crime and Desistance: Toward a Theory of Cognitive Transformation, *American Journal of Sociology*, 107: 990–1064.

Glaser, J. M. and Gilens, M. (1997) Interregional Migration and Political Resocialization, *Public Opinion Quarterly*, 61: 72–86.

Glaser, W. (1959) The Family and Voting Turnout, *Public Opinion Quarterly*, 23: 563–9.

Goffman, E. (1963) *Stigma*, Penguin Books, Harmondsworth, England.

Gottfredson, M. (1984) *Victims of Crime: Dimensions of Risk*, Home Office Research Study, 81, HMSO, London.

Gottfredson, M. and Hirschi, T. (1990) *A General Theory of Crime*, Stanford University Press.

Gottfredson, S. D. and Taylor, R. B. (1988) 'Community Contexts and Criminal Offenders', in Hope, T. and Shaw, M. (eds) *Communities and Crime Reduction*, HMSO, London.

Goulden, C. (2004) Beyond a Drug Trafficking Offence: No Way Forward?, *Probation Journal*, 51(2): 155–63.

Gove, W. (1985) 'The effect of age and gender on deviant behavior: A biopsychosocial perspective', in Rossi, A. S. (ed.) *Gender and the life course*, 115–44, Aldine, New York.

Graham, J. and Bowling, B. (1995) *Young People and Crime*, HMSO, London.

Grounds, A. and Jamieson, R. (2003) No Sense of an Ending, *Theoretical Criminology*, 7(3): 347–62.

Hagan, J. (1997) 'Crime and Capitalization: Toward a Developmental Theory of Street Crime in America', in Thornberry, T. (ed.) *Developmental Theories of Crime And Delinquency*, Transaction Press, New Brunswick.

Harding, D. J. (2003) Jean Valjean's Dilemma: The Management of Ex-convict Identity in the Search for Employment, *Deviant Behaviour*, 24: 571–95.

Harper, G. and Chitty, C. (2005) *The Impact of Corrections on Re-Offending: A Review of 'What Works'*, Home Office Research Study, 291, Home Office, London.

Hartless, J., Ditton, J., Nair, G. and Phillips, S. (1995) More Sinned Against than Sinning, *British Journal of Criminology*, 35(1): 114–33.

Henham, R. (1998) Human Rights, Due Process and Sentencing, *British Journal of Criminology*, 38(4): 592–610.

Henry, S. (1978) *The Hidden Economy: The Context and Control of Borderline Crime*, Martin Robertson, Oxford.

Hirschi, T. (1969) *Causes of Delinquency*, University of California Press, Berkeley.

Holden, (1986) Growing Focus on Criminal Careers, *Science*, 223: 1377–8.

Hollin, C. (1996) (ed.) *Working With Offenders*, John Wiley & Son, Chichester.

Home Office (2002) *Probation Statistics, 2001*, Home Office, London.

Home Office (2004) *Reducing Reoffending: National Action Plan* July, Home Office, London.

Hope, T. (2001) 'Crime Victimisation and Inequality in Risk Society', in Matthews, R. and Pitts, J. (eds) *Crime, Disorder and Community Safety*, Routledge, London.

Horney, J., Osgood, D. W. and Haen Marshall, I. (1995) Criminal Careers in The Short Term Intra-Individual Variability in Crime and Its Relation to Local Life Circumstances, *American Sociological Review*, 60: 655–73.

Hughes, M. (1997) An Exploratory Study of Young Adult Black and Latino Males and the Factors Facilitating Their Decisions to Make Positive Behavioural Changes, *Smith College Studies in Social Work*, 67(3): 401–14.

Hughes, M. (1998) Turning Points in the Lives of Young Inner-city Men Forgoing Destructive Criminal Behaviours: A Qualitative Study, *Social Work Research*, 22: 143–51.

Hunter, B. (2004) *The desistance of white-collar criminals: exploring processes of change amongst 'elite' offenders*, Unpublished MA dissertation, Criminology and Research Methods, Keele University.

Irwin, J. (1970) *The Felon*, Prentice Hall, New Jersey.

Jamieson, J., McIvor, G. and Murray, C. (1999) *Understanding Offending Among Young People*, The Stationery Office, Edinburgh.

Jamieson, R. and Grounds, A. (2003) No Sense of an Ending, *Theoretical Criminology*, 7(3): 347–62.

Janoski, T. (1998) *Citizenship & Civil Society*, Cambridge University Press, Cambridge.

Johnson, D. P. (1990) Security Versus Autonomy Motivation in Anthony Giddens' Concept of Agency, *Journal for the Theory of Social Behaviour*, 20(2): 111–30.

Johnson, D. R. and Booth, A. (1998) Marital Quality: A Product of the Dyadic Environment or Individual Factors?, *Social Forces*, 76: 883–904.

Johnson, J. and Kotarba, J. (2002) 'Postmodern Existentialism', in Kotarba, J. and Johnson, J. (eds) *Postmodern Existential Sociology*, Altamira Press, Oxford.

Johnson, J. and Ferraro, K. (1984) 'The victimized self: the case of Battered Women' in Kotarba, J. and Fontana, A. (eds) *The Existential Self in Society*, 119–30, University of Chicago Press, Chicago.

Jose-Kampfner, C. (1995) Coming to Terms With Existential Death: An Analysis of Women's Adaptation to Life in Prison, *Social Justice*, 17(2): 110–25.

Kakizawa, M. (2004) Counsellor Rehabilitation Bureau, Ministry of Justice, Japan. Presentation made to The Future of Crime and Punishment, International Probation Conference, London, 28–30 January 2004.

Kandel, D. B. (1980) Drug and Drinking Behavior Amongst Youth, *Annual Review of Sociology*, 6: 236–85.

Karatani, R. (2003) *Defining British Citizenship*, Frank Cass Publishers, London.

Karstedt, S. (2002) Emotions and Criminal Justice, *Theoretical Criminology*, 6(3): 299–317.

Karstedt, S. and Farrall, S. (forthcoming) *Respectable Citizens – Shady Practices: Crime, Social Change and the Moral Economy*.

Katz, J. (1988) *The Seductions of Crime*, Basic Books.

Kendall, K. (2004) 'Dangerous Thinking: A Critical History of Correctional Cognitive Behaviouralism', in Mair, G. (ed.) *What Matters in Probation*, Willan Publishing, Cullompton.

Knight, B. J. and West, D. J. (1975) Temporary and Continuing Delinquency, *British Journal of Criminology*, 15(1): 43–50.

Knight, B. J., Osborn, S. G. and West, D. J. (1977) Early Marriage And Criminal Tendency In Males, *British Journal of Criminology*, 17(4): 348–60.

Knowles, E. (2001) (ed.) *Oxford Dictionary of Quotations*, Oxford University Press, Oxford.

Kotarba, J. (1979) 'Existential Sociology', in McNall, S. G. (ed.) *Theoretical Perspectives in Sociology*, St. Martin's Press, New York.

Kotarba, J. (2002) 'Baby-Boomer Rock 'n' Roll Fans and the Becoming of Self', in Kotarba, J. and Johnson, J. (eds) *Postmodern Existential Sociology*, Altamira Press, Oxford.

Kotarba, J. and Bentley, P. (1988) Workplace Wellness Participation and The Becoming of Self, *Social Science & Medicine*, 26(5): 551–8.

Kotarba, J. and Fontana, A. (1984) (eds) *The Existential Self in Society*, Chicago University Press, Chicago.

Kotarba, J. and Johnson, J. (2002) (eds) *Postmodern Existential Sociology*, Altamira Press, Oxford.

Krienert J. and Fleisher, M. (2004) (eds) *Crime and Employment*, Altamira Press, Oxford.

Kruttschnitt, C., Uggen, C. and Shelton, K. (2000) Predictors of Desistance Among Sex Offenders: The Interaction of Formal and Informal Social Controls, *Justice Quarterly*, 17(1): 61–87.

Laub, J. H. and Sampson R. J. (2001) 'Understanding Desistance From Crime', in Tonry, M. H. and Norris, N. (eds) *Crime and Justice: An Annual Review of Research*, Vol. 26, pp. 1–78, University of Chicago Press, Chicago.

Laub, J. H. and Sampson, R. J. (2003) *Shared Beginnings, Divergent Lives*, Harvard University Press, Harvard.

Laub, J. H., Nagin, D. S. and Sampson, R. J. (1998) Trajectories of Change in Criminal Offending: Good Marriages and the Desistance Process, *American Sociological Review*, 63: 225–38.

Lauritsen, J., Sampson, R. J. and Laub, J. (1991) The Link Between Offending and Victimisation Among Adolescents, *Criminology*, 29(2): 265–92.

Lee, D. E. (1987) The Self-deception of the Self-destructive, *Perceptual and Motor Skills*, 65: 975–89.

Leibrich, J. (1993) *Straight To The Point: Angles On Giving Up Crime*, University of Otago Press, Otago, New Zealand.

Leibrich, J. (1996) 'The Role of Shame in Going Straight: A Study of Former Offenders', in Galaway, B. and Hudson, J. (eds) *Restorative Justice*, Criminal Justice Press, Monsey, NJ.

Lemert, C. C. (2000) 'Introduction', in Lemert, C. C. and Winter, M. F. (eds) *Crime and Deviance: Essays and Innovations of Edwin M. Lemert*, pp. 1–15, Rowman and Littlefield Publishers, Lanham, Maryland.

Lester, M. (1984) 'Self: Sociological Portraits', in Kotarba, J. and Fontana, A. (eds) *The Existential Self in Society*, Chicago University Press, Chicago.

Liker, J. K. (1982) Wage and status effects of employment on affective well being among ex-felons, *American Sociological Review*, 447: 264–83.

Loeber, R., Stouthamer-Loeber, M., Van Kammen, W. and Farrington, D. P. (1991) Initiation, Escalation and Desistance in Juvenile Offending and Their Correlates, *Journal of Criminal Law and Criminology*, 82(1): 36–82.

MacKenzie, D. L. and Brame, R. (2001) Community Supervision, Prosocial Activities and Recidivism, *Justice Quarterly*, 18(2): 429–45.

MacLeod, J. (1995) *Ain't No Makin' It*, Westview Press, Oxford.

MacQuarrie, K. (1972) *Existentialism*, Penguin Books, Harmondsworth.

Mair, G. (2004a) 'The Origins of What Works in England & Wales', in Mair, G. (ed.) *What Matters in Probation*, Willan Publishing, Cullompton, Devon.

Mair, G. (2004b) (ed.) *What Matters in Probation*, Willan Publishing, Cullompton, Devon.

Mann, M. (1986) *The Sources of Social Power, Vol 1*, Cambridge University Press, Cambridge.

Manning, P. K. (1973) Existential Sociology, *The Sociological Quarterly*, 14: 200–25.

Martinson, R. (1974) What works? Questions and Answers about Prison Reform, *The Public Interest*, 35: 22–54.

Maruna, S. (1997) Going Straight: Desistance From Crime and Life Narratives of Reform, *The Narrative Study of Lives*, 5: 59–93.

Maruna, S. (1998) *Redeeming One's Self: How Reformed Ex-Offenders Make Sense of Their Lives*, D. Phil dissertation, Northwestern University.

Maruna, S. (2000) Desistance From Crime and Offender Rehabilitation: A Tale of Two Research Literatures, *Offender Programs Report*, 4(1).

Maruna, S. (2001) *Making Good: How Ex-Convicts Reform and Rebuild Their Lives*, American Psychological Association Books, Washington DC.

Maruna, S. and Farrall, S. (2004) Desistance From Crime: A Theoretical Reformulation, *Kölner Zeitschrift für Soziologie und Sozialpsychologie*, 43.

Maruna, S. and Immarigeon, R. (2004) (eds) *After Crime and Punishment: Ex-Offender Reintegration and Desistance From Crime*, Willan Publishing, Cullompton, Devon.

Maruna, S. and LeBel, T. P. (2002) 'Revisiting Ex-prisoner Re-Entry: A Buzzword in Search of a Narrative', in Rex, S. and Tonry, M. (eds) *Reform & Sentencing*, Willan Publishing, Cullomption, Devon.

Maruna, S. and LeBel, T. P. (2003) Welcome Home?: Examining the Reentry Court Concept from a Strengths-based Perspective, *Western Criminology Review*, 4: 91–107.

Maruna, S., Porter, L. and Carvalho, I. (2004) The *Liverpool Desistance Study* and probation practice: Opening the dialogue, *Probation Journal*, 51(3): 221–32.

Matza, D. (1964) *Delinquency and Drift*, New York, Wiley.

May, C. (1999) *Explaining Reconviction Following A Community Sentence: The Role of Social Factors*, Home Office Research Study, 192, HMSO, London.

Mawby, R. I. and Walklate, S. (1994) *Critical Victimology*, Sage, London.

Mayhew, P. and Elliott, D. (1990) Self-reported Offending, Victimisation and the British Crime Survey, *Violence and Victims*, 5(2): 83–96.

McCulloch, T. (2005) Probation, Social Context and Desistance: Retracing the Relationship, *Probation Journal*, 51(2): 8–22.

McGuire, J. (1995) (ed.) *What Works?: Reducing Reoffending*, John Wiley & Son, Chichester.

McGuire, J. and Priestley, P. (1985) *Offending Behaviour*, Basford. London.

McKinnon, C. (2000) 'Civil Citizens', in McKinnon, C. and Hampsher-Monk, I. (eds) *The Demands of Citizenship*, 144–64, Continuum, London.

McNeill, F. (2000) 'Soft Options & Hard Cases: Public Attitudes, Social Exclusion and Probation', in Howard League for Penal Reform (eds) *Citizenship & Crime*, 9–12, London.

McNeill, F. (2003) 'Desistance-Focussed Probation Practice', in Chui, W. H. and Nellis, M. (eds) *Moving Probation Forward*, Pearson Education, London.

McNeill, F. (2004a) Desistance, Rehabilitation and Correctionalism: Developments and Prospects in Scotland, *Howard Journal of Criminal Justice*, 43(4): 420–36.

McNeill, F. (2004b) Supporting desistance in probation practice: A response to Maruna, Porter and Carvalho, *Probation Journal*, 53(3): 241–47.

McSweeney, T., Herrington, V., Hough, M., Turnbull, P. and Parsons, J. (2004) *From Dependency to Work*, The Policy Press, Bristol.

Meehan, E. (1999) 'Citizenship & Identity', in Holliday, I., Gamble, A. and Parry, G. (eds), *Fundamentals in British Politics*, 231–50, Macmillan, London.

Meisenhelder, T. (1977) An Exploratory Study of Exiting From Criminal Careers, *Criminology*, 15: 319–34.

Meisenhelder, T. (1982) Becoming Normal: Certification as a Stage in Exiting From Crime, *Deviant Behaviour*, 3: 137–53.

Meisenhelder, T. (1985) An Essay on Time and the Phenomenology of Imprisonment, *Deviant Behaviour*, 6: 39–56.

Mercier, C. and Alarie, S. (2002) 'Pathways Out of Deviance: Implications for Programme Evaluation', in Brochu, S., Da Agra, C. and Cousineau, M.-M. (eds) *Drugs & Crime Deviant Pathways*, Ashgate, Aldershot.

Messerschmidt, J. W. (1997) *Crime As Structured Action*, Sage, London.

Miller, R. L., Brickman, P. and Bolen, D. (1975) Attribution versus persuasion as a means of modifying behavior, *Journal of Personality and Social Psychology*, 31: 430–441.

Mischkowitz, R. (1994) 'Desistance From A Delinquent Way of Life?', in Weitekamp, E. G. M. and Kerner, H. J. (eds) *Cross-National Longitudinal Research on Human Development and Criminal Behaviour*, Kluwer, Academic Publishers.

Modell, J. (1994) Book review of 'Crime in the Making: Pathways and Turning Points through Life', *American Journal of Sociology*, 99: 1389–91.

Moffitt, T. (1993) 'Life-Course Persistent' and 'Adolescent-Limited' Antisocial Behaviour: A Developmental Taxonomy, *Psychological Review*, 100: 674–701.

Moffitt, T. E. (1997) 'Adolescence-Limited and Life-Course Persistent Offending: A Complementary Pair of Developmental Theories', in Thornberry, T. (ed.) *Developmental Theories of Crime and Delinquency*, Transaction Press, London.

Morgan, R. (2003) Review of Farrall, S. (2002) 'Rethinking What Works With Offenders', *British Journal of Criminology*, 43(4): 808–10.

Morrison, W. (1995) *Theoretical Criminology*, Cavendish Publishing, London.

Morton, A. (2001) *Gangland the Lawyers*, Virgin Publishing Ltd, London.

Mouzelis, N. (1997) Social and System Intergration: Lockwood, Habermas, Giddens, *Sociology*, 31(1): 111–19.

Mulvey, E. P. and Aber, M. (1988) 'Growing Out Of Delinquency: Development And Desistance', in Jenkins, R. L. and Brown, W. K. (eds) *The Abandonment of Delinquent Behaviour: Promoting The Turnaround*, Praeger, New York.

Mulvey, E. P. and LaRosa, J. F. (1986) Delinquency Cessation and Adolescent

Development: Preliminary Data, *American Journal of Orthopsychiatry*, 56(2): 212–24.

Murie, A. (1997) Linking Housing Changes to Crime, *Social Policy and Administration*, 31(5): 22–36.

New, C. (1994) Structure, Agency and Social Transformation, *Journal for the Theory of Social Behaviour*, 24(3): 187–205.

O'Brien, P. (2001) *Making It in the 'Free World'*, SUNY Press, New York.

O'Donnell, I. and Edgar, K. (1996a) *The Extent and Dynamics of Victimisation in Prisons*, Centre for Criminological Research, University of Oxford.

O'Donnell, I. and Edgar, K. (1996b) *Victimisation in Prisons*, Home Office Research Findings, 37, Home Office, London.

Oldfield, M. (1996) *The Kent Reconviction Survey*, Kent Probation Service, England.

Osborn, S. G. (1980) Moving Home, Leaving London and Delinquent Trends, *British Journal of Criminology*, 20(1): 54–61.

Ouimet, M. and Le Blanc, M. (1996) The Role of Life Experiences in the Continuation of the Adult Criminal Career, *Criminal Behaviour and Mental Health*, 6: 73–97.

Parker, H. (1976) 'Boys Will be Men: Brief Adolescence in a Down-Town Neighbourhood', in Mungham, G. and Pearson, G. (eds) *Working Class Youth Culture*, Routledge, London.

Pawson, R. and Tilley, N. (1997) *Realistic Evaluation*, Sage, London.

Peelo, M., Stewart, J., Stewart, G. and Prior, A. (1992) *A Sense of Justice: Offenders As Victims of Crime*, Association of Chief Officers of Probation, London.

Pezzin, L. E. (1995) Earning Prospects, Matching Effects and the Decision to Terminate a Criminal Career, *Journal of Quantitative Criminology*, 11(1): 29–50.

Plummer, K. (2003) *Intimate Citizenship*, University of Washington Press, London.

Pratt, M. W., Hunsberger, B., Pancer, M. and Alisat, S. (2003) A Longitudinal Analysis of Personal Values Socialization, *Social Development*, 12(4): 563–85.

Prewitt, K., Eulau, H. and Zisk, B. (1966) Political Socialization and Political Roles, *Public Opinion Quarterly*, 30: 569–82.

Putnam, R. (2000) *Bowling Alone*, Simon & Schuster, New York.

Quigley, B. M. and Leonard, K. E. (1996) Desistance of Husband Aggression in the Early Years of Marriage, *Violence and Victims*, 11: 355–70.

Quinney, R. (2002) *Bearing Witness to Crime and Social Justice*, SUNY Press, New York.

Rand, A. (1987) 'Transitional Life Events and Desistance From Delinquency and Crime', in Wolfgang, M. E., Thornberry, T. P. and Figlio, R. M. (eds) *From Boy To Man, From Delinquency To Crime*, University of Chicago Press, Chicago.

Ratcliffe, S. (2002) (ed.) *Oxford Dictionary of Phrase, Saying and Quotation*, 2nd edn, Oxford University Press, Oxford.

Ratcliffe, S. (2003) *Oxford Dictionary of Quotations by Subject*, Oxford University Press, Oxford.

Reiss, A. J. (1986) 'Why are communities important in understanding crime?', in

Reiss, A. J. and Tonry, M. (eds) *Communities and Crime*, University of Chicago Press, Chicago.

Retzinger, S. M. and Scheff, T. J. (1996) 'Strategy for Community Conferences: Emotions and Social Bonds', in Galaway, B. and Hudson, J. (eds) *Restorative Justice: International Perspectives*, 315–36, Criminal Justice Press, Monsey, NY.

Rex, S. (1999) Desistance from Offending: Experiences of Probation, *Howard Journal of Criminal Justice*, 38(4): 366–83.

Reynolds, B. (1995) *Crossing the Line: The Autobiography of a Thief*, Virgin Books Ltd, London.

Richards, S. and Jones, S. (2004) 'Beating the Perpetual Incarceration Machine', in Maruna, S. and Immarigeon, R. (eds) *After Crime and Punishment: Ex-Offender Reintegration and Desistance From Crime*, 57–82, Willan Publishing, Cullompton, Devon.

Ritchie, B. (2001) Challenges Incarcerated Women Face as They Return to Their Communities, *Crime and Delinquency*, 47: 368–89.

Rumgay, J. (2004) Scripts for Safer Survival: Pathways Out of Female Crime, *Howard Journal of Criminal Justice*, 43(4): 405–19.

Sampson, R. J. and Laub, J. H. (1993) *Crime In The Making: Pathways and Turning Points Through Life*, Harvard University Press, London.

Sampson, R. J. and Laub, J. H. (1997) 'A Life-Course Theory of Cumulative Disadvantage and the Stability of Delinquency', in Thornberry, T. (ed.) *Developmental Theories of Crime and Delinquency*, Transaction, London.

Sarre, P., Phillips, D. and Skellington, R. (1989) *Ethnic Minority Housing: Explanations and Policies*, Avebury, Aldershot.

Sartre, J.-P. (1943, trans 1958) *Being and Nothingness*, Routledge, London.

Seidler, V. J. (1998) 'Masculinity, violence and emotional life', in Bendelow, G. and Williams, S (eds) *Emotions in Social Life*, Routledge, London and New York.

Sherman, L. (1993) Defiance, Deterrence and Irrelevance: A theory of the criminal sanction, *Journal of Research in Crime and Delinquency*, 30: 445–73.

Sherman, L. W., Gartin, P. R. and Buerger, M. E. (1989) Hot spots of predatory crime: routine activities and the criminology of place, *Criminology*, 27: 27–55.

Shibutani, T. (1961) *Society and Personality*, Prentice Hall, Englewood Cliffs, NJ.

Shover, N. (1983) The Later Stages Of Ordinary Property Offender Careers, *Social Problems*, 31(2): 208–18.

Shover, N. (1985) *Aging Criminals*, Sage, Beverley Hills.

Shover, N. (1996) *Great Pretenders*, Oxford University Press, Oxford.

Shover, N. and Honaker, D. (1992) The Socially Bounded Decision Making of Persistent Property Offenders, *Howard Journal of Criminal Justice*, 31: 276–93.

Shover, N. and Thompson, C. (1992) Age, Differential Expectations And Crime Desistance, *Criminology*, 30(1): 89–104.

Sigel, R. S. and Hoskins, M. B. (1977) 'Perspectives on Adult Political Socilization – Areas of Research', in Renshon, S. A. (ed.) *Handbook of Political Socialization*, The Free Press, New York.

Simpson, C. (2004) When hope makes us vulnerable: a discussion of Patient-Healthcare Provider interactions in the context of Hope, *Bioethics*, 18(5): 428–7.

Singer, S. (1981) Homogeneous Victim-Offender Populations: A review and Some Research Implications, *Journal of Criminal Law and Criminology*, 72(2): 779–88.

Smith, D. (1986) *Crime, Space And Society*, Cambridge University Press, Cambridge.

Smith, D. A., Visher, C. A. and Jarjoura, G. R. (1991) Dimensions of Delinquency, *Journal of Research on Crime and Delinquency*, 28(1): 6–32.

Smith, L. G. and Akers, R. L. (1993) A Comparison of Recidivism of Florida's Community Control and Prison: A Five Year Survival Analysis, *Journal of Research into Crime & Delinquency*, 30: 267–92.

Sommers, I. and Baskin, D. (1998) *Casualties of Community Disorder: Female Violent Offenders*, Westview Press, Oxford.

Sommers, I., Baskin, D. R. and Fagan, J. (1994) Getting Out of The Life: Crime Desistance by Female Street Offenders, *Deviant Behaviour*, 15(2): 125–49.

Sparks, R., Bottoms, A. and Hay, W. (1996) *Prisons and The Problem of Order*, Clarendon Press, Oxford.

Stanko, E. (2002) Review of Katz, Jack, How Emotions Work, *Theoretical Criminology*, 6(3): 366–9.

Stones, R. (1991) Strategic Context Analysis: A New Research Strategy for Structuration Theory, *Sociology*, 25(3): 673–95.

Stones, R. (1996) *Sociological Reasoning*, Macmillan, Basingstoke.

Thamesdown Borough Council (1994) *Thamesdown Trends*, Swindon.

Thorogood, M., Arscott A., Walls P., Dunn N. and Mann, R. (2002) Matched controls in a case-control study. Does matching by doctor's list mean matching by relative deprivation? *International Journal of Social Research Methodology*, 5(ii): 165–72.

Thrift, N. (1985) 'Bear and Tree' or 'Bear and Mouse'?: Anthony Giddens' Reconstitution of Social Theory, *Sociology*, 19(4): 609–23.

Tolman, R. M., Edleson, J. L. and Fendrich, M. (1996) The Applicability of the Theory of Planned Behavior to Abusive Men's Cessation of Violent Behavior, *Violence and Victims*, 11(4): 341–54.

Trasler, G. (1979) Delinquency, Recidivism and Desistance, *British Journal of Criminology*, 19(4): 314–22.

Trice, H. M. and Roman, P. M. (1970) Delabeling, relabeling and Alcoholics Anonymous, *Social Problems*, 17: 538–46.

Tugade, M. M., Frederickson, B. L. and Fredman Barret, L. (2004) Psychological Resilience and Positive Emotional Granularity, *Journal of Personality*, 72(6): 1161–90.

Tyler, K. and Johnson, K. (2004) Victims and Offfenders, *Deviant Behaviour*, 25: 427–49.

Uggen, C. (2000) Work as a Turning point in the Life Course of Criminals: A Duration Model of Age, Employment and Recidivism, *American Sociological Review*, 67: 529–46.

Uggen, C. and Kruttschnitt, K. (1998) Crime in the Breaking: Gender Differences in Desistance, *Law and Society Review*, 32(2): 339–66.

Uggen, C. and Pilliavin, I. (1998) Asymmetrical Causation and Criminal Desistance, *Journal of Criminal Law and Criminology*, 88(4): 1399–1422.

Uggen, C., Manza, J. and Behrens, A. (2004) ' "Less Than the Average Citizen": Stigma, Role Transition and the Civic Reintegration of Convicted Felons', in Maruna, S. and Immarigeon, R. (eds) *After Crime and Punishment: Ex-*

Offender Reintegration and Desistance From Crime, 261–93, Willan Publishing, Cullompton, Devon.

Van Dijk, J. and Steinmetz, C. (1983) Victimisation Surveys: Beyond Measuring the Volume of Crime, *Victimology: An International Journal*, 8(1–2): 291–309.

Van Stokkom, B. (2002) Moral Emotions and Restorative Justice Conferences, *Theoretical Criminology*, 6(3): 339–60.

Walklate, S. (1992) 'Appreciating the Victim: Conventional, Realist or Critical Victimology?', in Matthews, R. and Young, J. (eds) *Issues in Realist Criminology*, Sage, London.

Walklate, S. (1996) 'Can There be a Feminist Victimology?', in Davies, P., Francis, P. and Jupp, V. (eds) *Understanding Victimisation*, Northumbria Social Science Press, Newcastle.

Walters, G. D. (1999) Human Survival and the Self-Destruction Paradox, *Journal of Mind and Behaviour*, 20(1): 57–78.

Warr, M. (1998) Life-Course Transitions and Desistance From Crime, *Criminology*, 36(2): 183–215.

Warren, C. and Ponse, B. (1977) 'The Existential Self in the Gay World', in Douglas, J. and Johnson, J. (eds) *Existential Sociology*, Cambridge University Press, Cambridge.

Weisburd, D., Waring, E. with Chayet, E. F. (2001) *White-Collar Crime and Criminal Careers*, Cambridge University Press, Cambridge.

Weitekamp, E., Kerner, H.-J., Stelly, W. and Thomas, J. (2000) 'Desistance from Crime: Life History, Turning Points and Implications for Theory Construction in Criminology', in Karstedt, S. and Bussmann, K.-D. (eds) *Social Dynamics of Crime and Control: New Theories for a World in Transition*, 207–28, Hart, Oxford.

West, D. (1955) *Homosexuality*, Penguin Books, Harmondsworth.

West, D. J. (1982) *Delinquency: Its Roots, Careers and Prospects*, Heinemann, London.

West, G. W. (1978) The Short Term Careers of Serious Thieves, *Canadian Journal of Criminology*, 20: 169–90.

Wilkins, C. (1999) 'Good Citizens': The Social & Political Attitudes of PGCE Students, *Oxford Review of Education*, 25(1 & 2): 217–30.

Willis, P. E. (1977) *Learning to Labour*, Gower, Aldershot.

Willis, P. E. (2003) Foot Soldiers of Modernity, *Harvard Education Review*, 73(3): 390–415.

Willmott, H. (1986) Unconscious Sources of Motivation in the Theory of the Subject: An Exploration and Critique of Giddens' Dualistic Models of Action and Personality, *Journal for the Theory of Social Behaviour*, 16(1): 105–21.

Wittebrood, K. and Nieuwbeerta, P. (1999) Wages of Sin? The Link Between Offending, Lifestyle and Violent Victimisation, *European Journal on Criminal Policy and Research*, 7: 63–80.

Wolfgang, M., Figlio, R. and Sellin, T. (1987) *Delinquency in a Birth Cohort*, University of Chicago Press, Chicago.

Worrall, A. (1990) *Offending Women*, Routledge, London.

Worrall, A. (1997) *Punishment in the Community: The Future of Criminal Justice*, Longman, London.

Worrall, A. & Hoy, C. (2005) *Punishment in the Community*, 2nd edn Willan Publishing, Cullompton, Devon.

Young, J. (1999) *The Exclusive Society*, Sage, London.
Zhang, L, Welte, J. and Wieczorek, W. F. (2001) Deviant Lifestyle and Crime Victimisation, *Journal of Criminal Justice*, 29: 133–43.

Index

As with the previous book that reported on this cohort, we provide an index of the individual cases in the sample. This allows readers to chart the progress of specific cases over time. Journal articles and chapters in edited collections follow the same numbering system.

212 Danny   : 141, 160
218 Gordon   : 161
223 Niall   : 106, 122–23, 163–64
227 Dominic   : 100–01, 117–18, 124, 125, 162

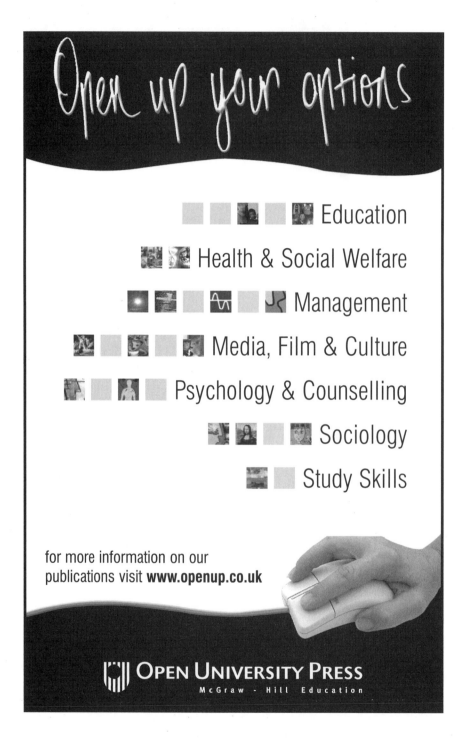